BUILDING SKILLS FOR THE TOEIC® TEST

TOEIC® is a registered trademark of Educational Testing Service

Gina Richardson
and Michele Peters

Longman

Pearson Education Limited,
Edinburgh Gate, Harlow,
Essex CM20 2JE, England
and Associated Companies throughout the world.

www.longman.com

First published 1995
Thirteenth impression 2002

Set in 11/14 point Plantin Light

Printed in Malaysia, PP

ISBN 0-17-556939-8

TOEIC® is a registered trademark of Educational Testing Service. There is no connection between Longman Group Ltd and Educational Testing Service, nor has this publication been endorsed by ETS.

TOEIC® directions and format are reprinted by permission of Educational Testing Service.

Acknowledgements

The publishers would like to thank the following for permission to reproduce copyright material. They have tried to contact all copyright holders, but in cases where they have failed will be pleased to make the necessary arrangements at the first opportunity:

American Airlines pages 133 (above), 170 (below); British Petroleum pages 94 (below), 96 (above and below), 101 (above), 140 (below), 175 (below); BT pictures page 177 (above); Citibank, N. A. pages 98, 141 (below); Alan Cummings page 178 (above); John Davis pages 13, 15, 101 (below), 178 (below), 179 (above and below); Educational Testing Service pages 9, 91, 131, 169; Louise Elkins pages 92 (below), 97 (below), 98 (above), 139 (above), 173 (above); Glaxo Holdings p.l.c. pages 135 (above), 171 (above and below), 173 (below); Sally and Richard Greenhill pages 17 (above and below), 19 (below), 95 (below), 137 (above), 140 (above), 170 (above), 174 (below), 176 (above); Hyatt International Hotels pages 132 (below), 134 (above), 136 (above and below), 172 (above), 174 (above); IBM page 172 (below); ICI page 11; Japan Information and Cultural Centre pages 92 (above), 93 (above and below), 95 (above), 132(above), 134 (below), 176 (below); Leyland DAF page 100 (above); McDonald's Restaurants Ltd page 18 (below); Mercury Communications Ltd page 99 (above); Nissan Motor (GB) Ltd pages 97 (above), 133 (below), 137 (below); Richard Powell pages 135 (below), 139 (below), 177 (below); Press Division of the Taipei Representative Office in the UK pages 94 (below), 100 (below), 138 (below), 141 (above), 175 (above); Damien Tunnacliffe pages 99 (below), 138 (above); The Wellcome Foundation Ltd pages 18 (above), 19 (above).

Contents

Introduction

About the TOEIC® Test

The Test of English for International Communication, TOEIC®, measures the English proficiency of adults. The test is not an academic test. It is an international test that covers the vocabulary and grammar adults might use anywhere in the world when they use English.

The TOEIC test has two sections: Listening Comprehension and Reading. Each section has several parts. The chart below shows the various parts of the test, the number of questions, and the total time you are given to work on each part.

Section		Questions	Time
Listening Comprehension			45 minutes
Part I	Pictures	20	
Part II	Question-Response	30	
Part III	Short Conversations	30	
Part IV	Short Talks	20	
Reading			75 minutes
Part V	Incomplete Sentences	40	
Part VI	Error Recognition	20	
Part VII	Reading Comprehension	40	
TOTAL		**200**	**120 minutes**

TOEIC scores run from 10 to 990. The score you receive for the Listening Comprehension section is added to the score you receive from the Reading section. Only your correct responses are counted toward the final score.

Section	Score
Listening Comprehension	5 to 495
Reading	5 to 495
TOTAL	**10 to 990**

The test is administered by regional representatives of the TOEIC offices of the Educational Testing Service in Princeton, New Jersey, USA. To take a TOEIC exam, you should contact your local representative or write to ETS at the address below:

TOEIC Service International
Educational Testing Service
Princeton, New Jersey 08541
USA

About *Building Skills for the TOEIC Test*

Building Skills for the TOEIC Test provides a clear, systematic approach to help you prepare for the TOEIC test step by step.

- You will hear, read, and analyze items like those on the TOEIC test.
- You will learn how to eliminate possible wrong answers; you will go from a 25% chance of choosing the correct answer to a $33\frac{1}{3}$% or even a 50% chance of choosing the correct answer.
- You will become familiar with the vocabulary used on the TOEIC. All presentations, activities, and practice tests contain vocabulary similar to that on the TOEIC test.
- You will learn how to Avoid the Trap. These are tricky items that can present problems to test takers.
- You will learn how to manage your time while taking the TOEIC test.
- You will most importantly improve your knowledge of English.

How to Find What you Want

The organization of this book is very simple. It is actually structured like the TOEIC test itself.

Chapter 1 Review

This chapter is divided into seven parts; each part represents a part of the TOEIC. Each part consists of a sample TOEIC item, focused review, exercises, and practice items to help you develop strategies to improve your score. Each TOEIC sample item is thoroughly explained in the text. Every practice item is explained in depth in the answer key at the end of the book.

Chapter 2 Practice Tests

There are three practice tests in this chapter. The format of the test is similar to the actual TOEIC test. For the Listening Comprehension section, there is an audio tape available. The tapescript is at the end of the book. Answer sheets and answer keys are also found there.

Appendix

The Appendix includes the tapescripts for the Listening Comprehension section of the Review chapter as well as the Listening Comprehension section of the three practice tests.

It also includes the answer keys for both the Review chapter and the three practice tests. Answer sheets are found at the end of the Appendix.

How to Use the Book

There are many ways to use this book depending on how much time you have and what your level of English proficiency is. Here are two methods you might try:

Method A

- Study all seven parts of the Review chapter carefully. Learn to focus on each part.
- Take a practice test.
- Note those parts where you missed the most questions.
- Review those parts in the book.
- Take another practice test.

Method B

- Take a practice test.
- Note those parts where you missed the most questions.
- Study those parts in the book.
- Take another practice test.

Please note that this book focuses on specific areas of the TOEIC exam; it is not a complete review of English grammar. When you read the explanatory answers for a practice test, write down the particular grammar item you missed. If you consistently make mistakes in a particular area of English grammar, use of conjunctions, for example, you should review that area in a standard grammar book.

A Final Word on Improving Your Score

After you have studied this book carefully, continue using English as much as you can. Go to movies in English; watch television in English; buy newspapers in English; correspond on e-mail with English speakers around the globe. The more you use English the better your score will be.

TEST TIP

REMEMBER, THE CORRECT ANSWER IS ONE OF FOUR CHOICES: (A), (B), (C), OR (D). YOU HAVE A 25% CHANCE OF GUESSING CORRECTLY! ELIMINATE ONE CHOICE, AND YOU HAVE A $33\frac{1}{3}$% CHANCE. ELIMINATE *ANOTHER* DISTRACTER, AND YOU HAVE A 50% CHANCE OF CHOOSING CORRECTLY.

1 Review

In the Listening Comprehension section of the TOEIC test, there are four different listening sections that give you the chance to show how well you understand spoken English. You will have approximately 45 minutes to answer 100 questions. The four parts to this section are:

- Part I: Pictures   20 questions
- Part II: Question-Response   30 questions
- Part III: Short Conversations   30 questions
- Part IV: Short Talks   20 questions

For all four parts, you will listen to an audiocassette. You will choose the correct answer from four written answers: (A), (B), (C), or (D) in Parts I, III and IV; and from three written answers in Part II.

Part I: Pictures

In Part I, you will see a picture in your test book. You will hear four short statements, but you will not see these four statements in your test book. The statements will be spoken just one time. Listen carefully to understand what the speaker says.

When you are listening to the four statements, look at the picture in your test book. Choose the statement that best describes the picture. Then, on your answer sheet, find the number of the question and mark your answer. You will have five seconds to answer each question.

Sample TOEIC Question

You will hear: (A) They're looking out the window.

             (B) They're having a meeting.

             (C) They're eating in a restaurant.

             (D) They're moving the furniture.

Choice (B), *They're having a meeting*, best describes what you see in the picture.

Therefore, you should choose answer (B).

Choice (A) is incorrect because they are by a window, not looking out of it. Choice (C) is incorrect because although you see coffee cups, they are not eating, and the setting is a conference room, not a restaurant.. Choice (D) is incorrect because they are not moving furniture.

Types of Statements

The statements in this section may have any of these five characteristics:

Characteristics	Examples
The statements are often in the present continuous tense.	The man is signing his name.
The statements often use pronouns instead of names.	She's watching television.
The statements are brief; they rarely use more than 5-6 words.	No, I don't.
Contractions are often used.	I think it's going to rain.
The definite article, *the*, is often used.	The cars are being towed.

Test Tips

You can improve your score on Part I by:
- looking for the main idea
- distinguishing similar sounds
- making assumptions

Skill 1: Looking for the Main Idea

Some TOEIC test questions ask for information about the main idea of the picture. The main idea is the general idea. It describes what is happening in the picture.

Sample TOEIC Question

You will hear: (A) They are having a discussion.
              (B) They are standing outside.
              (C) They are looking out the window.
              (D) They are delivering newspapers.

Choice (A), *They are having a discussion*, best describes what you see in the picture.

Choice (B) is incorrect because they are standing inside, not outside. Choice (C) is incorrect because they are talking, not looking out the window. Choice (D) is incorrect because you see newspapers, but they are not *delivering* newspapers.

Skill Focus

To find the main idea, look for the overall focus of the picture. Describe the scene of the picture to yourself. You may want to use the simple present or the present continuous form of the verbs in your descriptions.

Here are some examples of main idea statements.

- There are three people in the picture.
- They are standing inside.
- They are not looking out the window.
- They are looking at some pictures.
- There are newspapers in the picture.

Look at the other pictures in the book and describe each scene to yourself.

Exercises ⌾═══➤ p 224

Circle the main idea in the choices below. This will help you distinguish the main idea from the details.

1. (A) They're having a serious discussion.
   (B) They're wearing glasses.
   (C) Their suits are not clean.
   (D) They're holding glasses.

2. (A) The calendar shows May.
   (B) The clock shows 8:00 AM.
   (C) It's not a tidy office.
   (D) The plant is in the window.

3. (A) The plane is very crowded.
   (B) A man doesn't have a seatbelt on.
   (C) A passenger has her seat upright.
   (D) A flight attendant has long hair.

4. (A) There are puddles on the street.
   (B) There's an umbrella in the trash.
   (C) The weather has been stormy.
   (D) The windshield wipers are working.

5. (A) The doors arc opcn.
   (B) A man is stepping on the elevator.
   (C) A woman is holding the elevator door.
   (D) The people are riding an elevator.

Skill 2: Distinguishing Similar Sounds

On the TOEIC test, you may have to choose among statements that contain similar sounding words. Some English words have similar pronunciations. To distinguish similar sounding words, listen carefully for the differences in sounds. Then, think about what will make sense in the sentence.

Sample TOEIC Question

You will hear: (A) There is one person at the station.

(B) They're planning a vacation.

(C) She'll take a plane.

(D) The train is coming.

Choice (D), *The train is coming*, best describes what you see in the picture. You see a train arriving at a train station.

Choice (A) talks about a station, but it is incorrect because there are several people at the station in the picture. Choice (B) is incorrect because it confuses *vacation* with *station*. Also, you cannot tell by the picture if anyone is planning anything. Choice (C) is incorrect because it confuses the similar sounds *plane* and *train*. You should be able to hear the difference in the sounds *take a plane* and *take a train*.

Skill Focus

To learn how to distinguish similar sounds, you should hear the words pronounced in pairs. The pairs of words below all have similar sounds. Read these pairs of words aloud or listen as a friend reads them. Pay attention to the different sounds.

Words that sound similar at the beginning

personal	personnel
magnet	magnate
respectively	respectfully
than	then
devise	device

Words that sound similar at the end

hand	brand
cab	tab
large	charge
pay	say
place	pace
grain	drain
date	rate
then	yen
dine	fine
rest	guest

Words that sound similar when combined with other words

(they are)	they're	their
(he will)	he'll	hill
(we will)	we'll	well

Practice listening for different sounds. Reading aloud or listening to poetry that rhymes are good ways to practice.

Exercises ⊙━ p 224

Circle the word that doesn't have a similar sound. This will help you learn to distinguish different sounds in similar sounding English words.

1.	zip	tip	ship	pipe
2.	night	write	high	flight
3.	how	show	now	plow
4.	box	socks	locks	smokes
5.	trunk	brunch	hunch	lunch
6.	five	strive	glib	drive
7.	coast	most	cost	post
8.	chose	choose	close	those
9.	bin	dime	rhyme	time
10.	rat	bat	hat	cut

14

Skill 3: Making Assumptions

On the TOEIC test, you may be asked to make assumptions about the photos. When you make an assumption, you think ahead or think what might happen next. You may not SEE the action, but you can make a guess about the action. You must determine the facts presented in the photo and make assumptions accordingly.

Sample TOEIC Question

You will hear: (A) The waiter is changing his clothes.
               (B) He's about to give them change.
               (C) They are parking their car on the sidewalk.
               (D) Coffee beans are sold.

Choice (B), *He's about to give them change*, best describes what you see in the picture. The waiter has served them and could be looking for change. Therefore, the waiter is probably about to give the customers their change.

Choice (A) is incorrect because it confuses the related word *change* (money) with *changing his clothes*. Choice (C) is incorrect because you may see a *car* and a *sidewalk*, but the sentence doesn't make sense for the picture. Choice (D) is incorrect because it confuses the similar sound *coffee* with *café*.

15

Skill Focus

To make an assumption about the future, listen for the future tense of the verb. This will tell you which action is assumed to happen in the future. Remember that there are several structures that show future time in English. Review these structures below.

Structure for Future Tense	Examples
The auxiliary *will* + the base form of the verb is used.	He *will go.* They *will pay.* She *will shake* hands.
The verb (*to be*) + *going to* + the base form of the verb is used.	She's *going to ask* a question. They're *going to explain* the answer.
The phrase (*to be*) *about to* + the base form of the verb is used.	He *is about to speak.* They *are about to land.*
The verb (*to be*) + infinitive is used.	He *is to leave* at four o'clock. They *are to plan* the meeting.

Look at other pictures in this book. Make an assumption about what might happen next for each picture.

Exercises 🔑 p 224

Choose an assumption based on these descriptions of the photographs. This will help you make assumptions about what you see.

The photo shows:	Your assumption:
1. A cloudy sky	(A) The sun will shine soon. (B) It's going to rain. (C) The stars will come out. (D) There isn't a cloud in the sky.
2. Cars in a traffic jam	(A) The cars will move quickly. (B) The drivers will wait patiently. (C) Someone will be late. (D) No one is driving slowly.
3. People in line at an airport gate	(A) They're going to board a plane. (B) Their flight is delayed. (C) They're about to go home. (D) They're traveling on business.
4. Housekeeper entering a messy hotel room	(A) She will check into the hotel. (B) She's about to leave a tip. (C) She's going to clean the room. (D) She's going to go to bed.
5. A courier with a package going down a hall	(A) He will open the package. (B) He's about to deliver the package. (C) He's going to drop the package. (D) He's going to keep the package.

Practice: Part I p 224 ⬛ p 204

You will see a picture in your book and you will hear four statements. When you hear the four statements, look at the picture and choose the statement that best describes what you see in the picture.

1

2

3

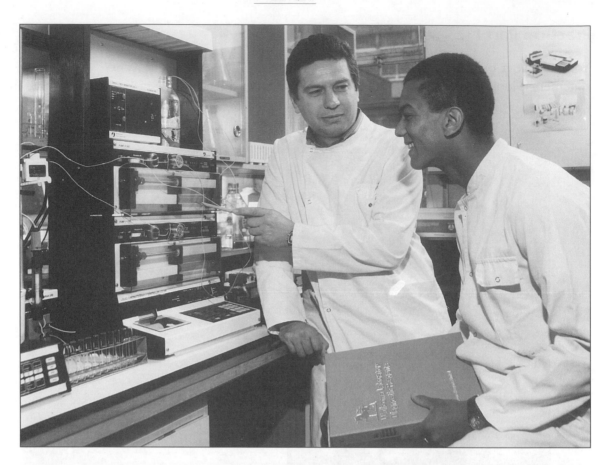

4

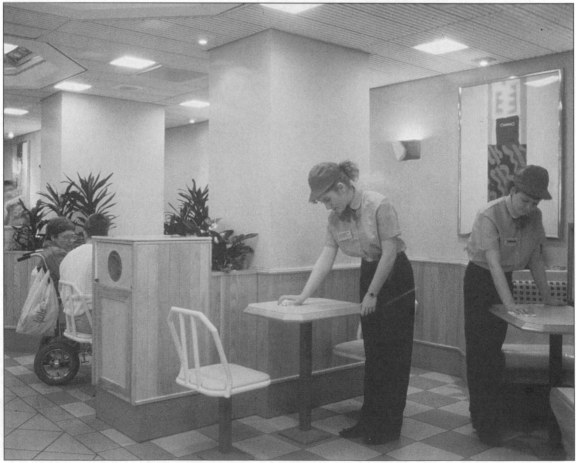

5

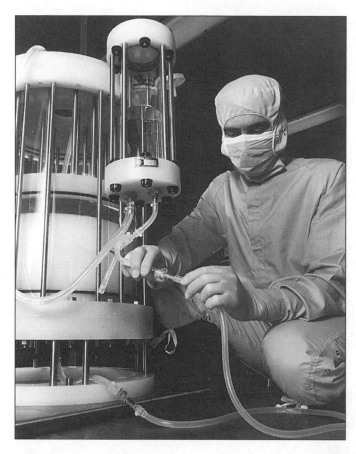

6

Part II: Question–Response

In Part II of the TOEIC test, you will hear a question and three responses. You will hear the question and the responses one time only. You will not be able to read them, so listen carefully and choose the best response to each question. You will have 5 seconds to answer each question.

Sample TOEIC Question

You will hear: How can I get to the airport from here?

You will also hear: (A) Take a taxi. It's just a short ride.
                       (B) No, I don't.
                       (C) You can get on easily.

Choice (A), *Take a taxi. It's just a short ride* is the best response to this Wh- question. Choice (A) directly answers the Wh- word *How*.

Choice (B) is incorrect because this is a response to a Yes/No question. Choice (C) is incorrect because it confuses the similar sound *get on* with *get to*.

Types of Questions

There are two types of questions in Part II: Wh- questions and Yes/No questions.

Wh- questions ask for information. These questions begin with Wh- words:

Wh- Words

Who ...?   What ...?   Where ...?   When ...?   How long ...?

Yes/No questions expect a *Yes* or *No* response. These questions begin with auxiliary verbs:

Auxiliary Verbs

Does he ...?   Can you ...?   Will she ...?   Have we ...?   Are they ...?

Test Tips

You can improve your score in Part II by:
- distinguishing Wh- and Yes/No questions
- identifying homophones
- recognizing negative meaning

Skill 1: Distinguishing Wh- and Yes/No Questions

On the TOEIC test you may have to determine the type of the question asked in order to choose the correct response. The wording of an answer has to be appropriate for the type of question asked. Make sure you can distinguish Wh- questions from Yes/No questions.

Sample TOEIC Question

When will the package arrive?
(A) Any minute.
(B) No, not yet.
(C) I'll pack it now.

Choice (A) is the correct answer because it has the correct form and answers the Wh-word *when*. Choice (B) is incorrect because its form is appropriate for answering Yes/No questions. It could be the correct answer if the question were Yes/No: *Has the package arrived?* Choice (C) is incorrect because it confuses the similar sounds *pack it* and *package*.

Skill Focus

The first words of a question are very important. They let you know immediately whether the question is Wh- or Yes/No. When you know what kind of question you have, you can predict the structure of your answer and the kind of information it should have.

Wh- Questions	Possible Responses
Who ...?	The sales director.
What ...?	A meeting.
Where ...?	On the second floor.
When ...?	At 10:00.
Why ...?	Because I was late.
How long ...?	For one hour.

Yes/No Questions	Possible Responses
Does he ...?	Yes, he does.
Can you ...?	No, I can't.
Will she ...?	Yes, she will.
Have we ...?	No, we haven't.
Should they ...?	Yes, they should.

Exercises ⊙⇒ p 225

Circle the question type. This will help you determine what kind of answer will fit the question.

Question	Question Type	
1. Who is talking?	Wh-	Yes/No
2. Are they prepared?	Wh-	Yes/No
3. Where are they?	Wh-	Yes/No
4. Have you ever been abroad?	Wh-	Yes/No
5. What will the tour be like?	Wh-	Yes/No

AVOID THE TRAP!

The answers to Yes/No questions begin with *yes* or *no*. Sometimes, the *yes* or *no* is understood but not spoken.

Skill 2: Identifying Homophones

On the TOEIC test you may have to recognize the different meanings of homophones. Homophones are words that sound alike, but have different meanings and different spellings. You cannot distinguish homophones by their pronunciation. You must distinguish them by the meaning of the sentence.

Sample TOEIC Question

You will hear: What will the weather be like tomorrow?

You will also hear: (A) He'll be here at seven.
                    (B) I think it's going to rain.
                    (C) She doesn't know whether she'll go.

Choice (B), *I think it's going to rain,* is the best response to the question. This Wh- question is asking for a weather forecast.

Choice (A) is incorrect because it confuses the similar sound *will the weather be* with *He'll be.* Choice (C) is incorrect because it confuses the homophones *whether* and *weather.*

Skill Focus

Homophones can always be distinguished by their meanings, even when you do not see them written down. Because each homophone in a pair has a different meaning, the words around a homophone in a sentence will indicate which homophone is being used. If the homophones are different parts of speech (and many of them are) the position of the word in the sentence will also help. You will see why this is true when you read the following questions and responses.

Homophones (meaning)	Examples
ad (advertisement)	Did you see this ad in the paper?
add (addition)	Did you add these numbers correctly?
allowed (permitted)	No one is allowed in the building after dark.
aloud (audible)	No one was willing to read aloud to the group.
band (orchestra)	The band gave a concert in the park.
banned (prohibited)	Dogs without leashes are banned from the park.
board (leaders of a firm)	The board is meeting in the conference room.
bored (uninterested)	Everyone got bored at the meeting.
cents (money)	It costs 50 cents to ride the bus.
sense (intelligence)	It makes sense to ride the bus.
sight (ability to see)	People's sight tends to change as they age.
site (location)	That site had three houses on it over the years.
fair (just, honest)	The decision should be fair for everyone.
fare (cost)	The fare has increased for everyone.
find (discover)	People sometimes find lost items when they are not looking for them.
fined (given a penalty)	People can be fined for crossing the street without a signal.

22

guessed (supposed)	Mr. Ho guessed that Mr. Yoder was visiting.
guest (visitor)	Mr. Ho knew that Mr. Yoder was our guest.
higher (above)	We must hang the banner higher so everyone can see it.
hire (employ)	We must hire more employees.
knew (past tense of *know*)	He knew where to buy a computer.
new (opposite of old)	He just bought a new computer.
mail (send by post)	The mail was delivered at 11:00.
male (opposite of female)	The person who delivered the package was male.
meat (food)	I don't eat much meat at lunch.
meet (to get acquainted with or spend time with someone)	I meet her every day for lunch.
overseas (abroad)	Ms. Dechaine is working on a project overseas.
oversees (supervises)	Ms. Dechaine oversees a new project at work.
pear (fruit)	I need to buy a pear at the vegetable store.
pair (two)	I need to buy a new pair of shoes.
road (street)	The country road needed to be repaired.
rode (past tense of *ride*)	He rode into the country to look at the scenery.
sale (low prices)	Mr. Sulka bought his boat on sale.
sail (travel by boat)	Mr. Sulka likes to sail his boat on weekends.
some (part)	You should get some help with those numbers.
sum (total of addition)	Your sum does not match the total.
suite (group of rooms of offices)	Please bring them to suite 110.
sweet (taste of sugar)	Please bring me something sweet.
wear (dress in)	What should I wear to the party?
where (tells place)	Where is the party taking place?
weigh (number of pounds)	I don't want to tell the doctor what I weigh.
way (direction)	I don't know the way to the doctor's office.
week (seven days)	She has been ill for a week.
weak (lack of strength)	She has been weak since her illness.

Exercises p 225

Read the following questions and responses. Circle the correct answer, and circle the homophones. This will help you see how homophones can be distinguished by their meanings.

1. You will hear: Do you know where we are to meet?
   (A) In the conference center.
   (B) Wear a suit.
   (C) I don't want meat.

2. You will hear: Where can I hire a guide?
   (A) I can make it lower.
   (B) Go to the tourist agency across the street.
   (C) It won't go higher.

3. You will hear: What's the total sum?
   (A) It's over a thousand.
   (B) We can't omit any of it.
   (C) Some of us are loyal.

4. You will hear: Did they raise the fare?
   (A) Yes. It costs 50 cents more.
   (B) It's not fair to anyone.
   (C) They razed the building.

5. You will hear: Do you prefer an aisle seat or a window seat for your guest?
   (A) He guessed correctly.
   (B) I'll see.
   (C) It doesn't matter.

AVOID THE TRAP!

There are words related to a homophone—like synonyms or antonyms—that could be used in the answer.

Example: The boat was at full sail.

I paid full price for the merchandise. (I didn't get it on sale.)

Skill 3: Recognizing Negative Meaning

Negation refers to making the meaning of a statement negative. You must determine whether the meaning of the statement you hear is positive or negative.

Sample TOEIC Question

You will hear: Why didn't the presentation start on time?

You will also hear: (A) That clock is never wrong.
(B) Nobody was late for the presentation.
(C) The microphone was not functioning.

Choice (C), *The microphone was not functioning*, is the best explanation for the presentation not starting on time.

Choice (A) is incorrect because *is never wrong* means *is always correct*. This does not explain why the presentation did not start on time. Choice (B) is incorrect because *Nobody was late* means *everyone was on time*. This does not explain why the presentation did not start on time.

Skill Focus

Usually, English sentences have only one negative word. Verbs are negative when they are used with the negative word *not*. Other words indicate other negative ideas (for example, *nobody* means *no people*). Review the negative expressions below. Remember that these expressions make the meaning of the sentence negative.

Negative Expressions

not	not all	never	nor	not at all	no one
no	neither	not ever	nobody		

Choose some positive statements from this book. Rewrite them so their meanings are negative.

Exercises 🔑 p 225

Circle the letter of the choice that matches the meaning of the sentence. This will help you understand the meanings of negative sentences.

1. There's no one in the office.
   (A) Only one person is there.
   (B) Nobody is there.

2. Neither Yoshi nor I knows.
   (A) We don't know.
   (B) I know.

3. He's not at all happy.
   (A) He's unhappy.
   (B) He's not unhappy.

4. She didn't recognize anybody.
   (A) She didn't recognize all the people.
   (B) She recognized no one at all.

5. Not all members participated.
   (A) Some members participated.
   (B) No one participated.

Practice: Part II 🔑 p 225 📼 p 204

You will hear a question spoken in English, followed by three responses. Listen carefully to what the speakers say. Choose the best response to each question.

1. Mark your answer on your answer sheet.

2. Mark your answer on your answer sheet.

3. Mark your answer on your answer sheet.

4. Mark your answer on your answer sheet.

5. Mark your answer on your answer sheet.

6. Mark your answer on your answer sheet.

7. Mark your answer on your answer sheet.

8. Mark your answer on your answer sheet.

9. Mark your answer on your answer sheet.

10. Mark your answer on your answer sheet.

Part III: Short Conversations

In Part III of the TOEIC test, you will hear 30 short conversations. The conversations are between two people. Listen to the conversations carefully. You will hear each conversation only once.

Then, in your test book, you will read a question about each conversation. You will also read four answer choices. Choose the best answer to the question. You will have eight seconds to answer each question.

Sample TOEIC Question

You will hear: *Man*   How was your trip to Manila?

             Woman I thought the tour of the port was most interesting.

             Man   They say it's one of the most active shipping centers in Asia.

You will read: What was interesting?

             (A) The harbor.

             (B) The airport.

             (C) The highway.

             (D) The tourist bus.

Choice (A), *The harbor*, is the best answer to the question *What was interesting?* This question is asking for specific information. There are three clues to help you make the correct answer choice. It's important to know the synonyms *port* and *harbor* to understand that the contraction *it's* refers to *port*. *Shipping* is a word related to *port*.

Choice (B) is incorrect because it confuses the similar sounds *port* and *airport*. Choice (C) is incorrect because although there is often a connection between a *trip* and a *highway*, it is not found in this conversation. Choice (D) is incorrect because although you hear *the tour of the port*, it confuses *the tour* with *tour*(ist) *bus*.

Types of Questions

In Part III of the TOEIC test, as in many parts of the TOEIC test, the questions ask either about the general idea of the conversation, or for specific information from the conversation. These questions have three common characteristics.

Characteristics	Examples
The questions are often very short.	Who is talking? Where are they?
The questions often ask for information. (The first words may be Wh- words)	When is the man's vacation? What does the client want?
The questions are often in the simple present or the present continuous tense.	Where are they going? Why is she changing her job?

Test Tips

You can improve your score on Part III of the TOEIC test by focusing on:

- listening for the main idea
- understanding Wh- questions
- understanding modal verbs

Knowing these characteristics will help you to predict the type of questions you might see. This will help you find the answer more quickly.

Skill 1: Listening for the Main Idea

On Part III of the TOEIC test, you may be asked questions about the main idea of the conversation. To answer these questions, you must focus on the whole conversation, not just part of the conversation.

Sample TOEIC Question

Woman   What seems to be the trouble?
Man   My car won't start.
Woman   There's a garage around the corner that has a very good mechanic.

What is the problem?
(A) He is lost.
(B) He needs a job.
(C) The car needs repair.
(D) The garage is closed.

Choice (C) is the correct answer. *His car won't start* means something is wrong with it and it needs to be repaired.

Choice (A) incorrectly infers that the man is lost from the fact that the woman gives him directions to a garage. Choice (B) confuses the idea of needing a job with the mention of a profession, a mechanic. Choice (D) is probably incorrect. Since the woman suggests the garage as a solution, she expects it to be open and helping motorists.

Skill Focus

It is very helpful to distinguish questions that ask for main ideas from other types of questions. If you know you have to answer a main idea question, you will know what kind of information to listen for. Review the examples below, which show some common main idea questions.

What are the speakers planning to do?
Where are the speakers?
What is the man going to do?
Where does this conversation take place?
What are the speakers talking about?

Exercises 🔑 p 226

Read the conversations below. Then, read questions (A) and (B). Circle the question that asks about the main idea. Then, think what the answer to the main idea question might be. This will help you identify the main idea of conversations.

1. *Man*   I have to stop by the Service Department to check an order.
   Woman   What's the trouble?
   Man   This order was delivered two weeks late.

   Which question asks the main idea?
   (A) How late was the order?
   (B) What is the man going to do?

2. *Woman*   Don't forget to stress the importance of design.
   Man   I won't. It's an important part of my presentation.
   Woman   And remember to illustrate your speech with good graphics.

   Which question asks the main idea?
   (A) What are the speakers talking about?
   (B) Why should the man use graphics?

3. *Woman*   She has ten years' experience, and she works well with people.
   Man   Yes. Let's recommend her for the job.
   Woman   I agree. We need her skills immediately.

   Which question asks the main idea?
   (A) What are the speakers planning to do?
   (B) How much experience does the woman have?

4. *Man*   Will we get what we want on this contract?
   Woman   Probably not. We disagree on some terms.
   Man   Let's do the best we can.

   Which question asks the main idea?
   (A) What do the speakers disagree on?
   (B) What are the speakers discussing?

5. *Woman*   Do you have exercise facilities at this hotel?
   Man   No, but we offer guests a courtesy pass for the gym next door.
   Woman   Great. I'd like one for tonight, please.

   Which question asks the main idea?
   (A) What is the woman inquiring about?
   (B) How many passes does the woman request?

Skill 2: Understanding Wh- Questions

On Part III of the TOEIC test, you may be asked information questions. Many information questions start with Wh- words. To answer information questions, focus on the meaning of the Wh- words: *What? Why? Who? Where? When? How much? How long?* These types of questions ask for either the main idea of the conversation or specific information from the conversation. These are examples of Wh- questions:

- What is Mr. Rozicer angry about?
- What are the men discussing?
- Who are the speakers talking about?
- Why is the man going by train?

Sample TOEIC Question

You will hear: *Woman*   I have tickets for the one o'clock flight.

            Man   I'm sorry. That flight has been delayed for two hours.

          Woman   Oh, no. That means I have a long wait.

You will read: How long has the flight been delayed?

           (A) Until one o'clock.

           (B) Until two o'clock.

           (C) For two hours.

           (D) For three hours.

Choice (C) is the correct answer. The man says the flight has been delayed for two hours.

Choice (A) gives the time that the flight was scheduled to leave. Choice (B) confuses *at two o'clock* with *for two hours*. Choice (D) confuses the time the flight will leave, *three o'clock*, with *three hours*. The plane was to leave at one o'clock, but there is a two hour delay. Now it will depart at three o'clock.

Skill Focus

Wh- words refer to specific information. Knowing how information is expressed by Wh-words helps you understand the meaning of Wh- questions. Read each statement below. Notice how each statement is changed into a Wh- question.

Statements	Wh- Questions
Ms. Gulbrandsen left a message.	Who left a message?
We should discuss the latest marketing report.	What should we discuss?
The project is due by 12 noon on the eighteenth.	When is the project due?
The office supply store is on State Street.	Where is the office supply store?
The picnic is postponed because it is raining.	Why is the picnic postponed?
You turn the machine on by pressing this button.	How do you turn this machine on?
I stayed at the party for three hours.	How long did you stay at the party?
My son is almost as tall as I am.	How tall is your son?

Exercises ⚷ p 226

Read each question below. Then circle the Wh- word that fits the meaning of the question. This will help you focus on the meaning of Wh- questions.

1. _____ will he look into the problem?
   (A) What
   (B) When

2. _____ are they discussing?
   (A) What
   (B) Where

3. _____ wasn't the shipment sent?
   (A) Why
   (B) Which

4. _____ is the man talking to?
   (A) Where
   (B) Who

5. _____ do I get to the Art Museum?
   (A) Where
   (B) How

Skill 3: Understanding Modal Verbs

In Part III of the TOEIC test, there are questions that use modal verbs: *should, can, could, will, may, might, must*. To answer these questions, focus on the meaning of the modals. A modal can express necessity, ability, possiblity, obligation, willingness, or intention. Knowing the meaning of the modal can help you understand the purpose of the conversation.

Sample TOEIC Question

You will hear: Woman   I have to catch a plane at six o'clock.
           Man   With this traffic jam, we can't get to the airport on time.
           Woman   I guess I'll have to take a later flight.

You will read: What must the woman do?
            (A) Catch a six o'clock flight.
            (B) Get out of the traffic jam.
            (C) Find a taxi.
            (D) Take a later flight.

Choice (D), *Take a later flight*, is the correct answer. The modal verb *must* indicates necessity. It is necessary for the woman to take a later flight because she will miss the six o'clock flight.

Choice (A) is incorrect because the woman cannot get to the airport in time for her six o'clock flight. Choice (B) is incorrect because it is usually not possible to get out of traffic jams once you are in them. Choice (C) is incorrect because the woman probably would not be able to find a taxi in a traffic jam, and she already has transportation. A taxi probably wouldn't be any faster. Notice that the ideas are explained by using *can* (*cannot*), the modal verb that expresses possibility.

Skill Focus

Modal verbs convey ideas about obligation and possibility. Because modal verbs are auxiliary verbs, they are used with main verbs. Sometimes the main verb can be deleted, but only if it is clearly understood (as in answer to Yes/No questions).

Modal Verbs	Meanings	Examples
can, could	ability, permission, or possibility	Can we meet in the small conference room? This loose screw could have been the problem.
will, would	intention or probability	Will you type this letter for me? On the train, we would see more scenery.
should	obligation or intention	We should mail this letter before the post office closes.
must	obligation or necessity	I must give Mr. Platig this urgent message.
may, might	possibility	I may be able to leave early today. Our company might bid on the contract.

Exercises 🔑 p 226

Read the conversation then circle the best response. This will help you focus on the meaning of the modals in questions on the TOEIC test.

1. *Woman* There are numerous new projects starting this spring.
 Man Our staff is working very hard now.
 Woman Let's think about hiring more staff.

 What should the speakers do?
 (A) Start new projects.
 (B) Plan more projects.
 (C) Hire more staff.
 (D) Work harder.

2. *Man* We need to submit the proposal by Monday.
 Woman I'll ask Mina to help research the case.
 Man Mina works in marketing. She can't move over to research.

 Why can't Mina help?
 (A) She has to submit the proposal by Monday.
 (B) She doesn't work in research.
 (C) She doesn't know the facts.
 (D) She hasn't been asked.

3. *Woman* Would you like to see the dessert list?
 Man Yes, please. And could you tell me where the telephone is?
 Woman Of course. It's to the left of the doorway.

 What will the woman do?
 (A) Give him the dessert list.
 (B) Leave the restaurant.
 (C) Make a telephone call.
 (D) Eat dinner.

4. *Man* Did you meet with the employees yesterday?
 Woman Yes. They are unhappy with the terms of the contract.
 Man That means they may walk off the job.

 What might happen?
 (A) The employees might be unhappy.
 (B) The woman might meet with the employees.
 (C) The employees might go for a walk.
 (D) There might be a strike.

5. *Woman* We have to trace last week's shipment. It was lost in transit.
 Man Did you check the paperwork?
 Woman Yes, and everything is in order.

 What must the speakers do?
 (A) Find the shipment.
 (B) Check the paperwork.
 (C) Lose the transfer.
 (D) Place an order.

Practice: Part III 🔑 p 226 📼 p 205

You will hear a conversation between two people. In your book, you will read a question about each conversation, followed by four answers. Choose the best answer to each question.

1. What are the speakers discussing?
   (A) A future meeting.
   (B) Wednesday's meeting.
   (C) An overseas meeting.
   (D) The employees' schedules.

2. Where does this conversation take place?
   (A) In an elevator.
   (B) At a receptionist's desk.
   (C) On the telephone.
   (D) In a parking lot.

3. How many questions were there?
   (A) Eight.
   (B) None.
   (C) Approximately twelve.
   (D) About five.

4. How does Mr. Ling feel about the deal?
   (A) He's unhappy.
   (B) He's uncertain.
   (C) He's confident.
   (D) He's mistaken.

5. What position does the woman want?
   (A) Secretary.
   (B) Office worker.
   (C) Receptionist.
   (D) Production manager.

6. What's the woman's opinion?
   (A) His department has failed.
   (B) The promotions hurt his department.
   (C) The schedules should be changed.
   (D) IIis department is successful.

7. What are the speakers discussing?
   (A) A problem.
   (B) A date.
   (C) A vacation.
   (D) A holiday.

8. What are the speakers planning to do?
   (A) Hand out paychecks.
   (B) Offer dessert.
   (C) Reward the employees.
   (D) Discuss morals.

9. What's the woman going to do?
   (A) Speak with the customer every day.
   (B) Call the customer.
   (C) Discuss the problem with the customer.
   (D) Make a telephone call.

10. What is the man's problem?
    (A) He is tall.
    (B) He has no appetite.
    (C) He's in a crowded room.
    (D) He doesn't know what to order.

Part IV: Short Talks

In Part IV of the TOEIC test, you will listen to short talks. These are not conversations. There are talks on the weather, advertisements, recorded announcements, etc. There is only one speaker. Each talk will be spoken only once. Listen carefully because the talk is not written out.

In your test book, you will find two or three questions about the talk. You will also read four answer choices. Choose the best answer to the question. There are 20 questions in Part IV. You will have eight seconds to answer each question.

Sample TOEIC Question

You will hear: In five minutes, for one hour only, women's coats and hats go on sale in our fifth-floor Better Fashions department. All merchandise is reduced by 25 to 40 percent. Not all styles in all sizes, but an outstanding selection nonetheless.

You will hear: When does the sale begin?

You will read: (A) In five minutes.
(B) In one hour.
(C) At 2:45.
(D) Tomorrow.

Choice (A) is the correct answer. The announcement states that the sale will begin in five minutes.

Choice (B) is incorrect because, although the phrase *In one hour* is grammatically correct, it confuses the meaning with *for one hour*. Choice (C) is incorrect because it confuses the similar sounding phrase *to forty* (percent) with *two forty-five*. Choice (D) is incorrect because although *tomorrow* could be a logical answer choice to a Wh- question that begins with *When*, there is no mention of *tomorrow* in the short talk.

Types of Questions

In Part IV, you may be asked questions about facts. Examples of factual questions are:

● What is going on sale?
● Who is attending the meeting?
● When does the increase go into effect?

These questions have three common characteristics.

Characteristics	Examples
The questions often begin with a Wh- word.	Who was disturbed? The passengers.
The questions are often in the present continuous tense.	What are the people doing? They're paying their bill.
The answers to the questions are usually short; the answer choices are made up of two to five words.	When is the ferry leaving? At noon.

Test Tips

You can improve your score on Part IV by:

● listening for answers to Wh- questions
● following the talk and questions in order
● making assumptions

Skill 1: Listening for Answers to Wh- Questions

As you listen to the short talks in Part IV, keep in mind the Wh- words. The answers to these questions are the specific facts found in the short talks.

Sample TOEIC Question

May I have your attention, please. Because our flight today is fully booked, we must require that passengers limit their carry-on items to one per person. If you have more than one carry-on item, please report to the counter now so that attendants may check your extra bags.

Who should report to the counter?
(A) Passengers who want to read.
(B) Passengers with two bags.
(C) Parents traveling with children.
(D) Attendants who are ready to leave.

Choice (B) is the correct answer. Passengers with more than one carry-on item should report to the counter. The announcement states that carry-on bags will be limited to one per person.

Choice (A) incorrectly associates *fully booked* with *read*. Choice (C) is a group of passengers with special concerns, but they are not mentioned here. Choice (D) is incorrect because the attendants are checking bags, not leaving work.

Skill Focus

Wh- question words appear in Parts II, III, IV, and VII of the TOEIC test. They tell you not only that specific information is required, but what kind of information to look for. Knowing what kind of information will answer each Wh- question word will help you listen for the right information. Review the common Wh- words below and the answer types they are associated with.

Wh- Words	Possible Answer Types	Examples
Who	name, title, identification	Ms. Engle, the manager, the man in the gray cap
What	object, idea, event	the computer, the manufacturing process, the theory, the banquet
When	time, day, month, year	1:00 on Tuesday, in the afternoon, in April, on the fifteenth, in 1996
Where	place, location	in the park, on the table, in a meeting
Why	reason, explanation	because the copier is broken, so that he will know how to get here
How	method, means, way	pull this handle, follow these directions, do this first
How + adj	length of object or time	11 inches, 3 hours
How + adv	quantity	4 pints, enough, some for everybody

Exercises 🔑 p 227

Circle the best response to each question. This will help you listen for information on the TOEIC test that answers Wh- words.

<u>Questions 1–2</u> refer to the following introduction.

I'd like to present Bob Atwood, the General Manager of Stansfield Company. We all know Stansfield Company as a compact disc manufacturing firm located outside of Sydney, Australia. Mr. Atwood has been on our Board of Directors for over ten years. We are honored to have Bob assigned here as consultant.

1. Who is being introduced?
    (A) Mr. Atwood.
    (B) Mr. Stansfield.
    (C) Sydney, Australia.
    (D) Stansfield Company.

2. Why is he assigned here?
    (A) He is the General Manager.
    (B) He is on the Board of Directors.
    (C) He wanted a vacation.
    (D) He is serving as a consultant.

<u>Questions 3–5</u> refer to the following advertisement.

How do you know which mutual fund to invest in this year? There are over three thousand mutual funds to choose from. If you can't stand the confusion, come to the trained experts at Townsend Fund for investment advice. There are four convenient Townsend locations to meet your needs. For over 25 years, the people of Townsend Fund have been successful at making your money work for you.

3. What kind of advisors does Townsend Fund have?
    (A) Trained.
    (B) Confused.
    (C) Busy.
    (D) Rich.

4. How many locations does Townsend have?
    (A) One.
    (B) Three.
    (C) Four.
    (D) Five.

5. How long has Townsend Fund been in existence?
    (A) A year.
    (B) A decade.
    (C) A quarter of a century.
    (D) A century.

Skill 2: Following the Questions Chronologically

In Part IV of the TOEIC test, try to skim the questions quickly before the talk begins. The questions are in the same order as the information presented in the talk. When the talk begins, go back to the first question for the talk. You can follow the talk by following the questions.

Sample TOEIC Question

Questions 1–3 refer to the following bulletin.

Kakuyama Parking Company announces an increase in the charges for monthly parking spaces in its lot. The changes will not go into effect until the first day of July of this year. The new fee will reflect a 7 percent increase on your current parking rate.

1. What kind of company is making the announcement?
   (A) Gardening.
   (B) Parking.
   (C) Car sales.
   (D) Banking.

2. When will the new rate start?
   (A) Immediately.
   (B) Next month.
   (C) July 1.
   (D) Next year.

3. How much will the increase be?
   (A) One percent.
   (B) Seven percent.
   (C) Seventeen percent.
   (D) Seventy percent.

1. Choice (B) is the correct answer. Kakuyama is a *parking* company.
   Choice (A) is not related to this talk. Choice (C), *car sales*, is incorrectly associated with the words *car*, *park*, *lot*, *rates*, and *increase*. Choice (D), *banking*, is incorrectly associated with the words *fee*, *rate*, *increase*, and *7 percent*.

2. Choice (C) is the correct answer. The announcement says the increase will start on the first day of July of this year.
   Choices (A), (B), and (D) are all contradicted by *the first day of July of this year*. For Choice (B), we CANNOT assume that next month is July.

3. Choice (B) is the correct answer. The announcement says the increase reflects a 7 percent increase on current rates.
   Choice (A) is not mentioned in any context. Choices (C) and (D) confuse *seven* with *seventeen* and *seventy* because of the similar sounds.

Skill Focus

Most of the talks will start out with general information and move on to specific information. Sometimes there may be a result or prediction at the end. The questions will follow this pattern, too. Knowing when to expect different kinds of questions can make it easier to follow the information in a talk. Review the questions below to see how questions can follow chronological order.

Question Type	Question	Listen for	Examples
General	Who is making this announcement? Where is this talk taking place? What is the discussion about?	the people or the setting a problem, object, or idea	teachers speak in classrooms; business people speak in meetings meeting a deadline, a menu, a marketing strategy
Specific	How much is the increase? When is it due?	answers to Wh- words	ten dollars next Friday
Result or Prediction	What will happen next? How will they probably solve the problem?	a logical or probable outcome	They will pay the bill. They will return the broken coffeemaker to the store.

Exercises 🔑 p 227

Circle the best answer for the questions below. This will help you follow the chronology of the short talks on the TOEIC test.

<u>Questions 1–2</u> refer to the following speech.

Welcome to our semiannual sales meeting, everyone. After lunch and a brief business meeting, a team from our Research and Development Department will join us and demonstrate our newest products. Each of you will have the chance to try samples from our new line and ask questions of the team. Now please help yourselves to the delicious buffet that has been set up in the adjoining dining room.

1. Who is attending the meeting?
   (A) Sales personnel.
   (B) Food Service staff.
   (C) Bank executives.
   (D) Factory workers.

2. What will people do first?
   (A) Try out some new products.
   (B) Eat a meal.
   (C) Visit the Research Department.
   (D) Discuss salaries.

Questions 3–5 refer to the following recorded message.

Thank you for calling Buffington's, the dependable retail store. Our hours are Monday through Saturday, nine o'clock to six o'clock. On Sundays, our hours are one o'clock to six o'clock. If you know the extension of the person you want to talk to, press the last three digits of the extension. If you want Customer Service, press two now. If you need an operator, stay on the line.

3. What is Buffington's?
   (A) A shopping mall.
   (B) A repair shop.
   (C) A store.
   (D) A bank.

4. When is Buffington's open?
   (A) Monday through Friday.
   (B) Monday through Saturday.
   (C) Saturday and Sunday only.
   (D) Every day.

5. What number do you press for Customer Service?
   (A) One.
   (B) Two.
   (C) Six.
   (D) Nine.

Skill 3: Making Assumptions

In Part IV of the TOEIC test, you may be asked questions for which you must make assumptions. These questions will not be about facts, but about assumptions.

Sample TOEIC Question

If you are ambitious and want to move ahead in your career, or if you want to enter a new field of business, we guarantee that you will gain a competitive edge by attending our seminars on professional development. The seminars are offered at many locations in the metropolitan area, at convenient evening hours. Choose the entire program of seminars, or select only the areas that interest you.

Who will be interested in this advertisement?

(A) Teachers.
(B) Farmers.
(C) Athletes.
(D) Business people.

Choice (D) is the correct answer. The seminars are for those interested in new fields of business and in professional development. They would probably work in the city during the day. All these ideas are associated with business.

Choice (A) makes an assumption about who will be giving the seminars, not who will be taking them. Choice (B) incorrectly interprets *new field*. Choice (C) draws an incorrect assumption from the phrase *competitive edge*.

Skill Focus

Questions about assumptions make you think about what is probable, based on the information in the talk. Questions about assumptions are often Wh- questions that ask about ideas or impressions conveyed in the passage. Review the questions below. They are examples of common questions about assumptions.

What will happen next?
Who is the intended audience?
What happened before?
What is the probable result?

Exercises 🔑 p 227

Make assumptions in response to the questions below, based on the information in the passage. This will help you make assumptions on the TOEIC test.

Questions 1–2 refer to the following report.

Those of you who are driving into the city from the northeast, please take notice that, because of highway construction on Route 312, traffic will be closed in the southbound lane at 9:30 tomorrow morning. That's Route 312, tomorrow morning at 9:30. You may want to find another route into the city tomorrow morning.

1. Who is this report for?
   (A) Commuters driving into work.
   (B) Construction workers.
   (C) Subway riders.
   (D) Joggers.

2. What is the announcer trying to prevent?
   (A) Highway construction.
   (B) A traffic jam tomorrow.
   (C) Train delays.
   (D) Accidents.

Questions 3–5 refer to the following talk.

We asked your customers about their favorite vacations. The majority said they preferred to travel in the months between June and September. Very few customers said they preferred to take vacations between the months of November and February. We think you could increase your business by offering more discounts during those low-activity months.

3. Who is the audience?
   (A) Travel agents.
   (B) Vacationers.
   (C) Students.
   (D) Pilots.

4. What is the speaker doing?
   (A) Giving advice.
   (B) Explaining a process.
   (C) Showing pictures.
   (D) Demonstrating a product.

5. What might happen next?
   (A) Vacations in November will increase.
   (B) The audience will ask questions.
   (C) Listeners will purchase tickets.
   (D) Customers will ask for discounts.

Practice: Part IV ⌗══ p 227 ▭ p 205

You will hear a short talk. In your book, you will read one or more questions about each short talk, followed by four answers. Choose the best answer to each question.

1. What kind of injury is mentioned?
    (A) Wrist injuries.
    (B) Injuries to the mouse.
    (C) Keyboard injuries.
    (D) Monitor problems.

2. What products are offered?
    (A) Computer operators.
    (B) Work habits.
    (C) Computer accessories.
    (D) Catalogs.

3. Who is the audience for this advertisement?
    (A) Computer operators.
    (B) Computer repairpersons.
    (C) Catalog salespersons.
    (D) Producers.

4. When will the event be held?
    (A) In Honolulu.
    (B) In September.
    (C) Last year.
    (D) For two weeks.

5. How many timeshares were sold last year?
    (A) Fifty percent.
    (B) Almost one hundred.
    (C) Five hundred.
    (D) Ten thousand.

Part V: Incomplete Sentences

Part V of the TOEIC tests your knowledge of both vocabulary and grammar. It consists of 40 incomplete sentences. Under each sentence, you will see four words or phrases, marked (A), (B), (C), and (D). You should choose the best word or phrase to complete the sentence.

Try not to spend more than 30 seconds per question. You will have only 75 minutes for all of Parts V, VI, and VII so you will want to use your time wisely.

Sample TOEIC Question

Before he joined our firm, Mr. Guzman _____ Maltex Corporation.
(A) was belonging to
(B) worked
(C) served
(D) was employed by

Choice (D) is the correct answer. The sentence should read, *Before he joined our firm, Mr. Guzman was employed by Maltex Corporation. Was employed by Maltex Corporation* is in the passive voice. It means the same thing as *Maltex Corporation employed Mr. Guzman.*

Choice (A) is incorrect because the verb, *belong*, does not indicate employment. In addition, stative verbs like *belong* are rarely used in the continuous form. Choice (B) is incorrect because the verb, *work*, is not followed by a preposition such as *worked at* or *worked for.* Choice (C) is not correct because the verb, *serve*, may be used with job positions, *served as marketing director*, but not with company names.

Test Tips

You can improve your score on Part V by:
- understanding prefixes
- understanding suffixes
- recognizing time markers
- understanding the passive voice
- identifying the correct prepositions
- using relative pronouns

Skill 1: Understanding Prefixes

On Part V, your knowledge of the meanings of prefixes will help you choose the word or phrase that matches the meaning of the sentence. A prefix is a word part that is added to the front of a word to change the meaning of the word.

Sample TOEIC Question

We should have that document on file, but it seems to have been _____.
(A) misplaced
(B) displaced
(C) replaced
(D) placed

Choice (A) is the correct answer. The sentence should read, *We should have that document on file, but it seems to have been misplaced.* The coordinating conjunction *but* adds contrasting information to the first part of the sentence. You should understand that the document is not on file. The prefix *mis-* adds a negative meaning to *place*. The document was *not placed* in the proper place; consequently it is not on file.

Choice (B) is incorrect because the prefix *dis-* means *lack of*; it usually refers to people. Choice (C) is incorrect because the prefix *re-* means *again*. Choice (D) is incorrect because *placed* should be followed by a location, *placed in the wrong file.*

Skill Focus

Prefixes increase vocabulary very efficiently, because they are a combination of a word part and a word whose meanings are already known. You can use this information to understand words that you have not seen before. Review the following list of common prefixes and their meanings. Then, look at the examples of words formed with the prefix. Think what the word probably means.

Prefix	Meaning	Examples
1. after-	after	afternoon, aftermath, afterward
2. ante-	before or in front of	antedate, antechamber, antecedent
3. anti-	against	antisocial, antibiotic, antidote
4. auto-	by itself or self	automobile, automatic, autobiography
5. bene-	good	benefit, beneficial, benign
6. bi-, bin-	two	bifocal, bicycle, binoculars
7. circu-	around	circulate, circular, circus
8. co-, col-	together	cooperate, coworker, collect
9. contra-	against	contradict, contrary, contrast
10. counter-	opposite	counteract, counterfeit, counterpart
11. dis-	lack of	disagree, disgrace, dishonest

Prefix	Meaning	Examples
12. hyper-	excessive	hypercritical, hyperbole, hypersensitive
13. hypo-	too little or beneath	hypoactive, hypodermic, hypoglycemia
14. il-	not	illogical, illegal, illegible
15. in-	not	incorrect, inhumane, inability
16. inter-	among or between	international, interaction, interfere
17. ir-	not	irresponsible, irregular, irrelevant
18. mal-	bad or wrong	malfunction, malpractice, malnourished
19. mis-	bad or wrong	misfortune, mistake, misplace
20. multi-	many or much	multilingual, multiple, multinational
21. omni-	all	omniscient, omnivorous, omnipotent
22. over-	too much	overactive, overflow, overdraw
23. poly-	many	polyglot, polygon, polytechnic
24. post-	after	postpone, postpaid, postscript
25. pre-	before	prefix, prefer, prehistoric
26. pro-	before or in favor of	prologue, procedure, pronoun
27. re-	again	rewrite, repeat, replace

Exercises 🔑 p 228

Classify prefixes by meaning. This will help you choose the word that matches the context on the TOEIC test.

1. Write eight prefixes from the list above that express a negative meaning.

_____   _____   _____   _____

_____   _____   _____   _____

2. Write two prefixes from the list above that express a positive meaning.

_____   _____

3. Write two prefixes from the list above that express a quantity.

_____   _____

4. Write four prefixes from the list above that express time.

_____   _____

_____   _____

AVOID THE TRAP!

Some prefixes look almost the same, but their meanings are different.

anti-
anti- means *against*

Example: anti-smoking means against smoking

ante-
ante- means *in front of*

Example: anteroom means a small room in front of a larger room

Skill 2: Understanding Suffixes

On Part V, your knowledge of suffixes will help you choose the word or phrase that matches the meaning of the sentence. A suffix is a word part that is added to the end of a word. Many suffixes change the part of speech of the word. Suffixes can help you determine whether the word is a noun, adjective, verb, or adverb. Suffixes can sometimes add meaning, too.

Sample TOEIC Question

Today office managers expect accuracy, efficiency, and _____ from those they supervise.
(A) dedication
(B) dedicated
(C) dedicatedly
(D) dedicate

Choice (A) is the correct answer. The sentence should read, *Today office managers expect accuracy, efficiency, and dedication from those they supervise.* The first two words, *accuracy* and *efficiency*, are nouns. We need to choose the same part of speech, a noun form, to complete the list. The suffix -*ation* indicates a noun. Choice (A), *dedication*, is the noun form of the verb *to dedicate*.

Choice (B) is incorrect because the suffix -*ed* indicates an adjective. Choice (C) is incorrect because the suffix -*ly* indicates an adverb. Choice (D) is incorrect because the word *dedicate* is a verb form.

Skill Focus

Suffixes increase vocabulary because they change the part of speech of a word. This means that you can turn the same idea into a noun, verb, adjective or adverb. You can use this information to understand words that you have not seen before. Review the following list of common suffixes and their meanings. Then, look at the examples of words formed with the suffix. Think what the word probably means.

Suffix	Meaning	Part of Speech	Examples
1. -al	relating to	adjective	influential, provincial, financial
2. -ance	state or quality of	noun	resistance, acceptance, extravagance
3. -ancy	state or quality of	noun	vacancy, pregnancy, redundancy
4. -ary	relating to	adjective	primary, secondary, fiduciary
5. -ate	to make	verb	activate, reciprocate, elevate
6. -ation, -tion	state or quality of	noun	inspiration, separation, deviation
7. -en	to make	verb	shorten, lengthen, fatten
8. -ency	state or quality of	noun	expediency, leniency, latency
9. -fy	to make	verb	beautify, clarify, specify
10. -hood	state or quality of	noun	childhood, adulthood, manhood

Suffix	Meaning	Part of Speech	Examples
11. -ic	relating to	adjective	economic, scientific, scenic
12. -ity	state or quality of	noun	authenticity, publicity, civility
13. -ize	to cause to become	verb	computerize, modernize, legalize
14. -ly	in the manner of at or intervals of	adverb	clearly, yearly, ordinarily
15. -ment	process or state of	noun	enjoyment, procurement, experiment
16. -ness	state or quality of	noun	kindness, darkness, likeness
17. -ous	full of	adjective	nervous, anxious, jealous
18. -ship	state or quality of	noun	friendship, relationship, kinship

Exercises ⊙━ p 228

Classify these suffixes by parts of speech. This will help you choose the part of speech that matches the context of a sentence on the TOEIC test.

1. Write eight suffixes from the list above that indicate noun forms.

_____   _____   _____   _____

_____   _____   _____   _____

2. Write four suffixes from the list above that indicate adjective forms.

_____   _____

_____   _____

3. Write one suffix from the list above that indicates an adverb form.

_____

4. Write four suffixes from the list above that indicate a verb form.

_____   _____   _____   _____

AVOID THE TRAP!

Some suffixes are spelled exactly the same, but represent different parts of speech.

-*ly* with adverb: When it is added to *week*, it becomes *weekly*. This is an adverb which means *every week*.

-*ly* with adjective: When it is added to *love*, it becomes *lovely*. This is an adjective which means *having pleasing qualities*.

Skill 3: Recognizing Time Markers

On Part V, your knowledge of time markers will help you choose the verb tense that matches the context of the sentence. Time markers are words that reflect the time of the verb.

Sample TOEIC Question

We usually _____ that brand available.
(A) has had
(B) have been having
(C) have
(D) are having

Choice (C) is the correct answer. The sentence should read, *We usually have that brand available.* The word *usually* is a time marker. It is an adverb of frequency that suggests habit. The verb tense should suggest habitual action.

Choice (A) is incorrect for two reasons: first, the present perfect tense does not carry the habitual idea of *usually*; and second, the subject *We* is a plural pronoun which does not agree in number with the singular verb, *has had.* Choices (B) and (D) are incorrect because *have* is rarely used in the continuous form when it indicates possession.

Skill Focus

Time markers can indicate different kinds of time. Some indicate periods of time, others indicate points of time, and still others indicate recurring time—things that happen repeatedly. This means that different kinds of time markers answer different kinds of time questions. Review the time markers below. Notice which kind of time question the different time markers answer.

Time Markers that Answer

When?	How long?	How often?
ago	since	usually
already	for	generally
before	until	often
after		rarely
during		weekly
next month		once a day

AVOID THE TRAP!

Since is sometimes used as a preposition with the present perfect tense, but it is also used to mean *because*.

Preposition:
Example: We have been here since 10 o'clock.

Subordinate conjunction:
Example: They didn't want to come since they weren't invited.

Exercises 🔑 p 228

Read the following sentences and circle the verb tense that matches the context of the sentence. This will help you recognize time markers on the TOEIC test.

1. How long has Mr. Block been working on the report?
   Mr. Block has been working on the report _____.

   (A) three hours ago
   (B) for three hours

2. When did the housekeeper clean the room?
   _____ we left the room, she cleaned it.

   (A) After
   (B) Usually

3. How long will Ms. Colinas fill in?
   Ms. Colinas will fill in _____ Ms. Irzel is out of the hospital.

   (A) until
   (B) already

4. When does the secretary take notes?
   The secretary takes notes _____ the meeting.

   (A) often
   (B) during

5. How do tourists prefer to see a new city?
   Visitors _____ prefer to start with a guided tour of the city.

   (A) generally
   (B) while

Skill 4: Understanding the Passive Voice

On Part V, your knowledge of the passive voice will help you choose the verb form that matches the context of the sentence. The passive voice is often used in formal and business communication. It is used when you do not need (or want) to mention who does the action.

Sample TOEIC Question

Before the dam _____ , the river overflowed its banks every spring.
(A) was built
(B) built
(C) was building
(D) builds

Choice (A) is the correct answer. The sentence should read, *Before the dam was built, the river overflowed its banks every spring.* The verb *was built* is in the past tense, passive voice. The emphasis is on the dam. It's not important who built the dam.

Choices (B), (C), and (D) are all incorrect because they are in active voice. That is, they all mean that the dam built something (which is illogical). We know that someone built the dam, so we require the passive voice. Choice (D) is illogical for another reason also. The main verb, *overflowed*, is in the past tense, so we cannot use the present tense in the subordinate clause, which begins with *before*.

Skill Focus

It is very helpful to know how to recognize the passive voice. When we think of the words in a sentence, we think of the grammatical structure—subject, verb, and object. But we can also think of these words in terms of their roles in the meaning of the sentence. In a basic sentence, the subject is the agent (the person who does the action); the verb is the action, and the object is the receiver (the thing that the action affects). In a passive sentence, the agent and the receiver have switched positions. Review the clues below for recognizing this pattern that identifies a passive sentence.

Clue 1   The subject of a passive sentence is NOT the agent (the person or thing that does the action).

Example: The letters were typed by the secretary.

Explanation: Who typed? Letters can't type, but a secretary can. The subject is not the agent; the object is the agent.

Clue 2   The object (agent) of a passive sentence has the preposition *by* in front of it.

Example: The announcement was made by the director.

Explanation: *By the director* means that the director is the agent.

Clue 3   The object (agent) of a passive sentence may be completely omitted from the sentence because it is understood, unknown, or unimportant.

Example 1:   The mail was delivered.

Explanation: We suppose the mail carrier delivered it. Everyone can guess this. It's not important.

Example 2:   The crime was committed at midnight.

Explanation: We don't know who committed the crime. The police don't know either. But we need to talk about the crime anyway.

Clue 4   The verb consists of a form of *be* and the past participle of the main verb.

Example: Our company has been mentioned in that magazine.

Explanation: The form of *be* indicates the subject does the action (is the agent). If *be* is left out, *Our company has mentioned*, it means the company mentioned the magazine. With *be*—*the company has been mentioned*—it means the magazine mentioned the company.

AVOID THE TRAP!

To be is used both in the passive voice and in the past continuous tense. Don't confuse them. Look at the whole sentence.

Passive Voice
Example: The reservations were confirmed.

Past Continuous Tense
Example: They were confirming the reservations when the phone went dead.

Exercises 🔑 p 228

Decide if an active or passive voice construction is needed. Knowing if the subject is the doer or the receiver of the action will help you determine if you need the active or passive voice on the TOEIC test.

1. The viewers _____ the opportunity to judge the performance.
   (A) were given
   (B) gave

2. The shipment must _____ carefully.
   (A) handle
   (B) be handled

3. The food manager _____ to eliminate theft.
   (A) was told
   (B) has told

4. The flight _____ on time.
   (A) was left
   (B) left

5. The proposal _____ now.
   (A) can be mailed
   (B) can mail

AVOID THE TRAP!

The past participle -ed is used in both the passive voice, the past tense, and as an adjective. Don't confuse them. Look at the whole sentence.

Passive Voice: Past Tense
Example: The meal was cooked before we came.

Active Voice: Past Tense
Example: They cooked the meal before we came.

Adjective
Example: The cooked food was on the table when we came.

Skill 5: Identifying the Correct Prepositions

On Part V, your knowledge of the context of the sentence will help you choose the correct preposition. Prepositions are words used to indicate phrases of time, place, or relationship. This section will review the common prepositions of time and place.

Sample TOEIC Question

We are so glad you could come. Welcome _____ Rome.
(A) in
(B) at
(C) to
(D) of

Choice (C) is the correct answer. The sentence should read, *Welcome to Rome.*

The combination of *Welcome* and *Rome* indicates that Rome is a destination. Destinations use the preposition of place, *to.*

Choice (A) is also a preposition of place, but is not used with destinations. Use it after you get there: *When I vacationed in Rome.* Choice (B) is a preposition of place (but not with cities) and time. Choice (D) is a preposition that shows possession.

Skill Focus

There are many prepositions in English. You must pay attention to the prepositions that you hear and read every day, because that is the best way to learn them. There are a few rules, however, about the use of prepositions. Review the prepositions below for common ways to express ideas of time and location. Notice the contrasts in the ways the prepositions are used.

Prepositional phrase	Use	Examples
to Rome	destination	I went to Rome.
in Rome	within a location	While I was in Rome, I saw many Roman ruins.
from Rome	direction away	I went from Rome to Vienna.
from Rome	source	I brought you this souvenir from Rome.
to the meeting	destination	I went to the meeting.
in the meeting	within a location	I was in the meeting all morning.
from the meeting	direction away	I went from the meeting to my office.
at the meeting	during	Some people got bored at (during) the meeting this morning.
at the airport	general location	I can catch a cab at the airport.
at 9:00	specific time	At 9:00, I arrived at work.

Prepositional phrase	Use	Examples
from 9:00 to (until) 10:00	boundaries of a time period	From 9:30 to 12:00, I attended a seminar.
for one hour	duration of time	I stopped for one hour to eat lunch.
since 10:00	time starting at a point and ending now	Since 1:00, I have been working on this report.
on February 6	with dates	I start my new job on February 6.
in one day	with days	I wrote the memo in one day.
in two weeks	with weeks	The package should arrive in two weeks.
in April	with months	His birthday is in April.
in the morning	with periods of the day	I ride the train in the morning.
at night	with night	It gets chilly at night.

AVOID THE TRAP!

The prepositions *for* and *since* are both prepositions of time. Don't confuse them. Look at the meaning of the verb and the length of time.

For shows a duration of time.
Example: We have been talking for an hour.

Since shows an exact point in time in the past.
Example: I've working here since 1994.

Exercises 🔑 p 228

Complete the sentence with the correct preposition from the list above. This will help you understand the context to choose the correct preposition on the TOEIC test.

1. Ms. Legesse is _____ a meeting right now.

2. Class starts _____ one month.

3. Meet me _____ noon.

4. The meeting continued _____ 5:30.

5. She's been the director _____ Mr. Lee retired.

Skill 6: Using Relative Pronouns

On the TOEIC test you may be asked to determine which relative pronoun correctly completes the sentence. Relative pronouns are words used to introduce subordinate clauses. The relative pronouns are *that, which, who, whose,* and *whom.*

Sample TOEIC Question

Mr. Wang spoke with the man _____ called yesterday.
(A) which
(B) who
(C) whose
(D) why

Choice (B) is the correct answer. The sentence should read, *Mr. Wang spoke with the man who called yesterday.* The relative pronoun *who* replaces *the man* in the subordinate clause *the man called yesterday.*

Choice (A) is incorrect because *which* is not used for people. Choice (C) is incorrect because you do not need to show possession. Choice (D) is incorrect because *why* is not a relative pronoun.

Skill Focus

It may help to remember that relative pronouns are called pronouns because, like other pronouns, they replace nouns. We can combine sentences with relative pronouns because they prevent us from repeating a noun. Review the relative pronouns below. Notice how the relative pronouns replace the nouns that are repeated.

1. Ms. Ling signed for the package.
   The package arrived this morning.
   Ms. Ling signed for the package the package arrived this morning.
   Ms. Ling signed for the package *which* arrived this morning.

2. This line is for the passengers.
   The passengers bought their tickets in advance.
   This line is for the passengers the passengers bought their tickets in advance.
   This line is for the passengers *who* bought their tickets in advance.

3. Ms. Riad received some letters.
   The letters were mailed last week.
   Ms. Riad received some letters the letters were mailed last week.
   Ms. Riad received the letters *that* were mailed last week.

4. The message is on your desk.
   I took the message for you.
   The message is on your desk I took the message for you.
   The message *that* I took for you is on your desk.

5. The director interviewed an applicant.
   The applicant's typing skills are strong.
   The director interviewed an applicant the applicant's typing skills are strong.
   The director interviewed an applicant *whose* typing skills are strong.

56

Exercises 🔑 p 228

Circle the correct relative pronoun for the sentences below. This will help you understand which relative pronoun to choose on the TOEIC test.

1. Here is the report _____ you wanted to read.
   (A) that
   (B) it

2. Mr. Peri is the chef _____ created this dish.
   (A) which
   (B) who

3. The person _____ computer is still on must be working late.
   (A) whose
   (B) why

4. The plants, _____ are rare and exotic, require meticulous care.
   (A) they
   (B) which

5. The tables _____ are by the window are the most popular.
   (A) who
   (B) that

AVOID THE TRAP!

A non-restrictive clause is a special kind of relative clause that begins and ends with a comma. It can use *who*, *whose*, *whom*, and *which*, but cannot use *that*.

Example: These chairs, *which* do not match the desks, must be replaced.
Always use *which* (instead of *that*) in a relative clause that begins and ends with a comma.

Practice: Part V 🔑 p 228

Choose the one word or phrase that best completes the sentence.

1. The restaurant _____ has just opened has a famous chef.
   (A) whose
   (B) who
   (C) it
   (D) that

2. Negotiations will take place _____ London.
   (A) at
   (B) in
   (C) by
   (D) to

3. We were in _____ with our supplier.
   (A) agree
   (B) agreeing
   (C) agreement
   (D) agreed

4. Mrs. Dubois is a _____ supervisor.
   (A) confident
   (B) confidence
   (C) confidentially
   (D) confidently

5. Our store gets more business _____ our new location.
   - (A) of
   - (B) to
   - (C) from
   - (D) in

6. The proposal _____ by messenger.
   - (A) delivered
   - (B) has delivered
   - (C) is delivered
   - (D) is delivering

7. On what date did you _____ the shipment?
   - (A) perceive
   - (B) deceive
   - (C) receive
   - (D) recede

8. Two weeks ago, Mr. Uto _____ his reservations.
   - (A) makes
   - (B) was made
   - (C) made
   - (D) has made

9. All the members have arrived _____ Mr. Sampson.
   - (A) accept
   - (B) without
   - (C) not
   - (D) except

10. She expressed her _____.
   - (A) appreciate
   - (B) appreciative
   - (C) appreciation
   - (D) appreciated

11. Eliza Donato _____ to Vice President in January.
   - (A) will promote
   - (B) will be promoting
   - (C) will be promoted
   - (D) promotes

12. Mr. Yung sent a reminder to customers _____ didn't pay their bills.
   - (A) what
   - (B) whom
   - (C) which
   - (D) who

13. Mr. Weber hired a new _____.
   - (A) assist
   - (B) assistance
   - (C) assisted
   - (D) assistant

14. Send a fax to _____ the prices.
   - (A) verily
   - (B) verify
   - (C) verifying
   - (D) verified

15. That product _____ until recently.
   - (A) wasn't invented
   - (B) invented
   - (C) didn't invent
   - (D) invented

16. We're sending Mary Sula to participate _____ the seminar.
   - (A) at
   - (B) to
   - (C) from
   - (D) in

17. The employees _____ by the director to give suggestions.
   - (A) are asking
   - (B) asking
   - (C) are asked
   - (D) be asked

18. Mr. Caputo usually _____ with a translator.
   - (A) is traveled
   - (B) travel
   - (C) is traveling
   - (D) travels

19. Her _____ employer gave her a good recommendation.
   - (A) prevalent
   - (B) prevent
   - (C) preview
   - (D) previous

20. Flight 201 will be arriving at Gate 7B _____ time.
   - (A) by
   - (B) on
   - (C) at
   - (D) within

Part VI: Error Recognition

Part VI of the TOEIC test contains 20 sentences which test vocabulary and grammar with four underlined words or four underlined phrases marked (A), (B), (C), and (D). Each of the 20 sentences contains one error. You are asked to find the one error in each sentence. If you try to determine which three underlined words are correct you can find the incorrect word or phrase by the process of elimination.

Try not to spend more than 30 seconds per question. You will have only 75 minutes for all of Parts V, VI, and VII so you will want to use your time wisely.

Sample TOEIC Question

<u>There will</u> be a <u>fifteen-minutes</u> <u>intermission</u> after the first <u>act</u>.
   A   B   C   D

Choice (B) is the correct answer. The sentence should read, *There will be a fifteen-minute intermission after the first act.* Choice (B) is hyphenated and is used as an adjective, modifying the noun, *intermission.* Remember that adjectives are not marked with the plural -*s* in English. As an adjective, the phrase should read ... *a fifteen-minute intermission.*

Choice (A) is a correct verb: the verb *will be* can be singular or plural, so subject and verb agreement is not a problem. The tense of the verb is not a problem, either. Choice (C) is a correct noun. There is a clue with the article *a* because *a* precedes singular countable nouns. Choice (D) is also a correct noun. Here it is the object of the preposition *after* and is preceded by an article, *the*, and an adjective, *first*.

Test Tips

You will improve your score on Part VI by:
- recognizing subject and verb agreement
- using the correct verb tense
- maintaining correct adjective placement
- recognizing questions in longer sentences
- identifying pronouns
- understanding conjunctions

Skill 1: Recognizing Subject and Verb Agreement

On the TOEIC test you may be asked to determine whether the subject and verb agree. The subject and verb must agree in number and person. This means if the subject is plural, the verb must be plural. If the subject is singular, the verb must be singular.

Sample TOEIC Question

Each <u>of the</u> machine parts <u>are</u> <u>guaranteed</u> <u>for</u> ninety days.
    A   B   C   D

Choice (B) is the correct answer. The sentence should read, *Each of the machine parts is guaranteed for ninety days*. The passive verb, *are guaranteed*, must agree with *Each*. We know that *each* is considered singular in number, so there is not agreement in this sentence.

Choice (A) is a correct preposition and article, part of the prepositional phrase *of the machine parts*. Choice (C) is a correct past participle, part of the passive verb construction *is guaranteed*. Choice (D) is a correct preposition of time describing the duration of the guarantee.

Skill Focus

In order to make the subject and verb in a sentence agree, you must be able to identify the subject, and you must know whether the subject is considered singular or plural. The subject and verb must agree in number (singular–plural) and in person (first person, second person, or third person).

The subject and verb may be separated by prepositional phrases, clauses, or adverbs.

Example: The *letters and faxes* on top of the cabinet in the storage room *are* ready to be filed.

The subject may have a singular form, but be considered plural.

Example: The *people are* interested in obtaining more information.

AVOID THE TRAP!

Third person singular in the simple present tense gives the most trouble. An *-s* must be added to the base form of the verb. Do not forget the *-s*.

Example: Mr. Lorca knows the program well.

Verb tenses with modals (*can, must, will, should*, etc.) are both singular and plural.

Examples: I can make the reservation. (singular)
              We can make the reservation. (plural)

Exercises 🔑 p 230

Circle the subject and rewrite the verb to match the subject. This will help you determine agreement between subjects and verbs on the TOEIC test.

1. The files in the file cabinet is all outdated.
2. The police always arrives quickly when there is a fire.
3. The man and woman who waited for the bus was late.
4. Ms. Pratowski's eyeglasses was broken in the accident.
5. My parents, who still lives in the same house in Santiago where I was born, met me at the airport.

Skill 2: Using the Correct Verb Tense

On the TOEIC test you may be asked to choose the correct tense for a verb within a sentence. When you analyze a verb in a sentence, you should try to determine if it is the correct tense. You can do this by understanding the context of the sentence. Check the sentence for a time marker or a phrase or clause that indicates time. If there is a second verb in the sentence, think whether the times indicated by the verbs make sense together.

Sample TOEIC Question

By June of next year, the <u>majority</u> of <u>blue-collar</u> workers <u>have gone</u> on strike at <u>least</u> once.
                    A   B   C   D

Choice (C) is the correct answer. The prepositional phrase, *By June of next year,* is a clue because it indicates a future time. We know that the word *by* is very important because it limits the time frame. When we talk about a future action, *workers will have gone on strike,* that is completed before a future reference point, *By June of next year,* we use the future perfect tense.

Choice (A) is a correct noun; note the article *the* which precedes it. Choice (B) is a correct adjective. Choice (D) is a correct adjective modifying *once.*

Skill Focus

There are four verb tense groups in English: simple, continuous, perfect, and perfect continuous. Each of these can be expressed in the past, present, or future. It can be helpful to remember that, except for the simple tenses, the verb tenses of English generally deal with relational time. That is, the tense of a verb is determined by its relationship to another verb (usually in the same sentence). This is why sentences often have two verbs in different tenses. One verb is a reference point for the tense of the other verb. The reference point can also be a time marker instead of a verb.

Review the tenses below. Notice the relationship of each tense to its reference point.

Simple tenses are used to mention an action, without particular emphasis on duration or relationship to other actions.

Examples:
Present: It rains every afternoon.
Past: It rained yesterday.
Future: It will rain tomorrow.

Continuous tenses emphasize that the action is happening or continuing.

Examples:
Present: It is raining right now.
Past: It was raining until 3:00.
Future: It will be raining when we leave work.

Perfect tenses emphasize that an action occurs before a reference point (another time or action).

Examples:
Present: It has rained every day for a week.
Past: It had rained every day while the weather was cold.
Future: It will have rained seven days by the end of this week.

Perfect continuous tenses emphasize the happening or continuing of an action that occurs before a reference point (another time or action) in the same time frame.

Examples:
Present: It has been raining for six hours now.
Past: It had been raining for six hours when the sun came out.
Future: It will have been raining long enough to set a record in two more hours.

Exercises 🔑 p 230

Circle the underlined word that is the verb and rewrite it in the correct tense. This will help you choose the correct verb tense on the TOEIC test.

1. Mr. Hana <u>slept</u> <u>soundly</u> in his bed <u>when</u> <u>the</u> telephone rang.
              A   B   C D

2. <u>Unless</u> she is off <u>next</u> week, Ms. Morea <u>has worked</u> all year <u>without</u> a vacation.
   A   B   C   D

3. <u>That</u> magazine <u>had been</u> late <u>every</u> month this <u>year</u>.
   A   B   C   D

4. <u>The</u> director <u>will have called</u> yesterday <u>about</u> the <u>annual</u> report.
   A   B   C   D

5. I always <u>am having</u> lunch <u>at</u> the <u>café</u> near <u>the</u> office.
              A   B   C   D

AVOID THE TRAP!

Some verbs in subordinate clauses must be in the simple present tense even though the main verb is in the future.

Example: The secretary <u>will announce</u> when Mr. Lee <u>arrives</u>.
The main verb *will announce* is in the future tense. The verb in the subordinate clause, *arrives*, is in the present.

Skill 3: Maintaining Correct Adjective Placement

On the TOEIC test, understanding adjectives may help you determine the meaning of the sentence. Adjectives that are in the wrong order can sometimes make the meaning of a sentence unclear.

Sample TOEIC Question

You <u>will have to</u> wait <u>one</u> more month before <u>ordering</u> the <u>new</u> expensive computer.
      A   B   C   D

Choice (D) is the correct answer. The sentence should read, *You will have to wait one more month before ordering the expensive new computer.*

Adjectives of age (new) come after general adjectives.

Choice (A) is a correct verb. Choice (B) is a correct number adjective. Choice (C) is a correct gerund (object of the preposition *before*).

Skill Focus

Many adjectives can be used together to modify the same noun. However, the nouns have to be in a certain order for the sentence to make sense. Review the chart below, which shows the order for common types of adjectives. Notice that general adjectives include those that describe size, shape, age, and color.

Article	Number adjective	General adjective	Participle as adjective	Origin adjective	Noun
the					statue table building
the	first second third				
the	first	usual small square new gray			statue
the	first	small	carved molded		statue
the	first	small	carved	French	statue

63

Exercises ⊙━━ p 230

Circle the adjectives and rewrite the sentences to put the adjectives in the correct order. This will help you spot adjectives that may make sentences unclear on the TOEIC test.

1. An Italian inexpensive restaurant has opened on the corner.

2. The boring long speech made everyone restless.

3. The white new paint makes the office seem brighter.

4. An American old movie is on television tonight.

5. This new conference table is better than the square old one.

Skill 4: Recognizing Questions in Longer Sentences

On the TOEIC test you may have to recognize questions that occur within longer statements or questions. The word order for questions within longer sentences is statement order (subject–verb) rather than question order (verb–subject).

Sample TOEIC Question

The employee asked when would he become eligible for promotion.
  A   B   C   D

Choice (C) is the correct answer. The sentence should read, *The prospective employee asked when he would become eligible for promotion.* The direct question would be: *When would (I) be eligible for ...?* Placed within a longer sentence, the word order changes to: *... when he would be eligible.*

Choice (A) is a correct subject. Choice (B) is a correct verb. Choice (D) is a correct prepositional phrase.

Skill Focus

The subject–verb order of the main clause of a sentence determines whether the sentence will be a statement or a question. Questions placed within longer sentences are not the main clause of the resulting sentence, so they must have subject–verb order. Review the statements and questions below. Notice that the words are in subject–verb order, except in the main clause of a question.

Mr. Hochul went to the meeting.
Did Mr. Hochul go to the meeting?
The secretary told me Mr. Hochul went to the meeting.

The flight was delayed.
Why was the flight delayed?
She did not know why the flight was delayed.

Dr. Latiba had planned to deliver the package by messenger.
How had Dr. Latiba planned to deliver the package?
I think Dr. Latiba had planned to deliver the package by messenger.

It is 10:00.
What time is it?
Can you tell me what time it is?

Exercises ⊙━ p 230

Make the questions below part of the longer sentence. This will help you understand questions that may appear in longer sentences on the TOEIC test.

1. When is the deadline?
   Do you know _____ ?

2. Why don't we have reservations?
   I would like to know _____ .

3. What is the name of the playwright?
   In the program it should say _____ .

4. Has the letter arrived?
   I hope _____ .

5. Who will be the next chairman?
   The committee will have to vote on _____ .

Skill 5: Identifying Pronouns

Knowing the different types of pronouns can help you understand how pronouns are used on the TOEIC test. Pronouns take the place of nouns. Different types of pronouns indicate different functions in the sentence. A closely related group of words is the group called pronominal adjectives. They replace the possessive form of nouns, and therefore, modify all nouns.

Sample TOEIC Question

<u>All</u> of <u>we</u> salesmen <u>work</u> <u>on</u> commission.
A   B   C   D

Choice (B) is the correct answer. The sentence should read, *All of us salesmen work on commission.* The word *of* is a preposition. The words following a preposition form the object of the preposition. Therefore, the pronoun must be in its object form, *us.* The subject of the sentence is *All.*

Choice (A) is a correct subject. Choice (C) is a correct verb. Choice (D) is a correct preposition.

Skill Focus

Pronouns must be like the nouns they replace. A pronoun must be singular or plural, and first, second, or third person, according to the noun. This is also true for pronominal adjectives. Review the pronouns and adjectives below. Notice that some pronouns have different forms for singular and plural, subject and object, while forms for other pronouns remain the same.

Pronouns as Subjects		Pronouns as Objects		Pronominal Adjectives of Possession	
Singular	Plural	Singular	Plural	Singular	Plural
I	we	me	us	my	our
you	you	you	you	your	your
he, she, it	they	him, her, it	them	his, her, its	their

Exercises ⊙⚷ p 230

Fill in the blanks below with the correct form of the pronoun. Other words in the sentence will indicate which pronoun you should use. This will help you understand the relationships among pronouns on the TOEIC test.

1. Even though we had a drop in sales, _____ overall profits remained high.

2. A guide will be waiting for _____ when we arrive at the hotel.

3. _____ will receive a special award for her accomplishments on the project.

4. You cannot spend all your time working unless work is rewarding for _____ .

5. The guests unpacked _____ luggage before _____ went down to the beach.

AVOID THE TRAP!

The contraction *it's* (it is) should not be confused with the pronominal adjective *its*.

The contraction *you're* (you are) should not be confused with the pronominal adjective *your*.

Skill 6: Understanding Conjunctions

Conjunctions are *combining* words. There are two types of conjunctions. Coordinating conjunctions combine words, phrases, or sentences. Subordinating conjunctions combine sentences and clauses. Knowing the meanings of conjunctions can help you understand sentences and reading passages found on the TOEIC test.

Sample TOEIC Question

Mr. Kokosinski is <u>happy</u> with <u>his</u> job, <u>because</u> the pay <u>is</u> low.
          A   B   C   D

Choice (C) is the correct answer. The sentence should read *Mr. Kokosinski is happy with his job, even though the pay is low.*

Because indicates a cause and effect relationship, meaning the low pay is the reason he likes his job. It makes more sense if he likes his job for other more important reasons, in spite of the fact that the pay is low. The conjunction *even though* shows a contrast in the ideas *is happy with his job* and *the pay is low.*

Although and *though* have the same meaning and function, and could also be used here.

Skill Focus

Conjunctions combine items by showing the relationship between them. The relationships they express fall into a few major groups: association, contrast, cause and effect, and time. Review the list of conjunctions and examples below. Notice the meaning that each conjunction has, and the meaning it conveys about the items joined.

Coordinating Conjunctions	Meanings	Examples
and	joins items	The manager and the vice president found a solution. Ms. Fleury brought cookies and Mr. Bomback provided lemonade.
or	gives a choice among items	We can meet at 1:00 or 2:00.
but	shows contrast among items	I would like to see a movie, but I have a lot of work to do.
both ... and	joins items	Both Mr. Abdalla and Ms. Olligher have offered to help.
not only ... but also	joins items	Mr. Sebree not only cooks wonderful meals, but also invites friends to share them.
either ... or	gives a choice between items	Either staying at home or going out will please me.
neither ... nor	excludes both items	Neither the book nor the movie was well done.
since	shows cause and effect	Since I leave work at 5:00, I can't be there before 6:00.
so that	shows cause and effect	The secretary keeps the telephone directory on her desk so that she can look up phone numbers quickly.
because	shows cause and effect	I brought an umbrella because it might rain.
while	shows cause and effect	Ms. Mudar typed the letter while Mr. Hull read the request.
when	shows time relationships	I will leave when I finish this phone call.
as soon as	shows time relationships	Let me know as soon as you reach a decision.
until	shows time relationships	The meeting will last until lunchtime.
even though	shows contrast of ideas	Even though he has little experience, he is good at his job.
although	shows contrast of ideas	She writes very well, although she does not enjoy it.
though	shows contrast of ideas	The seminar was interesting, though there was not enough time for the audience to ask questions.

Exercises 🔑 p 230

Find the conjunction in the sentences below. Rewrite the conjunction to make more sense in the sentence. This will help you understand the meanings of the conjunctions in sentences on the TOEIC test.

1. Ms. Albrecht got an apartment near the office while her commute would be shorter.

2. I will see either the play nor the movie this weekend.

3. The receptionist can take her lunch break until her replacement arrives.

4. The manager likes to write letters or does not like to type them.

5. Though Mr. Gacek is a talented artist, his paintings are on display at the City Gallery.

Practice: Part VI 🔑 p 230

Identify the one underlined word or phrase that should be corrected or rewritten.

1. Ms. Cescu <u>paid</u> her registration fee when <u>she</u> discovered that she would <u>not</u> be able to
       A   B   C
   attend <u>the convention</u>.
           D

2. The director <u>thought</u> that <u>either</u> the blue invitations and the green ones were <u>appropriate</u>
              A   B   C
   for <u>the seminar</u>.
         D

3. <u>By</u> the time the <u>final</u> report is due, the technicians <u>resolved</u> <u>their</u> problem.
  A   B   C   D

4. I <u>asked</u> the department secretary, <u>but</u> <u>she</u> did not know when <u>would</u> the managers take a
   A   B C   D
   break from their meeting.

5. Ms. Morisot lost <u>her</u> wallet while <u>he</u> <u>was</u> walking <u>in</u> the park at lunchtime.
                 A   B C   D

6. The shipment <u>of</u> machine parts <u>were</u> delayed <u>by</u> the workmen's <u>sudden</u> strike.
                A   B   C   D

7. The fast <u>first</u> train <u>leaves</u> for the city <u>at</u> 8:00 every <u>weekday</u> morning.
         A   B   C   D

8. Ms. Arnet asked <u>the manager</u> <u>how</u> late <u>will</u> the store be open <u>tonight</u>.
               A   B   C   D

9. <u>Because</u> <u>he</u> comes into the office <u>on</u> weekends, Mr. Fortescue <u>never</u> gets enough work done.
  A B   C   D

10. <u>Although</u> the article is <u>clearly</u> written, <u>she</u> contains factual information that <u>is</u> inaccurate.
    A   B   C   D

Part VII: Reading Comprehension

Part VII of the TOEIC test contains different types of reading materials. These readings are the kind you would find during the course of a normal day in an English speaking environment. These readings would include:

- advertisements
- announcements
- calendars
- charts
- fax forms
- forms
- graphs
- indices
- letters
- memos
- schedules
- bulletins

Each reading passage is followed by two to five questions. There are 40 multiple choice questions in Part VII. You must find the best choice—(A), (B), (C), or (D)—and mark your answer sheet. Try not to spend more than thirty seconds per question. You will have only 75 minutes for all of Parts V, VI, and VII so you will want to use your time wisely.

Sample TOEIC Question

Questions 1–4 refer to the following passage.

The White House, the official home of the President of the United States, was designed by the architect James Hoban, who is said to have been influenced by the design of a palace in Ireland. The building was begun in 1792 and was first occupied by the second President of the United States, John Adams, in November 1800. The house received its present name when it was painted white after being damaged by fire in 1814.

1. What is the main idea of the reading passage?
   (A) The White House has an interesting history.
   (B) President Adams was the first occupant of the White House.   Sample Answer
   (C) The architect of the White House was from Ireland.   ● (B) (C) (D)
   (D) The White House was damaged by fire.

Choice (A) is the correct answer. This is a main idea question. To find the main idea, you must look at the complete reading passage, not just one part, or one sentence. The reading passage states many facts. Choice (A) contains the most general, and true information.

Choices (B), (C), and (D) are true, but each contains only part of the information of the passage.

2. When was the White House first occupied?
   (A) 1776
   (B) 1792   Sample Answer
   (C) 1800   (A) (B) ● (D)
   (D) 1814

Choice (C) is the correct answer. This is a factual question. To find this specific fact, you should scan the passage for the specific date. The reading passage states: *The building ... was first occupied ... in November 1800*.

Choices (A), (B), and (D) are incorrect because the dates do not match the question.

3. Which of the following statements is probably true?
   (A) Palaces in Ireland are painted white.
   (B) All American presidents have lived in the White House.
   (C) John Adams was not President in 1800.
   (D) The White House was not white prior to 1814.

Sample Answer
(A) (B) (C) ●

Choice (D) is the correct answer. This is an inference question. The reader must infer the answer because the answer is not directly stated. The last sentence of the reading passage says that the White House *was painted white ... in 1814*. The last sentence implies that the official house of the President had been another color. But this information is not stated; it is only <u>implied</u>.

Choice (A) is incorrect because the design, not the color, of the White House was influenced by a palace (one palace, not several). Choice (B) is incorrect because the first President did not live in the White House. Choice (C) is incorrect because Adams was President when he moved into the White House in 1800.

4. What is the author's purpose?
   (A) To inform
   (B) To persuade
   (C) To criticize
   (D) To praise

Sample Answer
● (B) (C) (D)

Choice (A) is the correct answer. This question asks for the author's purpose in writing the passage. The purpose is not stated directly, so we must infer the answer. The information in the reading passage is general: we are informed what the White House is, who the architect was, what the design influences were, when it was begun, who the first occupants were, and how it received its name.

Choice (B) is incorrect because the author does not try to persuade us to believe or do something. Choices (C) and (D) are incorrect because there are no words of either criticism or praise. There are simply informative facts.

Types of Questions

There are basically two types of questions in Part VII of the Reading Comprehension Section of the TOEIC test. The questions in Part VII are based on what is <u>stated</u> (Main Idea and Factual questions) and what is <u>implied</u> (Inferential and Purpose questions).

Characteristics	Examples
Some questions ask for the main idea.	The main idea of this article is ... The main topic of this article is ... The author believes ...
Some questions ask for facts.	What happened ...? Who did what? How much ...? How many ...? How short ...? Which of the following is NOT mentioned? According to the article, what ...?
Some questions ask for an inference.	What does the author imply? What do you think ...? It can be inferred from the article that ... What can we infer from this passage?
Some questions ask for the purpose.	Why was this article written? What is the purpose of this article? Why did the author write this memo?

Test Tips

You will improve your score on Part VII by focusing on:

- recognizing the main idea
- understanding the facts
- predicting inferences
- understanding the purpose

Skill 1: Recognizing the Main Idea

On Part VII of the TOEIC test, you may be asked to determine the main idea of a reading passage. To answer these questions, you must focus on what the passage is about. Since the main idea tells the reader what the passage is about, it usually appears in the first paragraph.

Sample TOEIC Question

This question refers to the following announcement.

> The Marmax Group is a private family-held company that sells versions of the world's most treasured and expensive ladies' and men's colognes at a fraction of the original prices. Since our family started the business in 1993, we have been marketing our interpretations of famous perfumes under the brand name of "Aromas."

What is the main idea of the passage?
(A) The Marmax Group sells scents.
(B) Colognes are a fraction of Marmax's business.
(C) The company started in the 90s.
(D) The company has their own brand name.

Choice (A) is the correct answer. The company sells ladies' and men's colognes. The generic term for colognes and perfumes is *scent*. This is the main idea of the passage.

Choice (B) is incorrect, because (1) it is a detail and (2) the company sells colognes at a discount which are a fraction of the original cost, not a fraction of the total business. Choice (C) is incorrect, because it is a detail; when the company started business is not the main idea. Choice (D) is incorrect, because it is a detail. The article does not discuss the importance of a brand name.

Skill Focus

The main idea of a reading passage is not always in the same place in the passage. Sometimes you can best state the main idea exactly as it was stated in the passage. Other times, the main idea is best stated in slightly different words. But the main idea always appears early in the passage. Review these clues for finding the main idea. Notice that you may have to read several sentences before the main idea becomes clear.

Clue 1   The main idea may be in the first sentence of the passage, so the reader can know immediately what the passage is about.

Example: It is important to know how to write a good resume. A potential employer sees your resume before he or she ever meets you. Therefore, you must make sure your resume makes a good impression.

Main idea: It is important to know how to write a good resume.

Clue 2   The main idea may present a contrast to a statement in the first sentence (or first few sentences) of the passage, because the main idea is a reaction to the statement.

Example: Many people think that business is a complicated field. But the principles that guide successful businesses are actually quite simple.

Main idea: Business principles are simple.

Clue 3 The main idea may be a summary of details in the first sentence (or first few sentences) of a passage, because putting the details first may capture the reader's interest.

Example: The seats are comfortable, and the view outside the windows is lovely. The telephone, computer, printer, and fax machine are the latest models. It is obviously a luxury office. Like more and more offices these days, this one is in an automobile.

Main idea: The changing workplace includes offices in automobiles.

Exercises ⊙━━ p 232

The following groups of sentences contain one main idea and three supporting details. Choose the main idea from the sentences below. This will help you recognize the main idea in the reading passages in Part VII.

1. (A) This year 250 billion dollars was spent on dogs and cats.
   (B) Toys and clothes for pets are very popular.
   (C) Pet owners spend a lot of time and money on their pets.
   (D) There are doctors and even psychiatrists that specialize in pets.

2. (A) There were many famous military leaders in history.
   (B) Alexander the Great led his troops from Greece to India.
   (C) Genghis Khan's empire stretched from Mongolia to Eastern Europe.
   (D) General Eisenhower became President of the United States.

3. (A) The captain has to supervise the officers on the bridge.
   (B) One of the functions of the captain is to perform marriages at sea.
   (C) The captain is ultimately responsible for the safety of the passengers.
   (D) The captain of a ship has many duties.

4. (A) The hotel has a large fitness center with an indoor pool.
   (B) This hotel is the most luxurious in the city.
   (C) There is a concierge on every floor.
   (D) All rooms are suites with balconies.

5. (A) The modem transmits data at 14.4 bps.
   (B) The monitor is not in color.
   (C) My new computer does not have the latest technology.
   (D) The software programs have not been upgraded.

AVOID THE TRAP!

Don't mark a choice simply because it is true. There may be a choice that is true, but doesn't answer the question. Read the question carefully.

Skill 2: Understanding the Facts

On Part VII of the TOEIC test, you may be asked to find and determine the relationships among the facts in a reading passage. To answer factual questions, you must focus on the details in the passage. All factual statements are true and all are stated in the passage.

Sample TOEIC Question

This question refers to the following news article.

> RSX said its second quarter net income doubled to $6 million, even though the company had labor problems. An RSX spokesperson said the improved results showed a greater demand for its products. In its 20-year history, this is the most significant jump in earnings.

What was the net income of RSX in the first quarter?

(A) Three million dollars
(B) Six million dollars
(C) Twelve million dollars
(D) Twenty million dollars

Choice (A) is the correct answer. This fact is noted in the first sentence. In the second quarter the net income was double what it was in the first quarter. *To be doubled* means *to be twice as much.* This simple math makes the first quarter net income $3 million.

Choice (B) is the net income in the second quarter. Choice (C) is the net income if you doubled the second quarter income. Choice (D) is not mentioned as earnings, but *20* is mentioned as the number of years the company has been in business.

Skill Focus

Locating facts usually means paying attention to details. Although a fact may be clearly stated, it may also be hidden among other information or other words. Review the clues below for locating important facts in different forms.

Clue 1   The passage might state the fact explicitly.

Example: The company is 20 years old.

Fact: The company is 20 years old.

Clue 2   A sentence might "hide" a fact in a subordinate clause.

Example: No one believed the company would succeed when it began twenty years ago in a small town.

Fact: The company is 20 years old.

Clue 3   The same fact might be stated in different words in the passage.

Example: In the two decades since it opened its doors, the company has always been profitable.

Fact: The company is 20 years old. (Two decades means the same as 20 years and *opened its doors* means the same as *started.*)

Exercises ⊙⟿ p 232

Below you will read five general statements. Find two supporting facts in the list on the right and write their letters under the appropriate general statement. This will help you recognize the facts on the reading passages in Part VII.

General Statements

1. The ship's cabins are equipped for a passenger's safety and comfort.
   (1)
   (2)

2. Electronic mail is improving communication.
   (1)
   (2)

3. The weather is seasonably cold.
   (1)
   (2)

4. Medical research is under attack from animal rights groups.
   (1)
   (2)

5. Oil companies are investigating alternate sources of fuels.
   (1)
   (2)

Supporting Facts

(A) It was below freezing this morning.

(B) Life jackets are stowed under each bed.

(C) People find they write more often when they use e-mail.

(D) Protesters want to stop experiments on animals.

(E) All cabins have their own water purification system.

(F) Thousands of animal rights activists blocked the entrances to six research facilities.

(G) Oil, coal, and gas are limited resources.

(H) Correspondents from all over the world can send letters instantaneously via their computers.

(I) We expect more snow and ice later today.

(J) Solar energy may be one substitute for petroleum-based fuels.

AVOID THE TRAP!

Don't mark the first recognizable answer. Some test takers guess too quickly. They see a word from the passage, and assume it's the correct answer. Take time to analyze.

Skill 3: Predicting Inferences

On Part VII of the TOEIC test, you may be asked to make inferences about a reading passage. To make correct inferences, you must draw conclusions about what is likely or logical from information that is explicitly stated in the passage.

Sample TOEIC Question

This question refers to the following electronic index.

Where to GO	
On-line Index	
Business Data Plus	GO BUSDP
Business Demographics	GO BUSDEM
Executive News Service	GO ENS
Entrepreneur's Small Business Forum	GO SMALLBIZ
International Trade Forum	GO ITFORUM
PR and Marketing Archives	GO PRSIG

Who would most likely use this index?
(A) Hotel housekeepers
(B) Oil engineers
(C) Business people
(D) Airline pilots

Choice (C) is the correct answer. From the list of topics, you can infer that most of them concern business. In fact, the word *business* is in four of the six topics.

Choices (A), (B), and (D) are incorrect, because although these professions might possibly use this index, neither a hotel housekeeper, an oil engineer, nor an airline pilot would be the most likely user of a commercial index.

Skill Focus

Many different kinds of information can be a clue to predicting inferences. Clues may be found in the words used, in the way that the information is presented, and in probable occurrences, based on information given. Review the clues below, which show how different kinds of information can help predict inferences.

Clue 1   Clues to inferences may be found in terms that are repeated, or in the use of many words that are related to each other.

Example: Everyone wants to be with their families. Employees are happier if they have family time to take their children for bike rides, spend time with their parents, and go out to dinner with their spouse.

Inference: *Families, family, children, parents,* and *spouse* suggest that the idea of family is important to the passage.

Clue 2 Clues to inferences may be found in the way that information is combined, especially when steps seem to be left out.

Example: On the first day of work, new employees report to orientation. There will be sessions on company policy, employee benefits, and product history. On the fourth day, employees will be assigned to a trainer in their department.

Inference: The orientation sessions will last three days.

Clue 3 An inference may be the next logical outcome of a statement.

Example: Everyone will want to buy the product.

Inference: The manufacturer of the product will make a profit.

Exercises ⌦ p 232

Below there is a statement followed by three possible inferences that can be made from the first sentence. Circle the one sentence that is the most logical inference that can be made from the first sentence. This will help you recognize what is inferred on the reading passages in Part VII.

1. The politician lost the election.
   (A) She was absentminded.
   (B) Her policies weren't popular with the voters.
   (C) She was elected on the first ballot.

2. It took over an hour to drive just five miles.
   (A) The traffic was very heavy.
   (B) The distance was very long.
   (C) Our car is very fast.

3. Mozart could play the violin and the harpsichord when he was only five.
   (A) He was taught by his father.
   (B) He didn't want to play the trombone.
   (C) He was very precocious.

4. A knowledgeable consumer waits until items go on sale.
   (A) Smart shoppers like to save money.
   (B) If you know you need something, buy it now.
   (C) The best items are never on sale.

5. Company earnings would have been higher had there been no strike.
   (A) The workers will not go on strike.
   (B) The striking workers reduced the profitability of the company.
   (C) Earnings are always higher in the last quarter.

AVOID THE TRAP!

You won't find a direct answer to inferential questions in the reading passage.

Remember: You need to "read between the lines."

Skill 4: Understanding the Purpose

On Part VII of the TOEIC test, you may be asked to determine the purpose of a reading passage. To answer these questions, you must decide whether the purpose of the passage is to inform, persuade, criticize, amuse, praise, or apologize.

The purpose is not directly stated in the passage; you have to infer the purpose from the context. As you read, you should ask yourself: why was this passage written?

Sample TOEIC Question

This question refers to the following notice.

Here's an opportunity to put your sales ability to work as the owner of your own direct marketing agency. You'll sell ad services and have an international company behind you. Your income will increase and you will have more time to spend with your family. You will be able to take your vacations when YOU want to take them. Why work for others when you can work for yourself?

For more information, come to the Business Opportunity Show at the Carlton Hotel on July 23–24. No need to schedule an appointment. Just meet us at Booth 345.

What is the purpose of this notice?
(A) To give employees more time with their families
(B) To persuade you to come to the Business Opportunity Show
(C) To strengthen your sales ability
(D) To schedule an appointment

Choice (B) is the correct answer. The purpose of the notice is to persuade the reader to come to the Business Opportunity Show. If the person does come, he or she will be able to learn what is required to start a business that will make them wealthy, happy, and wise.

Choice (A) is incorrect, because having more time with your family is a result of having your own business. Choice (C) is incorrect, because the notice assumes the reader already has strong sales ability. Choice (D) is incorrect, because appointments are not required.

Skill Focus

When the reading passage is a chart, or form, it is usually easy to determine the purpose. The purpose is usually found in the title or heading of the form. When the reading passage is made up of one or more paragraphs, you may have to consider the passage carefully to decide the purpose. The clues below may help. Review these clues and the examples for determining the purpose of a reading passage.

Clue 1   An informative passage may contain several facts or figures. Such passages may be in the form of charts, graphs, or lists, as well as in paragraphs. Adjectives tend to be objective.

Example: The number of students seeking admission to the graduate business program has increased 20% over the past 18 months. Among the reasons for the increase are the opening of our new suburban classroom building last January and the 97%

excellence rating awarded to us by the accreditation board.

Explanation: The passage contains several facts and figures: *increased 20%, past 18 months, 97% excellence rating.* The only two adjectives that are not part of common phrases (such as *graduate business program* and *last January*) are *new* and *suburban.* Both of these are objective.

Clue 2   A persuasive passage usually recommends an action or a way of thinking. It typically gives the reasons for that position and the benefits of adopting it.

Example: The newly developed Warm 'n' Soft fabric may be the most comfortable winter fabric you have ever worn. It is 20% warmer than plain wool. It's also lightweight, which means that you won't be weighed down by a heavy coat. Warm 'n' Soft is water-resistant, too, so wet snow rolls right off. If you want to laugh at the cold weather this winter, make sure you choose a coat made of Warm 'n' Soft.

Explanation: The action recommended is the purchase of a Warm 'n' Soft coat. The reasons for recommending the purchase are that Warm 'n' Soft is warmer than wool, lightweight, and water-resistant. The benefit of purchasing a Warm 'n' Soft coat is that this coat will keep you warm, dry, and comfortable in wintertime.

Clue 3   A critical passage is usually a reaction to a stated idea or situation. It may present many contrasts and alternatives. It probably contains adjectives and other words that have both positive and negative meanings.

Example: The new Civic Center was a good idea for our city, but it has failed due to poor planning. Lack of parking and nearby restaurants has made the Center a place that is difficult to get to and uncomfortable to be in.

Explanation: This passage is a reaction to the first line, *a new Civic Center was a good idea for our city.* Notice that this is quite a positive statement, compared to the rest of the paragraph. The passage contrasts this good idea with the bad way the idea was carried out. It specifically mentions the effects of lack of parking and absence of nearby restaurants. It has positive words, *new* and *good,* and negative words, *failed, poor, lack of, difficult,* and *uncomfortable.*

Clue 4   A passage intended to amuse the reader may contain imaginative ideas. It may describe a situation, or present an image, that makes you smile. The facts presented are usually simple, rather than complicated.

Example: The Tasty Bakery is famous for making cakes in any shape or size. Among their most popular styles are cakes that look like roses, baskets of flowers, or footballs. They also make cakes to order, and some of the customers' requests have been unusual. One customer wanted a cake that looked like a hamburger. Another wanted a cake that looked like his dog. But the strangest request came from a mayor who wanted a replica of his town in cake for their Founder's Day celebration.

Explanation: The imaginative ideas presented in this passage are the many different shapes mentioned for the cakes. Certainly the images of these cakes that you make in your mind should make you smile. The facts mentioned are all quite simple and do not require you to make calculations or complicated associations. These facts are that the

Tasty Bakery is famous, they make cakes in different shapes and sizes, and some customer requests are unusual.

Clue 5   A passage in praise of something usually has many positive adjectives and words with positive connotations. It may show a positive result of a past action, or predict a positive outcome of a current or future action.

Example: The recently published *Guide to City Restaurants* will be a big help to visitors and residents who want to eat out. The guide gives clear, precise information about food, location, and prices. It is also well organized, so that information can be located quickly and easily.

Explanation: The many positive adjectives and other words in this passage indicate that its purpose is to praise the restaurant guide. The positive terms include *big help, clear, precise information, well organized, clearly,* and *easily*. It predicts a positive outcome of a future action, *will be a big help to visitors and residents who want to eat out*.

Clue 6   A passage intended to apologize for something acknowledges a mistake and expresses regret for the problems that the mistake might have caused. It also usually mentions some current or future action intended to rectify the mistake.

Example: This newspaper would like to announce that the sale price of Grip-Tight tires that appeared yesterday in the ad for Johnson's Garage was misprinted. The correct sale price of each tire is $90, as printed in today's ad. We regret any inconvenience that this error has caused Johnson's Garage and its customers.

Explanation: The mistake that is acknowledged is *the sale price of Grip-Tight tires that appeared yesterday in the ad for Johnson's Garage was misprinted*. The announcement expresses regret in the line *we regret any inconvenience that this error has caused Johnson's Garage and its customers*. The action to rectify the mistake is the explicit one that the newspaper has printed the ad with the correct price today, and the assumed one that they are correcting this mistake by printing the apology in the newspaper.

Exercises ◎══ p 232

Circle the purpose of the statements below. This will help you recognize the purpose of the reading passages in Part VII.

1. We want to congratulate Mr. Prahinski, who was responsible for the award-winning design of our new handheld personal communicator.

   What is the purpose of this statement?
   (A) To criticize
   (B) To persuade
   (C) To inform
   (D) To praise

2. I would like you to meet our new Front Desk Manager, Ms. Tamayo, who has been with our sister hotel in Rio.

   What is the purpose of this statement?
   (A) To amuse
   (B) To praise
   (C) To inform
   (D) To criticize

3. In the future, I hope that there will be more attention paid to our customers' needs and less time spent on your own personal affairs.

   What is the purpose of this statement?
   (A) To apologize
   (B) To praise
   (C) To criticize
   (D) To inform

4. There are 365 days in a year, except in a leap year, when there are 366.

   What is the purpose of this statement?
   (A) To inform
   (B) To persuade
   (C) To apologize
   (D) To praise

5. We apologize for the delay, but the severe weather patterns in the area have grounded all planes.

   What is the purpose of this statement?
   (A) To persuade
   (B) To apologize
   (C) To amuse
   (D) To criticize

AVOID THE TRAP!

Keep the main idea in mind as you determine the purpose. Most passages have details of several types. For example, a passage can praise part of an idea, but criticize most of the idea. You must look for the overall purpose of the passage.

Practice: Part VII

The questions below are based on a variety of reading material. Choose the one best answer to the questions.

<u>Questions 1–5</u> refer to the following page from an appointment calendar. p 232

MARCH

28 Monday

Meet train 6:42 at station

29 Tuesday

6:00 Tennis w/T. Kral

30 Wednesday

12:00 pm Lunch at Elizabeth's Café w/ Ms. Welby

31 Thursday

4:00 pm Teleconference

APRIL   **1** Friday

10:00 Staff meeting
11:00 Mr. James Gonsalves

2 Saturday

7:30am John Ling - golf course

3 Sunday

---

1. What is this calendar used for?
   (A) To schedule appointments
   (B) To organize ideas
   (C) To cancel appointments
   (D) To take notes

2. Where is the appointment with John Ling?
   (A) 7:30 P.M.
   (B) After the weekend
   (C) On the golf course
   (D) Saturday morning

3. What can be inferred from this page?
   (A) There will be a teleconference on Tuesday.
   (B) The staff meeting on Friday will not be longer than an hour.
   (C) There will be a tennis game on Thursday.
   (D) Ms. Welby is a vegetarian.

4. What schedule does this appointment calendar show?
   (A) A work week only
   (B) March 28 to March 31
   (C) A weekend only
   (D) Monday to Sunday

5. When is the appointment with Ms. Welby?
   (A) On Wednesday at midnight
   (B) At the train station on Monday evening
   (C) At noon
   (D) At Elizabeth's Café on Friday

Questions 6–8 refer to the following form.  p 232

Call 1-800-438-5459
to make a reservation

You have the opportunity to reserve these accommodations for next year. Send a non-refundable reservation fee (10%). The lease will be sent to you by November 15. Fill out this form and return it to our office as soon as possible.

Name & Address:
_____
_____

Phone: _____

Today's date: _____

10% paid by: _____

Reservation date: _____

Cash ☐   Check ☐

Reserved for office use:

Accommodations #:   Rec'd by:

6. What is this type of form used for?
   (A) To obtain insurance
   (B) To reserve accommodations
   (C) To pay a bill
   (D) To pay an invoice

7. Which of the following information is filled in at the office?
   (A) Name and address
   (B) Today's date
   (C) Phone number
   (D) Received by

8. Which of the following can NOT be used for payment?
   (A) Cash
   (B) Credit card
   (C) Personal check
   (D) Traveler's check

Questions 9–12 refer to the following newspaper article. p 232

RAISING RATES IN THE CITY—FOR THE TOURIST

WHEN TAXES ON hotel rooms in Washington, D.C. rise this summer, the city will go from having the 30th highest hotel taxes to having the 10th highest among the top tourist cities in the United States. This increase, from 11 percent to 13 percent, is a big one; however, the tax rate is much lower than hotel taxes charged in New York.

In addition to hotel taxes, there will be new restaurant taxes. Taxes at Washington restaurants will rise from 9 percent to 10 percent. This increase gives Washington the highest restaurant taxes in the country.

Although the new restaurant taxes will affect local citizens, the taxes will mostly affect tourists to the city. These tourists will pay both the new hotel taxes and the new restaurant taxes.

An organization based in San Francisco made a survey of "tourist taxes" in 50 most-visited cities. The study of hotel, restaurant, gasoline, car rental, and airfare taxes showed that the average family pays 14 percent of its vacation budget in taxes. "The tourist is the easiest target to tax because tourists don't vote where they spend," said the chairman of the organization.

9. What does this article primarily discuss?
   (A) The result of a survey
   (B) Tourist taxes
   (C) Washington, D.C.
   (D) Taxes in restaurants

10. Which taxes will increase by 2 percent?
   (A) Tourist taxes in San Francisco
   (B) Hotel taxes in Washington, D.C.
   (C) Restaurant taxes in Washington, D.C.
   (D) Tourist taxes in 50 most-visited cities

11. Which of the following is NOT true?
   (A) Hotel taxes in New York are higher than those in Washington, D.C.
   (B) Tourists and local citizens pay restaurant taxes
   (C) Taxes make up more than 10 percent of a family's vacation budget
   (D) New York has the highest restaurant taxes in the United States

12. Why are tourists "the easiest target to tax"?
   (A) Tourists are travelers; they don't stay to vote against politicians.
   (B) Tourists are easily found.
   (C) Tourists don't mind paying for fun.
   (D) Tourists usually don't spend a lot of money.

Questions 13–16 refer to the following message.  p 233

```
┌─────────────────────────────────────────────────┐
│  To:      Mr. Ramen                             │
│  Date:   12/08         Time:   10:15   (AM)PM   │
│  WHILE YOU WERE OUT                             │
│  Mr.     Sam Keng                               │
│  of      Hotel Service Corporation              │
│  Phone   (202) 555-1234  x341                   │
│  Area Code Number        Extension              │
│  ✔ TELEPHONED            ✔ PLEASE CALL          │
│  ☐ RETURNED YOUR CALL    ☐ WILL CALL            │
│                                                 │
│            Unable to make tomorrow s            │
│  Message _____         │
│            meeting; let s meet next             │
│                                                 │
│            Monday                               │
│                                                 │
│            Ms. Murohisa                         │
│            Operator                             │
└─────────────────────────────────────────────────┘
```

13. Who made the phone call?
   (A) Mr. Sam Keng
   (B) Mr. Ramen
   (C) Ms. Murohisa
   (D) Hotel Service Corporation

14. Who took the message?
   (A) Mr. Sam Keng
   (B) Mr. Ramen
   (C) Ms. Murohisa
   (D) Hotel Service Corporation

15. Why was the call made?
   (A) To cancel a meeting
   (B) To verify a meeting
   (C) To leave a message
   (D) To return a call

16. What will probably happen next?
   (A) Mr. Keng will call Mr. Ramen.
   (B) Mr. Keng and Mr. Ramen will meet on Monday.
   (C) Mr. Ramen will telephone Mr. Keng.
   (D) Ms. Murohisa will return Mr. Keng's call.

Questions 17–20 refer to the following form. p 233

CompuSys Conference

Secretaria Executiva
Av. Francisco Jose de Camargo Andrade, 34
13040-221 – Campinas, SP
Brazil

Telephone: (55) (192) 41-3204
Fax: (55) (192) 41-5432

Name _____
　　　　　　Last/Family　　　　　　　First　　　　　　　Middle

CompuSys Membership # _____

Company Name _____

Mailing Address _____

City/State/Zip/Country_____

Work Phone Number: Fax: _____ e-mail: _____

CONFERENCE: Please check appropriate fee(s). Advance Reservation Fees Until July 10, 19–	CompuSys Member Advance/Late or On-site	Non-Member Advance/Late or On-site
Full Conference Registration	☐ $330/ $420	☐ $430/ $530
Opening Ceremony	☐ $30/ $40	☐ $100/ $120
Day One of Conference (Oct.2)	☐ $100/ $120	☐ $110/ $135
Day Two of Conference (Oct.3)	☐ $100/ $120	☐ $110/ $135
Day Three of Conference (Oct.4)	☐ $100/ $120	☐ $110/ $135
Proceedings of the Conference	☐ $80/ $1000	☐ $110/ $135

Total (in U.S. dollars) $_____

Methods of Payment
☐ Payment Order
PAY TO: Banco do Brasil S.A., New York (USA)
　　SWIFT CODE: BRASUS44
　　CHIPS ABA: 0344
　　FED WIRE: ABA 0371-1466-8
　　FOR ACCT.: 128.141-6

☐ Credit Card
Card Holder Name _____
Card Number _____
Expiration Date_____

Authorized
Signature _____

---

17. What is this form for?
 (A) Customs declaration
 (B) Conference registration
 (C) Hotel reservation
 (D) Duty-free voucher

18. What is the cost for non-members to register for the opening ceremony on-site?
 (A) $30
 (B) $40
 (C) $100
 (D) $120

19. Where does the conference take place?
 (A) France
 (B) Switzerland
 (C) New York
 (D) Brazil

20. To save money, registration must be received no later than
 (A) July 10
 (B) October 2
 (C) October 3
 (D) October 4

Questions 21–25 refer to the following fax. p 233

SE
29th December 19—

Via Facsimile Number: 1-42-72-61-66

For the attention of: Mr. Armand Dubois

General Manager's Office
Grand Hotel Limited
Berkeley Square
London, W1A 2JQ
Telephone (0171) 518 7759
Telex 10761 Fax (0171) 518 1109

DUBOIS AND LEGER, L.L.P.
Attorneys At Law

Dear Mr. Dubois,

Thank you for your facsimile letter dated 28th December 1994, addressed to Ms. Anna Wong, Assistant Sales Manager, for whom I am replying.

It is with great pleasure that I reconfirm we have now reserved your one-bedroom suite from Sunday, 20th January until departure on Monday, 28th January 19—.

We will, of course, do our utmost to allocate your usual suite #301/2 for you. However, should this suite not be available, we will naturally provide a suitable alternative. I have noted that you require a non-smoking suite with a king-size bed with bed boards. This room will also be away from the room service waiter area or construction.

The daily rate for this accommodation is £500.00, inclusive of Service, excluding Value Added Tax at 17.5%.

I trust all is in order, and I look forward very much indeed to welcoming you back to the Grand. You may rest assured that we will do our utmost to ensure that your stay is as comfortable and as enjoyable as possible.

If you should feel I can be of any further assistance, please do not hesitate to contact me.

Yours sincerely,

Malcolm A. Ashton

Malcolm A. Ashton
General Manager

21. What was the purpose of the fax?
   (A) To promote the hotel
   (B) To confirm a reservation
   (C) To ask for legal advice
   (D) To change the arrival date

22. Who did Mr. Dubois originally write to?
   (A) Mr. Leger
   (B) The General Manager
   (C) Mr. Ashton
   (D) Ms. Wong

23. What can be said about Mr. Dubois?
   (A) He often stays at the Grand.
   (B) He likes to smoke.
   (C) He never stays longer than two nights.
   (D) He likes to be close to the waiter area.

24. What is included in the room rate?
   (A) Value Added Tax
   (B) Service
   (C) Breakfast
   (D) Airport transfers

25. What will the General Manager do if Suite 301/2 is occupied?
    (A) Refund £500
    (B) Clean it first
    (C) Offer a comparable suite
    (D) Add an extra bed

Questions 26–30 refer to the following fax. p 234

Visitors who want to see the city's attractions have several transportation options. The use of private cars is discouraged, since parking is limited and the streets of the historical district are narrow. Fortunately, excellent alternatives are available. The subway system provides fast, inexpensive transportation to all areas of the city, from 6:00 am to 12 midnight. Bus service operates 24 hours a day, for those who prefer to travel above ground and sneak in some extra sightseeing en route. Those of you who want to make sure that you see all the tourist attractions may be especially interested in our Visitor's Tour buses, which make stops at all points of interest throughout the city. For your convenience, special visitor's passes for all forms of public transportation are sold at hotels throughout the city, along with maps and schedules for transportation routes. Subway tickets may also be purchased at subway stops.

26. What is this announcement about?
    (A) Hotels
    (B) Visitors
    (C) Transportation
    (D) Attractions

27. What should visitors NOT do in the city?
    (A) Spend the night
    (B) Drive their cars
    (C) Walk alone
    (D) Travel at rush hour

28. Which service stops at midnight?
    (A) Bus service
    (B) Subway service
    (C) Tour service
    (D) Taxi service

29. Why may some people prefer traveling by bus?
    (A) People can see more of the city.
    (B) Buses are faster.
    (C) The subway is more expensive.
    (D) Bus routes are more convenient.

30. Where are tickets sold?
    (A) At special stands
    (B) On the buses
    (C) At some tourist attractions
    (D) At most hotels

PRACTICE TEST 1

Test of English for International Communication

General Directions

This is a test of your ability to use the English language. The total time for the test is approximately two hours. It is divided into seven parts. Each part of the test begins with a set of specific directions. Be sure you understand what you are to do before you begin work on a part.

You will find that some of the questions are harder than others, but you should try to answer every one. There is no penalty for guessing. Do not be concerned if you cannot answer all of the questions.

Do not mark your answers in this test book. <u>You must put all of your answers on a separate answer sheet</u> that you have been given. When putting your answer to a question on your answer sheet, be sure to fill out the answer space corresponding to the letter of your choice. Fill in the space so that the letter inside the oval cannot be seen, as shown in the example below.

Mr. Jones_____ to his accountant yesterday.

(A) talk
(B) talking
(C) talked
(D) to talk

Sample Answer
(A) (B) ● (D)

The sentence should read, "Mr. Jones talked to his accountant yesterday." Therefore, you should choose answer (C). Notice how this has been done in the example given.

Mark only <u>one</u> answer for each question. If you change your mind about an answer after you have marked it on your answer sheet, completely erase your old answer and then mark your new answer. You must mark the answer sheet carefully so that the test-scoring machine can accurately record your test score.

LISTENING COMPREHENSION

In this section of the test, you will have the chance to show how well you understand spoken English. There are four parts to this section, with special directions for each part.

Part I 🔑 p 235 📼 p 206

Directions: For each question, you will see a picture in your test book and you will hear four short statements. The statements will be spoken just one time. They will not be printed in your test book, so you must listen carefully to understand what the speaker says.

When you hear the four statements, look at the picture in your test book and choose the statement that best describes what you see in the picture. Then, on your answer sheet, find the number of the question and mark your answer. Look at the sample below.

Now listen to the four statements.

Sample Answer

(A) ● (C) (D)

Statement (B), "They're having a meeting," best describes what you see in the picture. Therefore, you should choose answer (B).

1

2

3

4

5

6

7

8

9

10

11

12

13

14

15

16

17

18

19

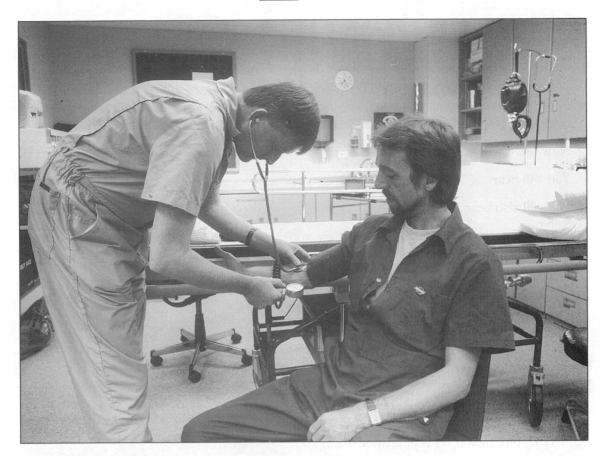

20

Part II 🔑 p 237 📼 p 207

Directions: In this part of the test, you will hear a question spoken in English, followed by three responses, also spoken in English. The question and the responses will be spoken just one time. They will not be printed in your test book, so you must listen carefully to understand what the speakers say. You are to choose the best response to each question.

Now listen to a sample question.

You will hear:

You will also hear:

<u>Sample Answer</u>

● (B) (C)

The best response to the question "How are you?" is choice (A), "I am fine, thank you." Therefore, you should choose answer (A).

21. Mark your answer on your answer sheet.

22. Mark your answer on your answer sheet.

23. Mark your answer on your answer sheet.

24. Mark your answer on your answer sheet.

25. Mark your answer on your answer sheet.

26. Mark your answer on your answer sheet.

27. Mark your answer on your answer sheet.

28. Mark your answer on your answer sheet.

29. Mark your answer on your answer sheet.

30. Mark your answer on your answer sheet.

31. Mark your answer on your answer sheet.

32. Mark your answer on your answer sheet.

33. Mark your answer on your answer sheet.

34. Mark your answer on your answer sheet.

35. Mark your answer on your answer sheet.

36. Mark your answer on your answer sheet.

37. Mark your answer on your answer sheet.

38. Mark your answer on your answer sheet.

39. Mark your answer on your answer sheet.

40. Mark your answer on your answer sheet.

41. Mark your answer on your answer sheet.

42. Mark your answer on your answer sheet.

43. Mark your answer on your answer sheet.

44. Mark your answer on your answer sheet.

45. Mark your answer on your answer sheet.

46. Mark your answer on your answer sheet.

47. Mark your answer on your answer sheet.

48. Mark your answer on your answer sheet.

49. Mark your answer on your answer sheet.

50. Mark your answer on your answer sheet.

Part III ☞ p 238 ▭ p 208

<u>Directions</u>: In this part of the test, you will hear several short conversations between two people. The conversations will not be printed in your test book. You will hear the conversations only once, so you must listen carefully to understand what the speakers say.

In your test book, you will read a question about each conversation. The question will be followed by four answers. You are to choose the best answer to each question and mark it on your answer sheet.

51. What are the speakers trying to do?
    (A) Go on a trip.
    (B) Finish a report.
    (C) Arrange a meeting.
    (D) Make a presentation.

52. Why can't the woman get the statement?
    (A) There are no profits.
    (B) It's still being typed.
    (C) It's confidential.
    (D) The woman is too late to get it.

53. What would the woman receive in the mail?
    (A) Bills for purchases.
    (B) A store credit card.
    (C) A price list.
    (D) Notices of upcoming sales.

54. What will the woman have?
    (A) Coffee.
    (B) Cream.
    (C) A roll.
    (D) A pastry.

55. Why will they break early for lunch?
    (A) The presentation is short.
    (B) They'll need lots of time.
    (C) There are too many people.
    (D) They can't be late.

56. What does the woman want the man to do?
    (A) Wait for the client.
    (B) Send the client up.
    (C) Call the woman.
    (D) Ask the client inside.

57. When can the woman go to the market district?
    (A) Before the tour starts.
    (B) During the tour.
    (C) At the end of the tour.
    (D) On a different tour.

58. What kind of seat would the woman prefer?
    (A) A window seat.
    (B) An aisle seat.
    (C) A center seat.
    (D) A comfortable seat.

59. What does the man suggest they see?
    (A) A concert.
    (B) A play.
    (C) A movie.
    (D) An opera.

60. What was the man doing wrong?
    (A) Putting the paper in too fast.
    (B) Giving it too much paper.
    (C) Using the wrong kind of paper.
    (D) Letting the paper get caught.

61. What will happen if the woman's book is overdue?
    (A) She will lose her library card.
    (B) She will have to pay a fine.
    (C) She will get to keep the book.
    (D) She will have to buy the book.

62. What is the problem with the meeting?
    (A) There is no time for the meeting.
    (B) Everyone is too busy for the meeting.
    (C) No available room is large enough for the meeting.
    (D) No one has prepared for the meeting.

63. Where did this conversation take place?
    (A) At an airport.
    (B) At a travel agency.
    (C) In a car repair shop.
    (D) In a hotel.

64. What does the man want to do?
    (A) Park his car.
    (B) Get his car repaired.
    (C) Find a park close by.
    (D) Buy a map.

65. What does the man do every morning?
    (A) Take the subway.
    (B) Give his brother a ride.
    (C) Think about work.
    (D) Use his computer.

66. What is the woman's profession?
    (A) Doctor.
    (B) Pharmacist.
    (C) Nurse.
    (D) Clerk.

67. What is the man doing?
    (A) Opening a window.
    (B) Ordering a cup of coffee.
    (C) Trying on shoes.
    (D) Shopping for a coat.

68. What does the man think about the woman?
    (A) She is not hungry.
    (B) She needs a break.
    (C) She has a nice voice.
    (D) She broke his computer.

69. What is the man expecting?
    (A) A package.
    (B) A letter.
    (C) Some pills.
    (D) Some checks.

70. What does the woman have to do?
    (A) Carry the bag on the plane.
    (B) Fit the bag under the seat.
    (C) Check the bag.
    (D) Weigh the bag.

71. Why shouldn't the man worry?
    (A) There's not enough time.
    (B) The letter can wait.
    (C) He can stay late.
    (D) The clock is wrong.

72. What does the woman advise the man to do?
    (A) Copy the memo.
    (B) Correct the error.
    (C) Answer the phone.
    (D) Fix the copier.

73. Why is the man disappointed?
    (A) The driver doesn't make change.
    (B) He will have to change buses.
    (C) The driver will send him a bill.
    (D) He will be late for class.

74. What is the man doing?
    (A) Preparing to type a letter.
    (B) Asking for a raise.
    (C) Working at his computer.
    (D) Applying for a job.

75. Why can the man lend the woman an umbrella?
    (A) He doesn't mind getting wet.
    (B) He'll wait until the rain stops.
    (C) He has two umbrellas.
    (D) He owes her a favor.

76. Where do these people probably work?
    (A) In an office.
    (B) At a hotel.
    (C) At a cafeteria.
    (D) In a market.

77. Why does the man need the woman's help?
    (A) He forgot his glasses.
    (B) He wants seafood.
    (C) He doesn't know how to read.
    (D) He dropped the tableware.

78. What does the man want to find?
    (A) The marketing department.
    (B) The water fountain.
    (C) The mail room.
    (D) The copy room.

79. Where will the woman eat?
    (A) Inside.
    (B) At home.
    (C) In the park.
    (D) On the patio.

80. What is the relationship between the speakers?
    (A) Boss and secretary.
    (B) Lawyer and client.
    (C) Teacher and student.
    (D) Clerk and customer.

Part IV 🗝 p 240 📼 p 210

<u>Directions</u>: In this part of the test, you will hear several short talks. Each will be spoken just one time. They will not be printed in your test book, so you must listen carefully to understand and remember what is said.

In your test book, you will read two or more questions about each short talk. The questions will be followed by four answers. You are to choose the best answer to each question and mark it on your answer sheet.

81. When should passengers approach the gate?
    (A) When their names are called.
    (B) When their boarding passes are ready.
    (C) When their bags are on board.
    (D) When their row number is called.

82. When can First Class passengers board?
    (A) Before everyone else.
    (B) After everyone else.
    (C) Any time.
    (D) During first-class boarding.

83. What should people NOT do before leaving the building?
    (A) Gather their personal belongings.
    (B) Move quickly to the exits.
    (C) Call the fire department.
    (D) Notify others.

84. How should people leave the building?
    (A) On the elevators.
    (B) By the stairways.
    (C) Through the windows.
    (D) From the roof.

85. This line provides information about
    (A) Restaurants.
    (B) Theaters.
    (C) Tours.
    (D) Shopping.

86. Which tour is NOT mentioned?
    (A) Museum.
    (B) Candlelight.
    (C) Walking.
    (D) Guided.

87. What business is advertised?
    (A) Cleaning services.
    (B) Delivery services.
    (C) Accounting services.
    (D) Printing services.

88. If customers place a large order, what will they offer them?
    (A) Special low rates.
    (B) Extra stationery.
    (C) Free advertising.
    (D) Guaranteed work.

89. Where are they located?
    (A) In the business district.
    (B) In the suburbs.
    (C) Throughout the city.
    (D) On the harbor.

90. What kind of weather is predicted for the next twenty-four hours?
    (A) Sunny.
    (B) Cloudy.
    (C) Mild.
    (D) Warm.

91. How will the wind change during the night?
    (A) It will increase.
    (B) It will decrease.
    (C) It will become dangerous.
    (D) It will become constant.

92. When is rain expected?
    (A) Late tonight.
    (B) Early tomorrow.
    (C) Around noon.
    (D) Late tomorrow.

93. This mail room is probably part of
    (A) The post office.
    (B) A large company.
    (C) A neighborhood.
    (D) The government.

94. What is NOT mentioned as a function of the mail room ?
    (A) Sorting mail.
    (B) Delivering mail.
    (C) Selling stamps.
    (D) Wrapping packages.

95. What kind of package should employees let the mailroom prepare?
    (A) Fragile packages.
    (B) Expensive packages.
    (C) Heavy packages.
    (D) Sturdy packages.

96. What is Dr. Yung's profession?
    (A) Scientist.
    (B) Medical doctor.
    (C) Professor.
    (D) Psychologist.

97. Where is this introduction most likely given?
    (A) In a classroom.
    (B) In a hospital.
    (C) At a banquet.
    (D) At a conference.

98. What does the news item discuss?
    (A) Banking practices.
    (B) The economy.
    (C) New car sales.
    (D) Automobile exports.

99. What is an explanation for the increase?
    (A) Old cars are wearing out.
    (B) It's easier to get a car loan.
    (C) Traffic is less congested.
    (D) People own more than one car.

100. What prompted more safety features on new cars?
    (A) The number of accidents.
    (B) Injuries to passengers.
    (C) Government regulations.
    (D) Consumer demand.

This is the end of the Listening Comprehension portion of the test. Turn to Part V in your test book.

READING

In this section of the test, you will have the chance to show how well you understand written English. There are three parts to this section, with special directions for each part.

Part V 🔑 p 241

Directions: This part of the test has incomplete sentences. Four words or phrases, marked (A), (B), (C), (D), are given beneath each sentence. You are to choose the one word or phrase that best completes the sentence. Then, on your answer sheet, find the number of the question and mark your answer.

Example	Sample Answer
Because the equipment is very delicate, it must be handled with _____ .	(A) (B) ● (D)

(A) caring
(B) careful
(C) care
(D) carefully

The sentence should read, "Because the equipment is very delicate, it must be handled with care." Therefore, you should choose answer (C).

Now begin work on the questions.

101. People _____ always willing to switch to a better product.

    (A) is
    (B) are
    (C) be
    (D) being

102. Our program is _____ selling software on the market.

    (A) the fast
    (B) fastest
    (C) faster
    (D) the fastest

103. Many companies hire consultants to give _____ on special projects.

    (A) advise
    (B) advertise
    (C) advice
    (D) adventure

104. Mr. Lee _____ his vacation after the project is completed.

    (A) will take
    (B) took
    (C) has taken
    (D) taking

105. Business travelers usually do paperwork _____ their flights.

    (A) during

    (B) while

    (C) when

    (D) as

106. The person _____ prepared this report has a real talent for writing.

    (A) which

    (B) who

    (C) whose

    (D) she

107. The restaurant will prepare any dish without salt if a guest _____ it.

    (A) will request

    (B) requests

    (C) requested

    (D) request

108. The Jones Company has a reputation for quality _____ service.

    (A) nor

    (B) but

    (C) and

    (D) or

109. The pharmacist needed the doctor _____ the prescription before she filled it.

    (A) verifying

    (B) verified

    (C) verifies

    (D) to verify

110. The radio advertisements will start airing _____ Friday.

    (A) of

    (B) in

    (C) on

    (D) at

111. Effective staff members _____ to instructions.

    (A) always listen carefully

    (B) carefully always listen

    (C) carefully listen always

    (D) listen always carefully

112. Mr. Golino has been worrying too much and _____ .

    (A) works too hard

    (B) worked too hard

    (C) working too hard

    (D) to work to hard

113. Both _____ must be on my desk by 3:00 this afternoon.

    (A) reporter
    (B) reports
    (C) reporting
    (D) report

114. _____ her innovative advertising ideas, she was not promoted.

    (A) Because of
    (B) Even though
    (C) Although
    (D) Despite

115. The offices in the Pacific region _____ their meeting for next month.

    (A) have scheduled
    (B) has scheduled
    (C) is scheduling
    (D) schedules

116. The _____ participants wanted the meeting to end soon.

    (A) boring
    (B) bores
    (C) bored
    (D) is boring

117. Ms. Wei returns all her phone calls _____ .

    (A) rarely
    (B) every day
    (C) never
    (D) always

118. The only room that is large enough is _____ large conference room.

    (A) the
    (B) a
    (C) an
    (D) it

119. The food must be served _____ it is prepared.

    (A) as soon
    (B) as soon as
    (C) soon as
    (D) sooner than

120. Mr. Stein _____ for the day when the phone call came.

    (A) has already left
    (B) already leaves
    (C) already left
    (D) had already left

121. The restaurant _____ overlooks the river is very popular.

   (A) it
   (B) that
   (C) whose
   (D) who

122. Please take extra soap and towels _____ Room 312.

   (A) at
   (B) of
   (C) to
   (D) in

123. The waitress suggested that we _____ the spicy chicken.

   (A) order
   (B) ordered
   (C) to order
   (D) ordering

124. The _____ argument caused everyone to vote in favor of the proposal.

   (A) convinced
   (B) convince
   (C) convincing
   (D) to convince

125. Although it seems unlikely, _____ sometimes influences business decisions.

   (A) politicians
   (B) politics
   (C) political
   (D) politicize

126. This long letter will require three _____ .

   (A) paper
   (B) papers
   (C) sheets of paper
   (D) sheet of paper

127. The hotel tries to have fresh flowers _____ the lobby.

   (A) out
   (B) of
   (C) to
   (D) in

128. Ms. Dubois is the head of our department of research and _____ .

   (A) developed
   (B) developing
   (C) development
   (D) develops

129. Both the TV ads _____ the newspaper ads will be withdrawn.

    (A) and
    (B) also
    (C) but also
    (D) nor

130. A company cannot survive if losses are always _____ profits.

    (A) great as
    (B) greater than
    (C) great than
    (D) the greatest

131. Guests may select a single room _____ a suite with a bedroom and office.

    (A) but
    (B) and
    (C) or
    (D) nor

132. Ms. Ajai can probably _____ a way for the computer to run the program.

    (A) devote
    (B) desire
    (C) device
    (D) devise

133. The new desk, _____ was delivered yesterday, looks wonderful in the reception area.

    (A) that
    (B) which
    (C) it
    (D) whose

134. If Mr. Chi _____ the project, it will be finished on schedule.

    (A) had managed
    (B) has managed
    (C) managing
    (D) manages

135. The chairwoman urged that we _____ a deal with the competitors.

    (A) making
    (B) to make
    (C) make
    (D) will make

136. The _____ highways in the area make commuting difficult.

    (A) crowded
    (B) crowding
    (C) crowds
    (D) crowd

137. The passengers _____ for a long time before they could be seated.

   (A) wished
   (B) wanted
   (C) waited
   (D) went

138. Ms. Barrios _____ to the convention if she can get time off.

   (A) has gone
   (B) had gone
   (C) will go
   (D) was going

139. The manager made his employees _____ the computer training classes.

   (A) attending
   (B) attend
   (C) to attend
   (D) attendance

140. The meeting will take place _____ 11:00.

   (A) in
   (B) on
   (C) for
   (D) at

Part VI ⚷ p 243

Directions: In this part of the test, each sentence has four words or phrases underlined. The four underlined parts of the sentence are marked (A), (B), (C), (D). You are to identify the one underlined word or phrase that should be corrected or rewritten. Then, on your answer sheet, find the number of the question and mark your answer.

Example   Sample Answer

All <u>employee</u> are required to <u>wear</u> their   ● (B) (C) (D)
    A   B

<u>identification</u> badges <u>while</u> at work.
    C   D

Choice (A), the underlined word "employee," is not correct in this sentence. This sentence should read, "All employees are required to wear their identification badges while at work." Therefore, you should choose answer (A).

Now begin work on the questions.

141. <u>Stores</u> must meet the expectations of today's consumer <u>who</u> <u>expects</u> quality, service, and
     A   B   C
    <u>not paying very much</u>.
           D

142. The guest <u>which</u> just arrived forgot <u>to sign</u> his name <u>in</u> the hotel register.
    A   B   C   D

143. <u>Automated</u> teller machines allow busy customers <u>making</u> deposits <u>and</u> to cash checks <u>whenever</u> it
     A   B   C   D
    is convenient.

144. <u>No one</u> knows <u>what</u> the ultimate <u>affect</u> of global pollution <u>will be</u>.
     A   B   C   D

145. <u>Sales</u> of the <u>newest</u> computer <u>have</u> doubled <u>since</u> the past eight months.
     A   B   C   D

146. <u>The</u> job status reports <u>are</u> printed <u>every month</u> out <u>on</u> the first Monday.
     A   B   C   D

147. The <u>better</u> treatment <u>for</u> eye strain <u>is</u> to look <u>away from</u> the computer screen every twenty
        A   B   C   D
    minutes.

148. The company insists that security guards <u>meeting</u> employees <u>at</u> the building exit <u>and</u> walk them
                                        A   B   C
    <u>to</u> their cars.
     D

149. The <u>best</u> seats <u>in</u> the theater <u>will be reserved</u> for <u>inviting</u> guests.
        A   B   C   D

150. Although they been advertising the position for six months, none of the people who have applied
     A   B   C   D

     for the job is qualified.

151. The members of the personnel committee has decided to revise the employee handbook.
                  A   B   C   D

152. Even though the hotel was already full, the manager did not have rooms for people who had been
     A   B   C

     stranded by the storm.
              D

153. If clients have trouble using a software, they can call our computer helpline.
     A   B   C   D

154. Ms. Do is on vacation, but both her assistant or the division manager can help you with your
                 A   B   C   D

     request.

155. The new machinery has been operating within six months, but that is not enough time to see any
                                        A   B   C

     increase in production.
                 D

156. The book had already been published by the time the error is discovered.
     A   B   C   D

157. The fish has become a popular item on the menus of most restaurants.
     A   B   C   D

158. The waiters at the new restaurant has not received proper training in food service.
                 A   B   C   D

159. A Consolidated Computers Company has announced the site of its new headquarters.
     A   B   C   D

160. Even though Mr. Huff expects his staff to work overtime, rarely he stays later than 5:30.
     A   B   C   D

Part VII

Directions: The questions in this part of the test are based on a variety of reading material (for example, announcements, paragraphs, and advertisements). You are to choose the <u>one</u> best answer, (A), (B), (C), or (D), to each question. Then, on your answer sheet, find the number of the question and mark your answer. Answer all questions following a passage on the basis of what is <u>stated</u> or <u>implied</u> in that passage.

Read the following example.

> The Museum of Technology is a "hands-on" museum, designed for people to experience science at work. Visitors are encouraged to use, test, and handle the objects on display. Special demonstrations are scheduled for the first and second Wednesdays of each month at 1:30 p.m. Open Tuesday–Friday, 2:30–4:30 p.m., Saturday 11:00 a.m.–4:30 p.m., and Sunday 1:00–4:30 p.m.

> When during the month can visitors see special demonstrations?

> (A) Every weekend

> (B) The first two Wednesdays

> (C) One afternoon a week

> (D) Every other Wednesday

<u>Sample Answer</u>

(A) ● (C) (D)

The passage says that the demonstrations are scheduled for the first and second Wednesdays of the month. Therefore, you should choose answer (B).

Now begin work on the questions.

Questions 161–162 refer to the following announcement. p 244

> Business trends around the world indicated a stronger global economy, a recent study suggests. Increases in sales, production, and employment have been consistent over the past six months. These are the highest levels since 1990. This study has been evaluating 9,000 companies in 112 countries to spot business trends.

161. What does this survey show?

    (A) People are out of work.

    (B) Stocks are going to fall.

    (C) Businesses are doing well.

    (D) Manufacturing is changing.

162. What aspect is NOT mentioned as reflecting this trend?

    (A) Employment

    (B) Production

    (C) Sales

    (D) Research

Questions 163–164 refer to the following subscription form. p 244

> Yes! I would like to order season tickets.
> **SIX-PLAY SERIES**
> | | |
> |---|---|
> | Tuesday–Thursday evenings | $56 per person |
> | Friday/Saturday evenings | $76 per person |
> | Sunday matinee | $66 per person |
>
> Please Print. _____
> Name _____
> Address _____
> City-State-Zip Code _____

163. What is this subscription for?

    (A) Plays

    (B) Movies

    (C) Magazines

    (D) Newspapers

164. What determines the price of the season tickets?

    (A) The location of the theaters

    (B) The time you attend

    (C) The number of plays you see

    (D) The kind of plays you see

Questions 165–168 refer to the following announcement.  p 244

MEMO

TO: All employees

FROM: Ron Starsky, Accounting

DATE: March 15, 19—

There has been an unprecedented increase in the amount of taxi fare indicated on the expense accounts of our business travelers. To help keep costs under control, please remember the following guidelines when using taxicabs in an unfamiliar city.

Be sure that the meter is turned on after, not before, you sit down in the cab. Request that you take the most direct route to your destination. Establish an approximate fare to your destination before the driver moves the cab. Always ask the taxicab driver for a receipt showing the driver's name, I.D. number, name of the cab company, destination, and the amount paid for the fare. This will enable us to verify the trip should the fare be disputed.

---

165. What is this memo about?

(A) Filling out travel vouchers.
(B) Learning your way around a city.
(C) Traveling safely.
(D) Saving cab costs.

166. Who should pay attention to this memo?

(A) Company employees
(B) Taxi drivers
(C) Accountants
(D) Cab companies

167. When should the driver turn on the meter?

(A) When you hail the cab
(B) Before you get in the cab
(C) After you are in the taxi
(D) After the driver puts bags in the trunk

168. Why should employees get a receipt from the driver?

(A) To prove where they went
(B) To verify the trip
(C) To give to accounting
(D) To obtain the driver's signature

Questions 169–171 refer to the following article. p 244

BUSY EXECUTIVES ARE always looking for more ways to squeeze time into their day. This effort has led them to start work even before they get to their offices at nine with what has become known as the power breakfast. The power breakfast is essentially a meeting between two or more powerful executives who consider themselves too busy to get together at any other time. Restaurants—particularly the ones at large hotels in large cities—go out of their way to accommodate these meetings. Some start serving full breakfasts in their most elegant dining rooms as early as 6:30 a.m., and most require reservations before 9:00 a.m.

169. What is one way business people get more work out of their day?

    (A) Have breakfast meetings
    (B) Work late
    (C) Hire more assistants
    (D) Move closer to the office

170. Who started this trend?

    (A) People who leave work early
    (B) People who can't cook
    (C) People who had to get to work early
    (D) People who are too busy to meet at other times

171. What is one sign that this has become common?

    (A) Restaurants have begun to serve breakfast.
    (B) Restaurants require reservations for breakfast.
    (C) Restaurants have hired more waiters to serve breakfast.
    (D) Restaurants give wake-up calls.

Questions 172–174 refer to the following article.  p 245

Companies who are looking to establish a new headquarters or other facility must consider location very carefully. The match, or lack of it, between the company's requirements and the available human and natural resources in the area can be crucial. A company's future growth and prosperity depends on a successful match of needs and resources.

Different companies, of course, have different needs. Some are looking for a good climate and sound infrastructure, like public transportation, schools, and other facilities for their employees. Others are seeking affordable office space and a large workforce. Still others want a low cost of living and access to cultural or outdoor activities to keep their employees happy. But the one common denominator must be a pro-business attitude in the community. If the citizens do not want commercial enterprises in their neighborhood, a company should consider another location.

172. What must companies look for when choosing a location?

   (A) Abundant natural resources
   (B) The desires of the board
   (C) A match between needs and resources
   (D) A range of different needs

173. What possible requirement is NOT mentioned in the article?

   (A) Affordable office space
   (B) Tax advantages
   (C) Sound infrastructure
   (D) Climate

174. What is essential for success in all cases?

   (A) Low cost of living
   (B) Access to cultural activities
   (C) A large workforce
   (D) A pro-business attitude

Questions 175–176 refer to the following graph.  p 245

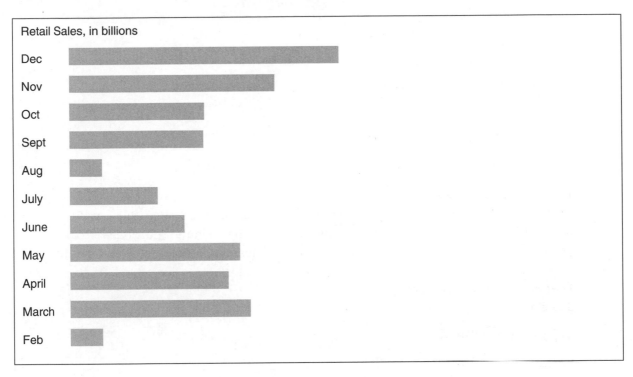

175. When does consumer spending peak?

   (A) March
   (B) January
   (C) December
   (D) June

176. Which months show the lowest retail sales?

   (A) February and August
   (B) April and May
   (C) July and August
   (D) November and March

Questions 177–179 refer to the following letter. p 245

408 Republic Avenue
Nogales, Mexico

Clothes by Mail Catalog
10 Lake Street
Springfield, Wisconsin 67032

To Whom it May Concern:
I am returning a pair of pants, item number 7042, because they did not fit. I would like my credit card, which was used for the original purchase, to be credited with the amount of the sale. I have enclosed the sales slip and credit receipt.
Thank you for your attention.
Sincerely,

Maria Gomez

Maria Gomez

177. What is the purpose of the letter?

(A) To get a catalog
(B) To check on some pants
(C) To return a purchase
(D) To order some clothes

178. How was the original purchase made?

(A) By credit card
(B) By check
(C) In cash
(D) As a gift

179. What does she request that the company do?

(A) Deliver the pants
(B) Refund her money
(C) Exchange the pants
(D) Credit her credit card

Questions 180–183 refer to the following article. ⊙🔑 p 245

Medical research has shown that mothers are right when they tell children to eat their vegetables. Fruits and vegetables have been shown to contain beneficial compounds that may encourage the body to stay healthy. Experts think that some of these compounds may even help fight off diseases such as cancer. They recommend that people consume a minimum of five servings of fruits and vegetables each day. Of course, for maximum benefit this should be combined with an overall reduction of dietary fat (including meats and cheeses) and a regular program of physical activity.

180. Which food groups does the article recommend?

   (A) Meat and eggs
   (B) Fruits and vegetables
   (C) Cheese and fish
   (D) Breads and cereal

181. What else do experts say about the compounds in these foods?

   (A) They have vitamins.
   (B) They contain fat.
   (C) They may fight disease.
   (D) They have calories.

182. How many servings of fruits and vegetables should people eat?

   (A) Two per day
   (B) Five per day
   (C) Five per week
   (D) Ten per week

183. What else should people do to stay healthy?

   (A) Cut down on fat
   (B) See the doctor
   (C) Eat meat
   (D) Drink water

Questions 184–187 refer to the following advertisement. p 245

> *If you plan your visit in October, don't miss the Harvest Festival. The festival offers a variety of activities for all age groups and interests. Children will enjoy listening to traditional stories and learning folk dances. Adults will enjoy the antique show and the crafts fair. Other attractions include a celebration of musical heritage and demonstrations of traditional skills such as candle making, butter churning, and bee keeping. The festival is held at the County Fairgrounds, ten miles outside of town on Highway 64 West. Space is available for you to park your car at the festival at no extra charge. The admission fee of $2 for adults and $1 for children is donated to the Preserve Our History Fund.*

184. What does this notice describe?

    (A) A lecture
    (B) A parade
    (C) A school
    (D) A festival

185. What activity is available for children?

    (A) Dancing
    (B) Painting
    (C) Ball playing
    (D) Singing

186. How does the advertisement assume that people get to the fairgrounds?

    (A) Walk
    (B) Fly
    (C) Take the subway
    (D) Drive a car

187. What happens to the admissions fee?

    (A) It is used to rent the fairgrounds.
    (B) It pays the performers.
    (C) It is donated to charity.
    (D) It pays for supplies.

Questions 188–191 refer to the following article.  p 245

Most people give little thought to the pens they write with, especially since the printers in modern homes and offices mean that very few items are handwritten. All too often, people buy a pen based only on looks, and wonder why they are not satisfied once they begin to use it. However, buying a pen that you will enjoy is not difficult if you keep a few simple tips in mind.

First of all, a pen should fit comfortably in your hand and be easy to manipulate. The thickness of the pen is the most important characteristic when determining comfort. If you have a small hand and thick fingers, you may be comfortable with a slender pen. If you have a larger hand and thicker fingers, you may prefer a fatter pen. The length of a pen can also influence comfort. A pen that is too long can easily feel top-heavy and unstable as you write.

Then, the writing point of the pen (called a nib on fountain pens) should allow the ink to flow evenly while the pen remains in contact with the paper. This will create a smooth line of writing, with no skips or gaps that indicate an irregular flow of ink within the pen. The point should also be sensitive enough to prevent ink from flowing when the pen is lifted from the paper. A point that does not seal off the flow may leave blots of ink at the end and beginning of each word, as you pick the pen up and put it down again.

Finally, the pen should make a bold, dark line. Fine-line pens may compensate for bad handwriting, but fine, delicate lines do not command attention next to printed text, as, for example, a signature on a printed letter. A broader line, by contrast, gives an impression of confidence and authority.

188. What does this article encourage people to do?

(A) Write more legibly
(B) Purchase better printers
(C) Write more things by hand
(D) Pay more attention to their pens

189. What is the most important characteristic to consider when determining the comfort of a pen?

(A) Thickness
(B) Length
(C) Weight
(D) Size

190. What might an irregular flow of ink cause?

(A) Smears
(B) Skips
(C) Blots
(D) Smudges

191. What is an advantage of fine-line pens?

(A) They are easier to write with.
(B) They convey confidence and authority.
(C) They can compensate for bad handwriting.
(D) They command attention.

Questions 192–195 refer to the following announcement. p 245

The Organization of Responsible Executives was founded five years ago to provide support and assistance for member executives who are looking for better ways to solve their problems. ORE concentrates on finding solutions that are environmentally and socially responsible. "If you need suggestions on non-polluting alternatives to chemicals, or want to know the pros and cons of setting up a day care center for your working parent, then we are the group to call," says director David Anderson. "If we don't have the information on hand, we'll find it for you." It is this kind of responsiveness that has made ORE the fastest-growing business organization to come along in years. It provides a one-source solution for executives who are trying help the company without hurting the world.

192. Who belongs to ORE?

(A) Secretaries
(B) Executives
(C) Parents
(D) Researchers

193. What is the purpose of ORE?

(A) To provide responsible solutions
(B) To introduce executives to each other
(C) To make lots of money
(D) To arrange mergers

194. How long has ORE been operating?

(A) For one year
(B) For two years
(C) For four years
(D) For five years

195. What shows that ORE is successful?

(A) It has large offices.
(B) It has high profits.
(C) It has grown fast.
(D) It has a good director.

Questions 196–198 refer to the following news item.  p 246

News Flash   News Flash   News Flash

Devastating floods along the coast have left many people homeless. People are asked to help by donating food, clothes, furniture, and other supplies to the Assistance Fund. Donations of bottled water are especially needed, since the floods have disrupted the local water supply. In addition, volunteers are needed to travel to the flooded area to help distribute the donations.

---

196. What does this notice concern?

   (A) Hazardous roads
   (B) Safety precautions
   (C) Help for flood victims
   (D) Warnings about weather

197. What kinds of supplies are NOT mentioned?

   (A) Medical supplies
   (B) Food
   (C) Clothing
   (D) Furniture

198. In addition to supplies, what is needed?

   (A) Teachers
   (B) New bridges
   (C) Places to stay
   (D) Volunteers

Questions 199–200 refer to the following guarantee. p 246

199. What happens if the workmanship is defective?

   (A) They will refund your money.
   (B) They will call a repairman.
   (C) They will replace parts.
   (D) They will give you a new appliance.

200. What kind of damage does the warranty NOT cover?

   (A) Poorly made parts
   (B) Abuse by the consumer
   (C) Bad motor design
   (D) Loose screws

> The manufacturer will replace all parts that fail due to defective workmanship. This warranty does not cover damage to this appliance resulting from dropping, crushing, burning, or operating in a manner not consistent with the directions in this manual.

Stop! This is the end of the test. If you finish before the time is called, you may go back to Parts V, VI, and VII and check your work.

PRACTICE TEST 2

Test of English for International Communication

General Directions

This is a test of your ability to use the English language. The total time for the test is approximately two hours. It is divided into seven parts. Each part of the test begins with a set of specific directions. Be sure you understand what you are to do before you begin work on a part.

You will find that some of the questions are harder than others, but you should try to answer every one. There is no penalty for guessing. Do not be concerned if you cannot answer all of the questions.

Do not mark your answers in this test book. You must put all of your answers on a separate answer sheet that you have been given. When putting your answer to a question on your answer sheet, be sure to fill out the answer space corresponding to the letter of your choice. Fill in the space so that the letter inside the oval cannot be seen, as shown in the example below.

Mr. Jones_____ to his accountant yesterday.

(A) talk
(B) talking
(C) talked
(D) to talk

Sample Answer
(A) (B) ● (D)

The sentence should read, "Mr. Jones talked to his accountant yesterday." Therefore, you should choose answer (C). Notice how this has been done in the example given.

Mark only one answer for each question. If you change your mind about an answer after you have marked it on your answer sheet, completely erase your old answer and then mark your new answer. You must mark the answer sheet carefully so that the test-scoring machine can accurately record your test score.

LISTENING COMPREHENSION

In this section of the test, you will have the chance to show how well you understand spoken English. There are four parts to this section, with special directions for each part.

Part I 🔑 p 246 📼 p 211

Directions: For each question, you will see a picture in your test book and you will hear four short statements. The statements will be spoken just one time. They will not be printed in your test book, so you must listen carefully to understand what the speaker says.

When you hear the four statements, look at the picture in your test book and choose the statement that best describes what you see in the picture. Then, on your answer sheet, find the number of the question and mark your answer. Look at the sample below.

Now listen to the four statements.

<u>Sample Answer</u>

(A) ● (C) (D)

Statement (B), "They're having a meeting," best describes what you see in the picture. Therefore, you should choose answer (B).

1

2

3

4

5

6

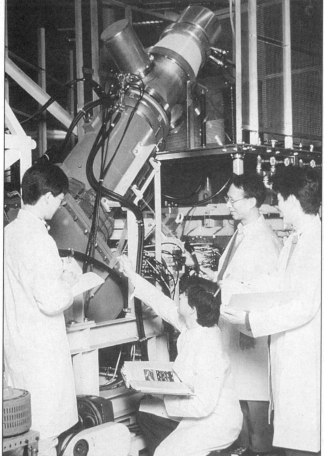

7

8

9

10

11

12

13

14

15

16

17

18

19

20

Part II 🔑 p 248 📼 p 212

<u>Directions</u>: In this part of the test, you will hear a question spoken in English, followed by three responses, also spoken in English. The question and the responses will be spoken just one time. They will not be printed in your test book, so you must listen carefully to understand what the speakers say. You are to choose the best response to each question.

Now listen to a sample question.

You will hear:

<u>Sample Answer</u>

You will also hear:

● (B) (C)

The best response to the question "How are you?" is choice (A), "I am fine, thank you." Therefore, you should choose answer (A).

21. Mark your answer on your answer sheet.

22. Mark your answer on your answer sheet.

23. Mark your answer on your answer sheet.

24. Mark your answer on your answer sheet.

25. Mark your answer on your answer sheet.

26. Mark your answer on your answer sheet.

27. Mark your answer on your answer sheet.

28. Mark your answer on your answer sheet.

29. Mark your answer on your answer sheet.

30. Mark your answer on your answer sheet.

31. Mark your answer on your answer sheet.

32. Mark your answer on your answer sheet.

33. Mark your answer on your answer sheet.

34. Mark your answer on your answer sheet.

35. Mark your answer on your answer sheet.

36. Mark your answer on your answer sheet.

37. Mark your answer on your answer sheet.

38. Mark your answer on your answer sheet.

39. Mark your answer on your answer sheet.

40. Mark your answer on your answer sheet.

41. Mark your answer on your answer sheet.

42. Mark your answer on your answer sheet.

43. Mark your answer on your answer sheet.

44. Mark your answer on your answer sheet.

45. Mark your answer on your answer sheet.

46. Mark your answer on your answer sheet.

47. Mark your answer on your answer sheet.

48. Mark your answer on your answer sheet.

49. Mark your answer on your answer sheet.

50. Mark your answer on your answer sheet.

Part III 🔑 p 249 📼 p 214

Directions: In this part of the test, you will hear several short conversations between two people. The conversations will not be printed in your test book. You will hear the conversations only once, so you must listen carefully to understand what the speakers say.

In your test book, you will read a question about each conversation. The question will be followed by four answers. You are to choose the best answer to each question and mark it on your answer sheet.

51. What will the man do for the woman?
    (A) Take notes.
    (B) Copy his notes.
    (C) Go to the meeting.
    (D) Help her search.

52. What does the clerk suggest?
    (A) A birthday present.
    (B) A pair of shorts.
    (C) Exercises in English.
    (D) Clothes for physical activity.

53. What does the woman think they should do?
    (A) Open windows.
    (B) Repair the old air conditioner.
    (C) Get a new air conditioner.
    (D) Turn on some fans.

54. Why was the man late?
    (A) They are building a new highway.
    (B) There was a traffic accident.
    (C) The man tried a new road.
    (D) The noise bothered him.

55. What kind of room did the customer request?
    (A) Single.
    (B) Double.
    (C) Smoking.
    (D) Non-smoking.

56. Where is the woman going?
    (A) The park.
    (B) The police station.
    (C) The courthouse.
    (D) Her home.

57. What is the couple going to eat?
    (A) Breakfast.
    (B) Lunch.
    (C) Salad.
    (D) Seafood.

58. What is the problem with the paper?
    (A) It should be in rolls.
    (B) It is covered with jam.
    (C) It is too thin.
    (D) It is too thick.

59. What does the woman think about the jacket?
    (A) The stain will come out.
    (B) It doesn't fit him.
    (C) He needs a new one.
    (D) The cleaners have ruined it.

60. Why doesn't the woman check out books from the library?
    (A) She doesn't like the books at the library.
    (B) She might lose them.
    (C) She is going away.
    (D) She already has enough books.

61. Why should the trip be canceled?
    (A) It won't be damp.
    (B) He shouldn't leave town.
    (C) The trip will be a hassle.
    (D) It will be too wet.

62. What is the problem?
    (A) He has too many clothes.
    (B) He doesn't wear the right clothes.
    (C) The closet is too wide.
    (D) All the clothes are out-of-date.

63. How often does the woman see the movie?
    (A) Only once.
    (B) Only last year.
    (C) Every year.
    (D) Once in a while.

64. How can the woman get a sofa to match the room?
    (A) Buy from a different store.
    (B) Select a different sofa.
    (C) Paint her living room.
    (D) Choose fabric from the catalogue.

65. Where does this conversation probably take place?
    (A) At home.
    (B) In a restaurant.
    (C) On a picnic.
    (D) At a banquet.

66. Why will they send the document by messenger?
    (A) It's faster.
    (B) It's cheaper.
    (C) It's safer.
    (D) It's clearer.

67. Why didn't the man take the job?
    (A) The pay was too low.
    (B) The work was too hard.
    (C) The description wasn't accurate.
    (D) The job was the same as his current one.

68. Where is the owner's daughter working?
    (A) In a school.
    (B) In the basement.
    (C) In the mail room.
    (D) At the post office.

69. Who is the man planning to see?
    (A) His mechanic.
    (B) His hairdresser.
    (C) His tailor.
    (D) His dentist.

70. Who spoke at the seminar?
    (A) The regular speaker.
    (B) A sick speaker.
    (C) A substitute speaker.
    (D) A better speaker.

71. What solution did the woman propose?
    (A) Hire temporary help.
    (B) Miss the deadline.
    (C) Delay the project.
    (D) Fire the manager.

72. What will they do for Ms. Greene?
    (A) Send flowers.
    (B) Give her a card.
    (C) Order balloons.
    (D) Call her.

73. What does the man think the tourists should do?
    (A) Drive into town.
    (B) Avoid rush hour.
    (C) Stop visiting the city.
    (D) Use the buses.

74. Why can't the woman return the call?
    (A) She has to go to a meeting.
    (B) He doesn't want to talk to her.
    (C) She is late for work.
    (D) He is out of town.

75. Why are they looking forward to the new restaurant?
    (A) They will save money.
    (B) They will have good food close by.
    (C) They can leave work early.
    (D) They can eat sandwiches.

76. What should the woman do before the meeting?
    (A) Make time to attend.
    (B) Get her notes ready.
    (C) Tell the moderator she wants to speak.
    (D) Say something important.

77. Why is the woman concerned about the reception?
    (A) She can't stay long.
    (B) She's going to be late.
    (C) She has to leave at 6:00.
    (D) She'll be in Toronto.

78. What have the speakers decided to do?
    (A) Change suppliers.
    (B) Order more supplies.
    (C) Check on the order.
    (D) Make up a list.

79. Why are postage costs up?
    (A) Employees are sending too much mail.
    (B) The company is paying too much for stamps.
    (C) Everyone is using overnight mail.
    (D) The cost of regular mail has gone up.

80. What will the woman do for the man?
    (A) Go to a concert.
    (B) Leave work early.
    (C) Write a check for the tickets.
    (D) Take a list to the purser.

Part IV 🗝 p 216 📼 p 251

Directions: In this part of the test, you will hear several short talks. Each will be spoken just one time. They will not be printed in your test book, so you must listen carefully to understand and remember what is said.

In your test book, you will read two or more questions about each short talk. The questions will be followed by four answers. You are to choose the best answer to each question and mark it on your answer sheet.

81. What is different about this sidewalk?
    (A) It is well-built.
    (B) It moves.
    (C) It is indoors.
    (D) It is crowded.

82. Where would this sidewalk most likely be found?
    (A) At a store.
    (B) In front of a building.
    (C) At a shopping mall.
    (D) In an airport.

83. When can members of the audience ask questions?
    (A) When the moderator says so.
    (B) After each speech is given.
    (C) When all speakers have finished.
    (D) After they submit written questions.

84. Where should they ask the questions?
    (A) From the speaker's platform.
    (B) At the front of the room.
    (C) From where you are sitting.
    (D) At the microphone.

85. What is being advertised?
    (A) Dishes.
    (B) Forks.
    (C) Glasses.
    (D) Bowls.

86. What can people NOT do with these products?
    (A) Cook in them.
    (B) Serve in them.
    (C) Freeze food in them.
    (D) Refrigerate food in them.

87. Why is this road important?
    (A) It doesn't need repairs.
    (B) It has nice scenery.
    (C) It leads into the city.
    (D) It goes to the business district.

88. How long will the construction take?
    (A) 24 hours.
    (B) A week.
    (C) A month.
    (D) A year.

89. What should drivers do to get into the business district?
    (A) Find another route.
    (B) Use the subway.
    (C) Ride with a friend.
    (D) Take the bus.

90. How is Madison House different from other houses on the tour?
    (A) It is newer and larger.
    (B) It is older and smaller.
    (C) It is more expensive.
    (D) It is more beautiful.

91. Why does Madison House have historical importance?
    (A) A famous crime took place there.
    (B) Famous people lived there.
    (C) It is the oldest house in town.
    (D) It shows the best design of its time.

92. What feature in particular is pointed out?
    (A) Interesting gardens.
    (B) Beautiful rugs.
    (C) Carved ceilings.
    (D) Spacious rooms.

93. What can people look forward to this
    weekend?
    (A) A long holiday.
    (B) Good weather.
    (C) A city celebration.
    (D) Time at the beach.

94. When will it get colder?
    (A) At night.
    (B) In the winter.
    (C) In November.
    (D) Next spring.

95. Where is this announcement probably heard?
    (A) In a cafeteria.
    (B) At an office.
    (C) On a train.
    (D) In a restaurant.

96. What is the announcement about?
    (A) Ticket sales.
    (B) Observation windows.
    (C) Station stops.
    (D) Seatings for dinner.

97. How many seatings are held?
    (A) None.
    (B) One.
    (C) Two.
    (D) Three.

98. What does this presentation discuss?
    (A) Retailers' plans.
    (B) Results of a survey.
    (C) Technological advances.
    (D) Salesclerk training.

99. What is the focus of the advertisements of
    most electronics stores?
    (A) Efficiency.
    (B) Quality.
    (C) Convenience.
    (D) Price.

100. What is more important to consumers than
     price?
     (A) Repair service.
     (B) Politeness.
     (C) Store location.
     (D) Type of advertisement.

This is the end of the Listening Comprehension
portion of the test. Turn to Part V in your test
book.

READING

In this section of the test, you will have the chance to show how well you understand written English. There are three parts to this section, with special directions for each part.

Part V ☞ p 252

Directions: This part of the test has incomplete sentences. Four words or phrases, marked (A), (B), (C), (D), are given beneath each sentence. You are to choose the one word or phrase that best completes the sentence. Then, on your answer sheet, find the number of the question and mark your answer.

Example   Sample Answer

Because the equipment is very delicate,   (A) (B) (C) ●
it must be handled with _____ .

(A) caring
(B) careful
(C) care
(D) carefully

The sentence should read, "Because the equipment is very delicate, it must be handled with care." Therefore, you should choose answer (C).

Now begin work on the questions.

101. The housekeeping department needs to order _____ uniform for its new employee.

    (A) an
    (B) a
    (C) the
    (D) some

102. The director _____ for his vacation and will not return until next week.

    (A) leaving
    (B) had left
    (C) has left
    (D) will have left

103. The _____ document describes the new regulations.

    (A) enclosed
    (B) enclose
    (C) enclosing
    (D) to enclose

104. The receptionist refused to _____ the package.

    (A) except
    (B) exception
    (C) affect
    (D) accept

105. The man _____ hat blew off in the wind chased it across the park.

    (A) his
    (B) whose
    (C) who
    (D) that

106. The solution they suggested requires _____ the entire department.

    (A) reorganization
    (B) reorganize
    (C) to reorganize
    (D) reorganizing

107. Ms. Sirichanya _____ the package when she discovered the address was wrong.

    (A) had mailed
    (B) has mailed
    (C) will mail
    (D) would mail

108. The captain's solutions are usually quite _____ .

    (A) sensitive
    (B) sense
    (C) sensible
    (D) senses

109. The convention is being held _____ the Greenwood Conference Center.

    (A) on
    (B) in
    (C) of
    (D) at

110. If Mr. Hu does not arrive soon, we _____ without him.

    (A) left
    (B) is leaving
    (C) will leave
    (D) had left

111. People in urban areas _____ credit cards for major purchases.

    (A) uses
    (B) use
    (C) to use
    (D) using

112. Ms. Quistorf felt hungry, _____ there was nothing at the snack bar she wanted to eat.

    (A) only
    (B) or
    (C) nor
    (D) but

113. The chef greets each of his cooks _____ .

    (A) every day
    (B) always
    (C) rarely
    (D) never

114. She is a good manager _____ biggest asset is her ability to organize a project.

    (A) who
    (B) her
    (C) whose
    (D) it

115. The driver decided to take a detour _____ there was an accident on the highway.

    (A) whether
    (B) because
    (C) although
    (D) where

116. The research division announced it has made _____ toward an effective vaccine.

    (A) progress
    (B) a progress
    (C) the progress
    (D) one progress

117. Trying to cut costs by 8% may be _____ task the team has faced yet.

    (A) a hard
    (B) as hard as
    (C) the hardest
    (D) harder than

118. Ms. Rios is interested in learning about the company and _____ her business skills.

    (A) to improve
    (B) improving
    (C) improve
    (D) improved

119. The engineer _____ can devise a way to overcome this problem will receive a bonus.

    (A) he
    (B) she
    (C) who
    (D) whom

120. The _____ statement shocked the board members.

    (A) surprising
    (B) surprised
    (C) surprise
    (D) had surprised

121. Television advertising costs _____ print advertising.

    (A) most than
    (B) as much
    (C) more as
    (D) more than

122. Consumers' desire for low-fat foods _____ the current health trend in the food industry.

    (A) start
    (B) has started
    (C) had started
    (D) is starting

123. The new design failed because it was not _____ the original one.

    (A) as convenient as
    (B) more convenient
    (C) convenient than
    (D) most convenient

124. Mr. Atari was getting ready to leave the hotel when he _____ a phone call.

    (A) receives
    (B) had received
    (C) is receiving
    (D) received

125. Unless the factory can increase _____ , headquarters will consider closing it.

    (A) produce
    (B) producing
    (C) production
    (D) productive

126. Because traffic is heavy, I suggest _____ for the airport early.

    (A) leaving
    (B) to leave
    (C) will leave
    (D) am going to leave

127. Mr. Kam _____ night classes for the past three months.

    (A) is attending
    (B) has been attending
    (C) will attend
    (D) had attended

128. Limited space forced the writer _____ his article shorter.

    (A) making
    (B) make
    (C) makes
    (D) to make

129. The manager will have a meeting _____ the client this afternoon to discuss the problem.

    (A) for
    (B) to
    (C) with
    (D) as

130. The scientist will postpone the test if he _____ any problems.

    (A) anticipates
    (B) anticipated
    (C) will anticipate
    (D) has anticipated

131. The board _____ about the merger by the time the new president takes over.

    (A) decides
    (B) decided
    (C) has decided
    (D) will have decided

132. Bags checked by a passenger _____ sent to security.

    (A) is
    (B) are
    (C) was
    (D) am

133. Ms. Ni always arrives early _____ her long commute.

    (A) because of
    (B) because
    (C) in spite of
    (D) since

134. The copy machine was reduced to even _____ the sale price.

    (A) less than
    (B) more than
    (C) as much as
    (D) least as

135. The passengers were not allowed to board _____ the crew was cleaning the cabin.

    (A) during
    (B) while
    (C) for
    (D) whether

136. Ms. Kezmarsky is known not only for her intelligence _____ for her efficiency.

    (A) but also
    (B) also
    (C) and
    (D) so

137. The hole in the side indicated that the crate had been _____ during shipment.

    (A) hurt
    (B) injured
    (C) damaged
    (D) wounded

138. I _____ her for help whenever my department is understaffed.

    (A) ask
    (B) asks
    (C) asked
    (D) had asked

139. Mr. Nakara added the figures quickly _____ accurately.

    (A) and
    (B) but
    (C) or
    (D) nor

140. _____ the chairman gets his exercise by walking to work.

    (A) Rarely
    (B) Each morning
    (C) Never
    (D) Always

Part VI 🔑 p 254

Directions: In this part of the test, each sentence has four words or phrases underlined. The four underlined parts of the sentence are marked (A), (B), (C), (D). You are to identify the <u>one</u> underlined word or phrase that should be corrected or rewritten. Then, on your answer sheet, find the number of the question and mark your answer.

Example	Sample Answer

All <u>employee</u> are required to <u>wear</u> their   ● (B) (C) (D)
    A   B

<u>identification</u> badges <u>while</u> at work.
    C   D

Choice (A), the underlined word "employee," is not correct in this sentence. This sentence should read, "All employees are required to wear their identification badges while at work." Therefore, you should choose answer (A).

Now begin work on the questions.

141. The store's annual <u>sell</u> is held <u>the</u> first two weeks <u>in</u> January <u>every year</u>.
                  A   B   C   D

142. <u>Because</u> the survey produced <u>unexpecting</u> results, <u>the</u> team decided <u>to test</u> the questions again.
      A   B   C   D

143. <u>The</u> vice-president particularly <u>likes</u> the <u>simple</u> <u>of</u> the new management plan.
    A   B   C   D

144. <u>Our</u> international office <u>had be</u> located <u>in</u> Singapore <u>since</u> 1978.
    A   B   C   D

145. The park <u>across</u> <u>the</u> street <u>is</u> quiet and <u>there is peace</u>.
             A   B   C   D

146. <u>An new</u> account representative <u>who</u> was <u>hired</u> last week <u>will be starting</u> work today.
      A   B   C   D

147. <u>Since</u> we have two <u>qualified</u> candidates, it is difficult <u>to decide</u> <u>whose</u> should get the promotion.
      A   B   C   D

148. <u>The</u> new hotel they <u>are building</u> is twice <u>large as</u> the old one <u>on</u> Main Street.
    A   B   C   D

149. The secretary <u>has</u> made <u>rarely</u> mistakes <u>in</u> typing letters <u>for</u> his boss.
              A   B   C   D

150. <u>The</u> sales representatives <u>in</u> the western region <u>has received</u> the award for <u>the highest</u> sales.
    A   B   C   D

151. <u>When</u> employees do <u>an</u> excellent job, it <u>is</u> wise of the company to <u>rewards</u> them.
      A   B   C   D

152. That building, <u>its</u> architect <u>is</u> very famous, <u>has become</u> a national landmark <u>for</u> our country.
              A   B   C   D

153. There <u>are</u> any tables available <u>never</u> at this restaurant <u>when</u> it is time <u>for</u> dinner.
     A   B   C   D

154. Mr. LoMonte decided <u>to order</u> <u>a lamb</u> for dinner <u>because</u> he <u>was</u> very hungry.
                 A   B   C   D

155. The <u>elderly</u> client suggested that we <u>got</u> her a chair <u>while</u> she <u>waited</u> for her appointment.
     A   B   C   D

156. The police <u>is</u> closing the street <u>so</u> that workmen <u>can repair</u> the <u>broken</u> water main.
          A   B   C   D

157. <u>Security</u> for <u>the</u> project forbids visitors <u>going</u> into that section <u>of</u> the facility.
   A   B   C   D

158. The receptionist <u>took</u> a message <u>as</u> Ms. Goa while <u>she</u> was <u>on</u> the phone.
            A   B   C D

159. <u>A</u> company <u>that</u> prints our stationery <u>is going</u> out <u>of</u> business.
  A   B   C   D

160. <u>Although</u> she did not feel <u>tired</u>, Ms. Chin fell asleep <u>while</u> the <u>boring</u> presentation.
   A   B   C   D

Part VII

Directions: The questions in this part of the test are based on a variety of reading material (for example, announcements, paragraphs, and advertisements). You are to choose the <u>one</u> best answer, (A), (B), (C), or (D), to each question. Then, on your answer sheet, find the number of the question and mark your answer. Answer all questions following a passage on the basis of what is <u>stated</u> or <u>implied</u> in that passage.

Read the following example.

> The Museum of Technology is a "hands-on" museum, designed for people to experience science at work. Visitors are encouraged to use, test, and handle the objects on display. Special demonstrations are scheduled for the first and second Wednesdays of each month at 1:30 p.m. Open Tuesday–Friday, 2:30–4:30 p.m., Saturday 11:00 a.m.–4:30 p.m., and Sunday 1:00–4:30 p.m.

> When during the month can visitors see special demonstrations?

> (A) Every weekend

> (B) The first two Wednesdays

> (C) One afternoon a week

> (D) Every other Wednesday

Sample Answer

(A) ● (C) (D)

The passage says that the demonstrations are scheduled for the first and second Wednesdays of the month. Therefore, you should choose answer (B).

Now begin work on the questions.

Questions 161–162 refer to the following notice.  p 255

NOTICE TO CUSTOMERS

Due to the high volume of customers at our spring sale, we cannot guarantee that all items pictured in this advertisement will be available in all sizes and colors at all stores. We appreciate your understanding, and encourage you to shop early for the best selection.

---

161. What does this disclaimer tell customers?

(A) The guarantee is good.
(B) The store closes early.
(C) The sale is over.
(D) Items may sell quickly.

162. What should customers do?

(A) Shop early
(B) Avoid the store
(C) Pay higher prices
(D) Go to the mall

Questions 163–164 refer to the following instructions. p 255

To open the child-resistant cap on this medicine bottle, match the arrow on the cap with the arrow on the bottle. Press down to release. Then, twist cap to the right to open bottle.

---

163. What kind of cap is on the bottle?

(A) Easy-open
(B) Child-resistant
(C) Waterproof
(D) Metal cap

164. What does a person have to do before twisting the cap off?

(A) Turn upside down.
(B) Twist to the left.
(C) Press downward.
(D) Lift upward.

Questions 165–167 refer to the following letter. p 255

Davis & Reeves

16 Salisbury Road,
Tsinshatsui Kowloon,
Hong Kong
Tel: (852) 03 721 1121   Fax: (852) 03 739-4466

    Dr. Li Han
    Enviro-Chemicals, Inc.
    7499 Hannam-dong
    Yongsan-ku
    Seoul, Korea

Dear Dr. Han:

We have received your registration for our annual conference. Information about hotels and transportation are found in the enclosed conference brochure.

    If you need further assistance in arranging your trip, please call our conference coordinator in Hong Kong at (852) 03 721 1121.

We look forward to seeing you at the conference.

        Sincerely,

        Le Zhaolie

        Le Zhaolie
        Conference Registration

---

165. What is the purpose of this letter?

(A) To get money for the conference
(B) To invite speakers to the conference
(C) To acknowledge conference registration
(D) To make travel arrangements

166. What is enclosed with the letter?

(A) A registration form
(B) A brochure about the conference
(C) Tickets for the conference
(D) An invitation to the conference

167. Who should Dr. Han contact if she has other questions?

(A) The conference coordinator
(B) Le Zhaolie
(C) Davis & Reeves
(D) A ticket agent

Questions 168–170 refer to the following announcement. p 255

> ## NOTICE:
>
> To make your shopping at Harold's as easy as possible, you are invited to use our concierge services at the Concierge Desk. The Concierge Desk is located on the main level, beside the Gourmet Food Shop. We offer a range of shopper services including public transportation schedules, direct lines to taxi services, and package mailing. We also have a complete database of merchandise in our stores, so that we can direct you to the store that will best suit you needs. You may visit the Concierge Desk in person, or you may call from the direct-line telephone at any of the lighted directory maps in the mall.

168. What does the Concierge Desk provide?

    (A) Directions to tourist attractions
    (B) Advice on fashion
    (C) Information for the hotel guest
    (D) Services for the shopper

169. Where is the Concierge Desk located?

    (A) In a hotel
    (B) By the Gourmet Food Shop
    (C) At the tourist bureau
    (D) In an airport

170. What is one way to get in touch with the Concierge Desk?

    (A) Stop one of their representatives
    (B) Page them from a store
    (C) Write a letter
    (D) Use the direct phone

Questions 171–174 refer to the following article.  p 256

TWENTY YEARS AGO WHEN THE PERSONAL computer hit the business world, experts predicted the advent of the paperless office. But time has proved them wrong. Offices have more paper than ever. People can easily print out a personal copy of a document for anyone who needs to see it. Programs such as spelling and grammar checkers, as well as improved computer graphics, have led people to expect perfection in their documents, and to keep printing copies until they get it. The simple truth is that most people simply prefer paper. Scientific studies have shown that paper copies are easier for people to read and to edit than is text on a screen. And many people are still nervous about documents being accidentally deleted from a computer—if not through their own fault, through a computer system failure or a power outage. In short, although office paper may be significantly reduced, the paperless office is unlikely to become a reality.

171. What does this article discuss?

(A) The advantages of computers
(B) The failure of the typewriter
(C) The paperless office
(D) The efficiency of printers

172. When was the paperless office first predicted?

(A) When office computers became common
(B) When people realized the need to recycle
(C) When paper became too expensive
(D) When printers failed to work as advertised

173. How have computer programs generated more paper?

(A) They use lots of paper.
(B) They print multiple copies.
(C) They make documents easy to prepare.
(D) They connect easily to printers.

174. Why will offices probably always use paper?

(A) Paper can be signed.
(B) Paper is traditional.
(C) Paper is easier to mail.
(D) Many people prefer paper.

Questions 175–179 refer to the following article.  p 256

Economists have pointed to the reduction in small airline commuter flights as a sign that the airline industry is in financial trouble once again. A careful review of the relevant facts, however, reveals that nothing could be further from the truth, as the following analysis indicates. The first point often cited to support the idea of failure is the recent reduction in the number of commuter flights. Certainly it is obvious to anyone who looks at the figures that the number of commuter flights has fallen by 20% over the past five years. This drop, however, is due to reasons that actually reflect growth, rather than decline, in the airline industry. Many former commuter flights have been absorbed into the schedule of regular commercial flights due to increased passenger demand on those routes. Thus, though commuter flights have decreased, non-commuter flights have increased, reflecting an overall increase in passengers. Second, some former commuter routes were designated as such only because the smaller airports at the destination could not accommodate larger planes. But many growing cities have improved and expanded their airport facilities in recent years to encourage business and tourism in their regions. These physical improvements to the airports have eliminated the need for all flights in these areas to be made in small commuter planes. It is questionable whether such flights should ever have been described as commuter flights, since in these cases the label applied to airport restriction, rather than flight distance or passenger demand. Finally, increased numbers of passengers for short flights have made flying larger planes more economical for the airlines, which means that due to plane size alone these flights are no longer officially considered commuters. Thus, the commuter flight is alive and well, and bigger than it has ever been before.

175. Why do some economists think the airline industry may be in trouble?

(A) Commuter flights have decreased.
(B) The number of passengers is down.
(C) The rate of complaints is higher.
(D) Many pilots have resigned.

176. Why has the number of commuter flights fallen recently?

(A) Fewer people want to fly them.
(B) They have been merged with regular flights.
(C) Commuter planes are not safe.
(D) There are not enough planes.

177. How have improvements at airports influenced commuter flights?

(A) They have made passengers more comfortable.
(B) They can handle many more flights.
(C) There are now more airports.
(D) They can accommodate larger planes.

178. Why are airlines flying larger planes on these routes?

(A) It is more economical.
(B) It is easier.
(C) It is safer.
(D) It is faster.

179. What does this say about commuter flights?

(A) They have increased.
(B) They have changed.
(C) They are more expensive.
(D) They are quicker.

Questions 180–182 refer to this graph. p 256

Reasons for Return of Clothing Gifts

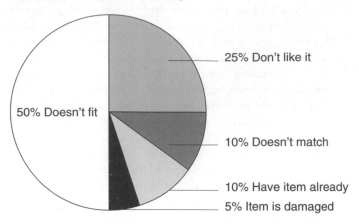

180. Why are most clothing gifts returned?

    (A) They do not match other clothes.

    (B) They are too expensive.

    (C) They do not fit.

    (D) They are ugly.

181. What percentage of people do not like the gift they received?

    (A) 15%

    (B) 20%

    (C) 25%

    (D) 50%

182. What is the least common reason for clothing to be returned?

    (A) It is not expensive enough.

    (B) There is something wrong with it.

    (C) The quality is poor.

    (D) It did not arrive on time.

Questions 183–186 refer to the following advertisement. p 256

The Historical District, just minutes away from downtown, is the best place to stay while visiting our city. The charming gardens and historical houses provide a restful environment for relaxing. But when business or sightseeing calls, we have easy access to downtown, with five subway stations in the District and excellent taxi service. Over 1,000 hotel rooms at various hotels and inns offer a range of prices and tour packages. Excellent restaurants and stores are conveniently located.

Call for a free visitor's guide.

---

183. What does this advertisement want people to do?

    (A) Plan a business trip

    (B) Visit the city

    (C) Stay in the District

    (D) Take the subway

184. What features of the District provide a restful atmosphere?

    (A) Music and food

    (B) Trees and flowers

    (C) Pools and lakes

    (D) Houses and gardens

185. Why is the District appropriate for business travelers?

    (A) There is a good taxi service.

    (B) It is convenient to downtown.

    (C) There are offices in the area.

    (D) It costs less to stay there.

186. How does a potential visitor find out more about the District?

    (A) Request a visitor's guide

    (B) Visit the area

    (C) Reserve a room at a hotel

    (D) Write a letter

Questions 187–189 refer to the following article.  p 256

187. What has dropped during the third quarter?

(A) Production
(B) Manufacturing
(C) Consumer purchases
(D) Construction industry figures

188. Who prepared the report?

(A) Business people
(B) New home buyers
(C) The government
(D) The construction industry

189. What accounted for most of the decrease?

(A) Unemployment
(B) The economy
(C) Rebuilding
(D) New construction

The national construction industry figures continued to drop during the third quarter, and may drop further in the next few months, according to a government report. Figures fell from 57.9 percent to 49.3 percent as overall construction reached its lowest level in three years. New construction, the most reliable indicator, accounted for most of the decrease.

Questions 190–192 refer to the following advertisement.  p 256

The Financial Planning Office is offering a **Family Budget Guide** (No. 1063X) to help members collect and analyze information about their income and spending habits. It includes guidelines for setting budget goals, saving for college, and planning for retirement. Price: $25 for 50 copies.

190. What is the Financial Planning Office offering?

(A) A new publication
(B) A new service
(C) A new product
(D) A new job

191. What guidelines are NOT mentioned?

(A) Setting budget goals
(B) Saving for college
(C) Selecting an insurance plan
(D) Planning for retirement

192. What is the minimum number of copies that can be ordered?

(A) 1
(B) 10
(C) 25
(D) 50

Questions 193–196 refer to the following article. p 256

People's concern about keeping their diets healthy has reached a peak in recent years. Everyone is trying to eat foods that are low in fat and high in fiber. They watch their intake of salt, sugar, and calories. They shun food additives and shop for organic fruits and vegetables. It should not be surprising, then, that these health concerns have now been extended to the diets of their pets. In the past, owners simply gave their pets leftover food from family meals or bought whatever dog food was on sale. Now, these choices are considered to be lacking in necessary nutrients for proper animal growth and development. The emphasis has shifted to health and nutritional value.

Gourmet stores that have traditionally sold rare and imported foods are beginning to sell gourmet dog and cat foods alongside their "people" food. Specialty pet shops are opening, offering foods with healthier ingredients such as rice and lamb, even though such ingredients are not traditionally considered suitable for pets. There are even specific lines of food for pets with special needs. Some lines are based on the age of the pet. These include high-energy varieties for puppies or kittens, vitamin-enriched styles for adult animals, and low-calorie and high-fiber food for elderly animals.

Other lines of pet food are designed in consideration of the health problems of the animals (or health concerns of their owners). Brands may be salt-free to combat high blood pressure, additive-free to fight allergies, and fat-free to prevent excessive weight gain. There are even animal drinks for pets in special circumstances. For example, drinks containing electrolytes, which help the body maintain a proper balance of fluids, can be helpful for animals who live in hot, dry climates where dehydration is a potential problem. All of these new pet foods claim to be recommended by veterinarians and scientifically developed to address the nutrition and health needs of that special pet.

193. Whose diets are people now concerned about?

(A) Their children's
(B) Their parents'
(C) Their pets'
(D) Their own

194. Where can pet owners find these new pet foods?

(A) Cookbooks
(B) Gourmet food stores
(C) Grocery stores
(D) Catalogues

195. Why are the new foods supposed to be better?

(A) They are healthier.
(B) They taste better.
(C) Pets like them better.
(D) Owners have confidence in them.

196. What special line of food is NOT mentioned?

(A) Salt-free
(B) Puppy food
(C) Additive-free
(D) Vegetarian

Questions 197–200 refer to the following article. p 257

Almost every office is looking for additional space. One easy way to get it is to use moveable partitions instead of, or in conjunction with, the solid interior walls of your existing office space. These walls provide several important benefits. First, they let you take maximum advantage of existing space. No more conflicts where one office is just a little too small and another is just a little too big—just move the partition over a foot to adjust the space for everyone. Second, you can change the positions of the partitions as your business needs change. If one project ends and another begins, you can easily change the office space to accommodate project needs. Finally, new materials make these walls both sound-absorbant and lightweight, so they provide the privacy of built-in walls with the advantages of flexible space.

197. What is this article about?

(A) Office redecoration
(B) Moveable partitions
(C) Improving efficiency
(D) Renting new offices

198. Why do partitions create space?

(A) They are cheaper than real walls.
(B) They are narrower than real walls.
(C) You can move them where you need them.
(D) They have shelves on them.

199. Why are partitions a good choice for businesses with different projects?

(A) They can be easily stored.
(B) They make the office look different.
(C) They help you organize information.
(D) You can change the space for different projects.

200. How do the partitions provide privacy?

(A) They absorb sound.
(B) They reach the ceiling.
(C) They do not have windows.
(D) They do not have doors.

Stop! This is the end of the test. If you finish before time is called, you may go back to Parts V, VI, VII and check your work.

PRACTICE TEST 3

Test of English for International Communication

General Directions

This is a test of your ability to use the English language. The total time for the test is approximately two hours. It is divided into seven parts. Each part of the test begins with a set of specific directions. Be sure you understand what you are to do before you begin work on a part.

You will find that some of the questions are harder than others, but you should try to answer every one. There is no penalty for guessing. Do not be concerned if you cannot answer all of the questions.

Do not mark your answers in this test book. <u>You must put all of your answers on a separate answer sheet</u> that you have been given. When putting your answer to a question on your answer sheet, be sure to fill out the answer space corresponding to the letter of your choice. Fill in the space so that the letter inside the oval cannot be seen, as shown in the example below.

Mr. Jones _____ to his accountant yesterday.

(A) talk
(B) talking
(C) talked
(D) to talk

Sample Answer

(A) (B) ● (D)

The sentence should read, "Mr. Jones talked to his accountant yesterday." Therefore, you should choose answer (C). Notice how this has been done in the example given.

Mark only <u>one</u> answer for each question. If you change your mind about an answer after you have marked it on your answer sheet, completely erase your old answer and then mark your new answer. You must mark the answer sheet carefully so that the test-scoring machine can accurately record your test score.

LISTENING COMPREHENSION

In this section of the test, you will have the chance to show how well you understand spoken English. There are four parts to this section, with special directions for each part.

Part I 🔑 p 257 📼 p 217

<u>Directions</u>: For each question, you will see a picture in your test book and you will hear four short statements. The statements will be spoken just one time. They will not be printed in your test book, so you must listen carefully to understand what the speaker says.

When you hear the four statements, look at the picture in your test book and choose the statement that best describes what you see in the picture. Then, on your answer sheet, find the number of the question and mark your answer. Look at the sample below.

Now listen to the four statements.

<u>Sample Answer</u>

(A) ● (C) (D)

Statement (B), "They're having a meeting," best describes what you see in the picture. Therefore, you should choose answer (B).

1

2

3

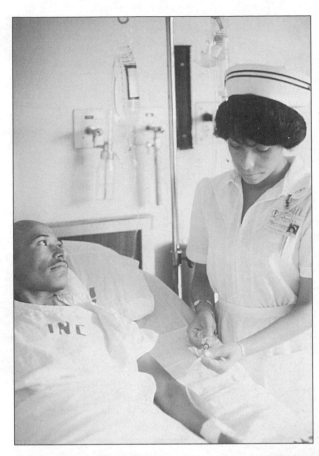

4

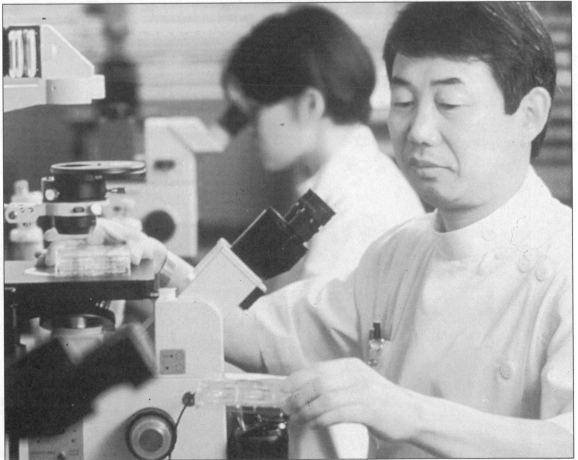

5

6

7

8

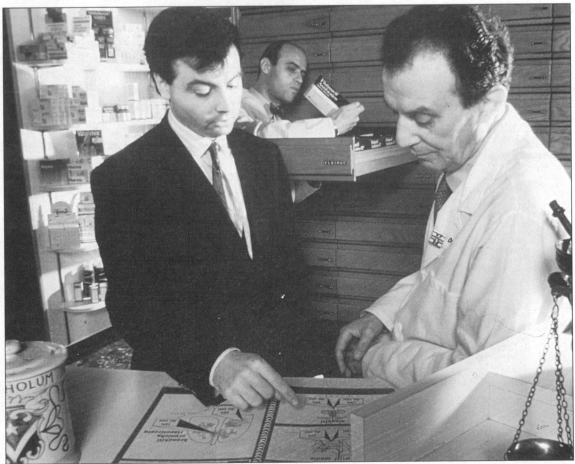

9

10

11

12

13

14

15

16

17

18

19

20

Part II 🔑 p 259 📼 p 219

<u>Directions</u>: In this part of the test, you will hear a question spoken in English, followed by three responses, also spoken in English. The question and the responses will be spoken just one time. They will not be printed in your test book, so you must listen carefully to understand what the speakers say. You are to choose the best response to each question.

Now listen to a sample question.

You will hear:

You will also hear:

<u>Sample Answer</u>

● (B) (C)

The best response to the question "How are you?" is choice (A), "I am fine, thank you." Therefore, you should choose answer (A).

21.   Mark your answer on your answer sheet.

22.   Mark your answer on your answer sheet.

23.   Mark your answer on your answer sheet.

24.   Mark your answer on your answer sheet.

25.   Mark your answer on your answer sheet.

26.   Mark your answer on your answer sheet.

27.   Mark your answer on your answer sheet.

28.   Mark your answer on your answer sheet.

29.   Mark your answer on your answer sheet.

30.   Mark your answer on your answer sheet.

31.   Mark your answer on your answer sheet.

32.   Mark your answer on your answer sheet.

33.   Mark your answer on your answer sheet.

34.   Mark your answer on your answer sheet.

35.   Mark your answer on your answer sheet.

36.   Mark your answer on your answer sheet.

37.   Mark your answer on your answer sheet.

38.   Mark your answer on your answer sheet.

39.   Mark your answer on your answer sheet.

40.   Mark your answer on your answer sheet.

41.   Mark your answer on your answer sheet.

42.   Mark your answer on your answer sheet.

43.   Mark your answer on your answer sheet.

44.   Mark your answer on your answer sheet.

45.   Mark your answer on your answer sheet.

46.   Mark your answer on your answer sheet.

47.   Mark your answer on your answer sheet.

48.   Mark your answer on your answer sheet.

49.   Mark your answer on your answer sheet.

50.   Mark your answer on your answer sheet.

Part III 🔑 p 260 📼 p 220

Directions: In this part of the test, you will hear several short conversations between two people. The conversations will not be printed in your test book. You will hear the conversations only once, so you must listen carefully to understand what the speakers say.

In your test book, you will read a question about each conversation. The question will be followed by four answers. You are to choose the best answer to each question and mark it on your answer sheet.

51. When will the people have lunch?
    (A) Tomorrow.
    (B) When she's done the report.
    (C) Another time.
    (D) At the restaurant.

52. Where does this conversation probably take place?
    (A) At the cleaners.
    (B) At the office.
    (C) At a clothing store.
    (D) On a plane.

53. How did the waiter solve the problem?
    (A) Turned out the lights.
    (B) Moved the table.
    (C) Moved the customers.
    (D) Closed the curtains.

54. Why does the desk clerk warn the woman?
    (A) Reservations are expensive.
    (B) There may be no room in any hotel.
    (C) The location of the hotels is inconvenient.
    (D) Theirs is the only hotel in town.

55. What is the man's problem?
    (A) He doesn't know how to reduce the image.
    (B) He can't start the copier.
    (C) He has too many pages.
    (D) He can't read the print.

56. How will the mechanic let the man know about his car?
    (A) He will wait at the garage.
    (B) He will phone him later.
    (C) He will come by after work.
    (D) He will leave a message.

57. What is their complaint about the director?
    (A) He is always late.
    (B) He doesn't like his employees.
    (C) He won't listen to suggestions.
    (D) He is rarely available.

58. What is the woman trying to do?
    (A) Repair a hole.
    (B) Buy a sweater.
    (C) Exchange a sweater.
    (D) Make a sweater.

59. What problem are they discussing?
    (A) The office is too loud.
    (B) The office is too small.
    (C) They need to hire more people.
    (D) The chairs aren't comfortable.

60. What does the woman dislike?
    (A) Standing up.
    (B) Driving.
    (C) Commuting.
    (D) Watching the news.

61. What are the speakers trying to do?
    (A) Make a doctor's appointment.
    (B) Meet a client.
    (C) Close a sale.
    (D) Set up a meeting.

62. What does the man want to do?
    (A) Eat.
    (B) Cook.
    (C) Go home.
    (D) Be late.

63. What are the speakers discussing?
    (A) The fish he caught.
    (B) His vacation.
    (C) Hiking.
    (D) The scenery.

64. What is the best way to describe the coffee?
    (A) New.
    (B) Expensive.
    (C) Different.
    (D) Good.

65. Why is the woman concerned?
   (A) She wants to go.
   (B) The printer is slow.
   (C) There are many more pages.
   (D) She's been waiting for ages.

66. What advantage does the man think the woman possesses?
   (A) Good eyesight.
   (B) A firm handshake.
   (C) The ability to handle details.
   (D) Lots of self-confidence.

67. What does the woman ask the man about?
   (A) His airline carrier.
   (B) His weight.
   (C) His travel plans.
   (D) His luggage.

68. What does the woman think the man should do?
   (A) Wear gloves.
   (B) See a doctor.
   (C) Play ball.
   (D) Exercise his fingers.

69. What do people in the town do for fun?
   (A) Have parties.
   (B) Go to concerts.
   (C) Visit museums.
   (D) Learn to cook.

70. How does the man think the woman should spend her day?
   (A) Working.
   (B) Testing.
   (C) Sleeping.
   (D) Running.

71. How does the man think people should learn to cook?
   (A) By taking classes.
   (B) By cooking a lot.
   (C) By using good recipes.
   (D) By studying with chefs.

72. Why does the man want good news in the newspapers?
   (A) It will teach people to solve problems.
   (B) It will make people buy newspapers.
   (C) It will make it harder to report bad news.
   (D) It will make people feel good.

73. Why is the woman going to the site?
   (A) To give advice about the project.
   (B) To keep the project on schedule.
   (C) To speed the project up.
   (D) To learn about the project.

74. How did the woman try to improve the report?
   (A) By asking someone else to read it.
   (B) By asking the man to rewrite it.
   (C) By getting someone to explain it.
   (D) By making suggestions about it.

75. Why is the man upset?
   (A) He can't tour the houses.
   (B) There are no more guidebooks.
   (C) He misplaced his guidebook.
   (D) He wanted to go to the Tourist Center.

76. Why are the melons bad this year?
   (A) There was too much rain.
   (B) There was not enough rain.
   (C) They were harmed during shipping.
   (D) The growing season was too short.

77. Why shouldn't he mail the information?
   (A) It's unnecessary.
   (B) It's too slow.
   (C) It's too expensive.
   (D) It's too complicated.

78. What will the man probably do?
   (A) Take fewer clothes.
   (B) Stop wearing his jacket.
   (C) Pack cooler clothes.
   (D) Buy clothes when he gets there.

79. Why is the man concerned?
   (A) The receptionist is late.
   (B) No one is working at the front desk.
   (C) He wants to hire a delivery service.
   (D) The company needs security guards.

80. Where does this conversation likely take place?
   (A) A shopping center.
   (B) An office complex.
   (C) A movie studio.
   (D) A museum.

Part IV 🔑 p 262 📼 p 222

<u>Directions</u>: In this part of the test, you will hear several short talks. Each will be spoken just one time. They will not be printed in your test book, so you must listen carefully to understand and remember what is said.

In your test book, you will read two or more questions about each short talk. The questions will be followed by four answers. You are to choose the best answer to each question and mark it on your answer sheet.

81. Where would a person hear this announcement?
    (A) At a university.
    (B) In a restaurant.
    (C) At a train station.
    (D) At a museum.

82. What is the purpose of this announcement?
    (A) To give a track change.
    (B) To announce a delayed arrival.
    (C) To announce an early departure.
    (D) To give notice of repairs.

83. What information did they get wrong?
    (A) The identity of the victim.
    (B) The name of the bus driver.
    (C) The location of the accident.
    (D) The profession of the rescuer.

84. Why did they make this statement?
    (A) To report the accident.
    (B) To correct an error.
    (C) To warn the public.
    (D) To save the victim.

85. What kind of weather is predicted?
    (A) Rain.
    (B) Snow.
    (C) Hail.
    (D) Thunder.

86. What should people be prepared for?
    (A) Food shortages.
    (B) Power blackouts.
    (C) Bad driving conditions.
    (D) Delays in mail delivery.

87. If someone hears this recording, who is he or she calling?
    (A) The newspaper.
    (B) The telephone company.
    (C) A radio station.
    (D) A cable TV service.

88. Which category is NOT mentioned?
    (A) Ordering new service.
    (B) Billing inquiries.
    (C) Changing current service.
    (D) Requesting repairs.

89. What can the caller do to talk to a person directly?
    (A) Press 4.
    (B) Dial another number.
    (C) Stay on the line.
    (D) Call another company.

90. What special service is the county providing?
    (A) Raking leaves.
    (B) Offering bags for leaves.
    (C) Trash collection.
    (D) Garden maintenance.

91. What will happen to the leaves?
    (A) They are put in a landfill.
    (B) They are combined with other trash.
    (C) They are thrown away.
    (D) They are turned into fertilizer.

92. Who can get the fertilizer?
    (A) Anyone with leaves.
    (B) Anyone in the area.
    (C) Residents of the county.
    (D) People who have bags.

93. What is the topic of this report?
   (A) Food safety.
   (B) Picnics.
   (C) Summer fun.
   (D) Using containers.

94. What kinds of food should people avoid on a picnic?
   (A) Food that is very fresh.
   (B) Food that is too sweet.
   (C) Food that is hard to eat.
   (D) Food that spoils easily.

95. What is essential for transporting food?
   (A) A car.
   (B) A cooler.
   (C) Children.
   (D) Baskets.

96. Why was the plane delayed?
   (A) They needed to repair it.
   (B) The weather was bad.
   (C) The runway was crowded.
   (D) The pilot was late.

97. How are they boarding the passengers?
   (A) By ticket type.
   (B) By seat number.
   (C) By zone.
   (D) By row.

98. Why are they requesting passengers to board in this manner?
   (A) It makes the passengers safer.
   (B) It is easier to stow luggage.
   (C) It requires less supervision.
   (D) It is faster.

99. When will regular service resume?
   (A) Right away.
   (B) When the track is cleared.
   (C) In two more hours.
   (D) After repairs are completed.

100. Why can't commuters board the first few trains?
   (A) They won't stop at the station.
   (B) They will be filled with other passengers.
   (C) They are going out of the city.
   (D) They are moving too fast.

This is the end of the Listening Comprehension portion of the test. Turn to Part V in your test book.

READING

In this section of the test, you will have the chance to show how well you understand written English. There are three parts to this section, with special directions for each part.

Part V ⊙══ p 263

Directions: This part of the test has incomplete sentences. Four words or phrases, marked (A), (B), (C), (D), are given beneath each sentence. You are to choose the one word or phrase that best completes the sentence. Then, on your answer sheet, find the number of the question and mark your answer.

Example   Sample Answer

Because the equipment is very delicate,   (A) (B) ● (D)
it must be handled with _____ .

(A) caring
(B) careful
(C) care
(D) carefully

The sentence should read, "Because the equipment is very delicate, it must be handled with care." Therefore, you should choose answer (C).

Now begin work on the questions.

101. You should read the operating instructions _____ you use new appliances.

   (A) before
   (B) after
   (C) because
   (D) although

102. The police _____ the area near company headquarters.

   (A) to patrol
   (B) patrolling
   (C) patrols
   (D) patrol

103. _____ I am tired, I will work late tonight.

   (A) Or
   (B) Even though
   (C) Because
   (D) So that

104. Mr. Han _____ his bags when he found out his flight was canceled.

    (A) packed
    (B) were packing
    (C) was packing
    (D) has packed

105. The manager had _____ his assistant about the changes before he announced them to the other employees.

    (A) said
    (B) told
    (C) talked
    (D) explained

106. You'll find the papers _____ the file cabinet on the left.

    (A) at
    (B) of
    (C) out
    (D) in

107. The accountant demands that his clerks _____ their work carefully before submitting it.

    (A) check
    (B) will check
    (C) to check
    (D) checking

108. The competitor's product is neither as efficient _____ as inexpensive as ours.

    (A) or
    (B) but
    (C) nor
    (D) either

109. Employees are paid _____ .

    (A) rarely
    (B) twice a month
    (C) always
    (D) never

110. Although Ms. Kent _____ reservations, the hotel did not have a room for her.

    (A) had made
    (B) has made
    (C) made
    (D) makes

111. The wildlife preserve is _____ tourist attraction in the city.

    (A) as popular as
    (B) more popular than
    (C) most popular
    (D) the most popular

112. The waiter poured us some water _____ forgot to give us menus.

    (A) and
    (B) but
    (C) or
    (D) nor

113. The customers in the store _____ the beautiful holiday displays.

    (A) has liked
    (B) liking
    (C) like
    (D) likes

114. The final report on the project needs to be completed _____ possible.

    (A) as quickly as
    (B) quickly as
    (C) quickly than
    (D) more quickly

115. The food at the banquet was good, and the _____ was even better.

    (A) entertain
    (B) entertained
    (C) entertaining
    (D) entertainment

116. The hotel needs _____ better training for its front desk staff.

    (A) provides
    (B) will provide
    (C) to provide
    (D) provide

117. A _____ draft of the report was sent to the editor.

    (A) competed
    (B) completed
    (C) competent
    (D) complained

118. _____ her vacation she toured every museum in the city.

    (A) During
    (B) While
    (C) Because
    (D) Although

119. You can buy stamps at the post office _____ from a vending machine.

    (A) nor
    (B) but
    (C) or
    (D) neither

120. Ms. Fili _____ for us for 30 years by the time she retires.

    (A) will work

    (B) has worked

    (C) has been working

    (D) will have been working

121. Always _____ the shipment before you sign for it.

    (A) examined

    (B) examines

    (C) examine

    (D) will examine

122. The trade fair will start _____ Monday of next week.

    (A) in

    (B) on

    (C) over

    (D) with

123. I _____ to work on time if the bus is late.

    (A) cannot get

    (B) could not get

    (C) have gotten

    (D) had gotten

124. The _____ newspaper article puzzled readers.

    (A) confuse

    (B) to confuse

    (C) confused

    (D) confusing

125. Mr. Ngo _____ a trip to the islands until he realized it was hurricane season.

    (A) planned

    (B) has planned

    (C) had been planning

    (D) plans

126. Ms. Demera knows how to get _____ the client's office.

    (A) about

    (B) to

    (C) under

    (D) of

127. Ms. Yi _____ on her secretary to plan her schedule.

    (A) depends

    (B) depending

    (C) dependent

    (D) dependence

128. I prefer to pay by _____ .

    (A) bill
    (B) payment
    (C) check
    (D) balance

129. If we _____ earlier, there would have been tickets available.

    (A) have inquired
    (B) inquired
    (C) will inquire
    (D) had inquired

130. Each item reflects our effort to _____ the highest quality in our products.

    (A) preserve
    (B) reserve
    (C) deserve
    (D) persevere

131. The head of the division will be going to the convention _____ an emergency arises.

    (A) when
    (B) unless
    (C) because
    (D) since

132. The rider _____ left his umbrella on the bus can claim it by calling lost-and-found.

    (A) he
    (B) his
    (C) who
    (D) which

133. Mr. Biancheri could not find his telephone directory, so he _____ one from Ms. Rocher.

    (A) loaned
    (B) sent
    (C) lent
    (D) borrowed

134. I suggest _____ an attorney before proceeding with a lawsuit.

    (A) consult
    (B) consulting
    (C) to consult
    (D) will consult

135. _____ the company throws a party for its employees.

    (A) Rarely
    (B) Never
    (C) Seldom
    (D) Once a year

136. The company _____ not yet answered our complaint.

   (A) has
   (B) does
   (C) will
   (D) is

137. The Royal Hotel offers _____ accommodations in the city.

   (A) better than
   (B) best than
   (C) the best
   (D) as good as

138. The furniture, _____ is being replaced as we redecorate, will be donated to charity.

   (A) that
   (B) which
   (C) it
   (D) whose

139. Every room should have clean sheets, fresh towels, _____ new bars of soap each morning.

   (A) and
   (B) nor
   (C) or
   (D) but

140. Area businesses are encouraged _____ office paper.

   (A) recycles
   (B) recycling
   (C) recycle
   (D) to recycle

Part VI ⊙━━ p 265

<u>Directions</u>: In this part of the test, each sentence has four words or phrases underlined. The four underlined parts of the sentence are marked (A), (B), (C), (D). You are to identify the <u>one</u> underlined word or phrase that should be corrected or rewritten. Then, on your answer sheet, find the number of the question and mark your answer.

Example

Sample Answer

All <u>employee</u> are required to <u>wear</u> their
    A   B

● (B) (C) (D)

<u>identification</u> badges <u>while</u> at work.
    C   D

Choice (A), the underlined word "employee," is not correct in this sentence. This sentence should read, "All employees are required to wear their identification badges while at work." Therefore, you should choose answer (A).

Now begin work on the questions.

141. The secretary checked the <u>spelling</u> and <u>verify</u> the figures <u>before</u> sending the brochure <u>to</u> the printer.   A   B   C   D

142. <u>The</u> president came to the <u>concluding</u> <u>that</u> he should <u>restructure</u> the company.
  A   B   C   D

143. This new software <u>for</u> accounting <u>and</u> money management is <u>the more</u> comprehensive program
                A   B   C
<u>on</u> the market.
 D

144. <u>Scarcely</u> Ms. Mandia had gotten <u>to</u> her office <u>when</u> the phone <u>began</u> to ring.
    A   B   C   D

145. <u>The</u> manager of the <u>sales</u> department <u>plans</u> to work both nights <u>or</u> weekends to finish the project.
   A   B   C   D

146. There <u>is</u> time <u>still</u> to mail your letter <u>before</u> the session <u>starts</u>.
      A   B   C   D

147. Anyone <u>who</u> has pain <u>after</u> meals should consider <u>seek</u> medical <u>attention</u>.
         A   B   C   D

148. People <u>is</u> <u>sometimes</u> skeptical of the claims <u>advertising</u> makes <u>about</u> new products.
      A   B   C   D

149. The <u>raise</u> in <u>prices</u> has caused <u>many</u> customers <u>to reconsider</u> unnecessary purchases.
      A   B   C   D

150. Ms. Li <u>seldom</u> eats beef; she <u>prefers</u> to have <u>a fish</u> or some <u>vegetables</u>.
         A   B   C   D

151. <u>The</u> applicant <u>left</u> the interview not <u>knowing</u> <u>also</u> she would get the job.
  A   B   C D

152. The table <u>who</u> looks so <u>good</u> in the lobby <u>is</u> an antique <u>donated</u> by our family.
     A   B   C   D

153. The contractors urged city officials <u>approve</u> the building <u>permit</u> for the <u>construction</u> of <u>the</u> new
               A   B   C   D
office complex.

154. Mr. Nyeong did not <u>get</u> the promotion <u>because</u> he had <u>worked</u> hard <u>for</u> it.
       A   B   C   D

155. The <u>reassured</u> financial report made the stockholders <u>much</u> happier about their investments <u>than</u>
  A   B   C
they <u>had been</u>.
  D

156. <u>A captain</u> <u>of</u> our ship has decided <u>to retire</u> <u>next</u> year.
 A B   C D

157. The caterer <u>who</u> was hired for the office party <u>provided</u> beautiful decorations <u>and</u> delicious <u>foods</u>.
    A   B   C   D

158. If it rains, we <u>had to</u> cancel <u>the</u> parade <u>scheduled</u> for today.
 A   B   C   D

159. Mr. Vasko <u>wants</u> the money <u>but not</u> the <u>responsible</u> <u>that</u> comes with a promotion.
    A   B   C   D

160. <u>Computerized</u> word processing is much <u>fastest</u> than <u>typing</u> on <u>a</u> typewriter.
  A   B   C D

Part VII

Directions: The questions in this part of the test are based on a variety of reading material (for example, announcements, paragraphs, and advertisements). You are to choose the one best answer, (A), (B), (C), or (D), to each question. Then, on your answer sheet, find the number of the question and mark your answer. Answer all questions following a passage on the basis of what is stated or implied in that passage.

Read the following example.

> The Museum of Technology is a "hands-on" museum, designed for people to experience science at work. Visitors are encouraged to use, test, and handle the objects on display. Special demonstrations are scheduled for the first and second Wednesdays of each month at 1:30 p.m. Open Tuesday–Friday, 2:30–4:30 p.m., Saturday 11:00 a.m.–4:30 p.m., and Sunday 1:00–4:30 p.m.

When during the month can visitors see special demonstrations?

(A) Every weekend
(B) The first two Wednesdays
(C) One afternoon a week
(D) Every other Wednesday

Sample Answer
(A) ● (C) (D)

The passage says that the demonstrations are scheduled for the first and second Wednesdays of the month. Therefore, you should choose answer (B).

Now begin work on the questions.

Questions 161–162 refer to the following announcement.  p 266

> The Kyler International Center for Professional Education provides a broad spectrum of training for business executives. We will also work with you to tailor programs for your specific needs. Programs can be held at the Kyler Conference Center if scheduling allows, or can be held at a location of your choice. To discuss what we can do for you and your organization, please contact the Program Director.

161. What is this announcement about?

   (A) An upcoming seminar
   (B) Training possibilities
   (C) A new conference center
   (D) A schedule of classes

162. Who should people contact if they want to know more?

   (A) Mr. Kyler
   (B) The university
   (C) The Program Director
   (D) The Conference Center

Questions 163–165 refer to the following label. p 266

163. Why should consumers be careful with this product?
   (A) It can be fattening.
   (B) It can be harmful.
   (C) It can cause stains.
   (D) It can soften skin.

164. What should consumers do if they get this product in their eyes?
   (A) Rinse with water for 15 minutes.
   (B) Keep their eyes closed.
   (C) Wash their eyes with soap.
   (D) Blink rapidly.

165. How should this product be stored?
   (A) In a dry place
   (B) With the lid tightly closed
   (C) At a low temperature
   (D) With other chemicals

> **Warning:** Keep this product away from small children. This product can cause irritation. Do not get in eyes or on skin. In case of eye contact, immediately rinse eyes with plenty of cool water for at least 15 minutes. In case of skin contact, wash with plenty of soap and water. If irritation persists, seek medical attention. Keep securely closed.

Questions 166–167 refer to the following letter. p 266

Assensuej 513
5642 Millinge
Denmark

Bittman Bookstore
Lange Voorhout 50-52
2574 EG The Hague
The Netherlands

To whom it may concern:

Please send me 2 copies of the book How to be a
Billionaire. I have enclosed a check for $34 to cover
the cost of two books and $4 for shipping and
handling costs.

Please send the books to me at the address above.

Yours truly,

Ann-Marie Berns

Ann-Marie Berns

---

166. How much does each book cost?
   (A) $4
   (B) $15
   (C) $30
   (D) $34

167. Where should the books be sent?
   (A) To The Hague
   (B) To Bittman Bookstore
   (C) To The Netherlands
   (D) To Denmark

Questions 168–170 refer to the following article.  p 267

Managers in the business world have been taught to think in terms of control. The good manager is one who oversees every aspect of his department and makes the decisions about what goes on. But some companies are beginning to take a different approach to management style. Such tight control, many believe, leads not to good business, but to an over-stressed manager. Now, managers are encouraged to think in terms of empowerment, that is, giving some control for everyday decisions to others. Advocates of empowerment say that it keeps more managers happy and on the job and gives employees a reason to take pride in their work.

168. What word characterizes the new management style?
(A) Empowerment
(B) Control
(C) Stress
(D) Pride

169. How is it different from earlier ideas about management?
(A) The manager makes decisions.
(B) Managers do all the work.
(C) Employees make decisions.
(D) Each employee knows his job.

170. What benefit does this have for employees?
(A) They feel proud of their work.
(B) They like the manager more.
(C) They get more vacations.
(D) They receive higher salaries.

Questions 171–172 refer to the following graph. p 267

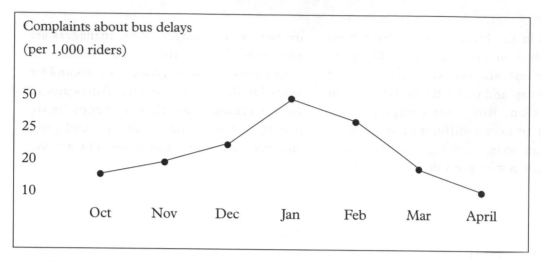

Complaints about bus delays
(per 1,000 riders)

171. During what month do complaints peak?
    (A) April
    (B) October
    (C) February
    (D) January

172. When are the fewest complaints received?
    (A) December
    (B) April
    (C) January
    (D) November

Questions 173–177 refer to the following article.  p 267

DO YOU HAVE shooting pains in your forearm? Do you notice weakness in your fingers? Do you get an unpleasant, tingling sensation in your hands? Is it painful to move your wrist? The cause of these complaints may be a seemingly harmless device you use every day—your computer. Doctors are reporting increased numbers of patients with a disorder known as carpal tunnel syndrome, a painful injury of the hands and arms (carpal refers to the bones in the wrist).

Carpal tunnel syndrome has been relatively common in patients with inflammatory diseases such as rheumatoid arthritis, but is uncommon among the general population, except as a result of direct trauma. The sudden rise in carpal tunnel syndrome among the healthy, otherwise uninjured people was puzzling at first, but doctors soon traced it to its source. Although carpal tunnel syndrome can be caused by a variety of repetitive hand movements, its most common cause is constant use of improperly positioned computer keyboards and equipment.

Unfortunately, little is known about treating or curing this injury. Braces that support the wrist and forearm can help, as can resting the affected muscles. If carpal tunnel syndrome is ignored, it can even lead to long-term disability. It is therefore important that people who use computers every day should try to prevent this condition by taking some basic precautions.

First, make sure that both your chair and the height of your computer table are adjustable. Raise or lower your chair so that you can sit with both feet flat on the floor. Your knees should be even with, or just below, the level of your lap to ease strain on the back and shoulder muscles. Next, adjust the level of the computer keyboard so that it is at about the same height as your elbows when you are sitting in the chair. This enables you to type on the keyboard without reaching up and over, the position that invites the most injury. Then check the viewing distance between your eyes and the keyboard. It should be a minimum of 18 inches to avoid eye strain. Place the monitor so that you look across or slightly downwards at the computer screen, rather than upwards. Make sure that the size of the type on the screen, the brightness, and the contrast are set so that you can read the screen easily without leaning forward. Finally, work for no more than two hours at a time.

During these breaks, it is important to rest your muscles from the constant repetition. That is, use movements that you do not use at the computer. Get up from your chair. Walk around the office; stretch by leaning gently from side to side and backwards. Lift your arms over your head. Change your field of vision by staring out a window at a distant object. Do not return to work at your computer for at least half an hour. With these precautions, the chances of sustaining a carpal tunnel injury are greatly reduced.

173. What kinds of injuries will this advice help readers avoid?
(A) Repetitive motion injuries
(B) Knee injuries
(C) Back strain
(D) Neck strain

174. What feature should office furniture have?
(A) It should be attractive.
(B) It should be soft.
(C) It should be adjustable.
(D) It should be high.

175. Where should the computer keyboard be?
(A) On your knees
(B) At about elbow height
(C) On top of the table
(D) Close to the screen

176. What should be a minimum of 18 inches apart?
(A) The floor and your feet
(B) Your knees and the table
(C) The keyboard and your elbows
(D) Your eyes and the computer screen

177. How long should people work without taking a break?
(A) One hour
(B) Only two hours
(C) Just four hours
(D) Six hours

Questions 178–180 refer to the following article.  p 267

178. Why do people like cellular phones?
   (A) They can use them in the office.
   (B) They fit in a briefcase.
   (C) They like technology.
   (D) They can take them anywhere.

179. What is the disadvantage of cellular phones?
   (A) The sound is not clear.
   (B) They do not ring loudly.
   (C) They are expensive.
   (D) They work only in one city.

180. If people visit another city often, what is the simple solution to make their cellular phone work?
   (A) Get a second number in that city
   (B) Use a regular telephone
   (C) Communicate by fax
   (D) Buy a beeper

Technology has come to the rescue of those who hate to be out of touch. First there were beepers; now there are cellular phones. These small telephones can go anywhere with you. Anyone who may need to reach you, can simply call your cellular number. Of course, the numbers for most cellular phones work only in a specific city. Some companies have formed networks with other cellular phone services in other cities to try to make numbers work for their customers no matter where they are. But customers who travel frequently to the same city have come up with their own solution— they simply get a second cellular phone number for the second city.

Questions 181–183 refer to the following card.  p 267

Please make checks payable to Computer Training Seminars, Inc.

☐ Check enclosed   ☐ Bill my company (purchase order enclosed)

Credit card authorization

Charge to (credit card name) _____

Credit card number _____

Expiration date _____

Cardholder name _____

Authorizing signature _____

181. Which is NOT a way to pay for the seminar?
   (A) Check
   (B) Bill
   (C) Credit card
   (D) Cash

182. What must be enclosed if the company should be billed?
   (A) A purchase order
   (B) A note from accounting
   (C) A letter from the manager
   (D) A check from the company

183. If people pay by check, who should the check be made out to?
   (A) Computer Training Seminars, Inc.
   (B) Their company
   (C) The credit card company
   (D) The bank

Questions 184–186 refer to the following article. p 267

When you travel by air, your luggage can sometimes get lost. This is most likely to happen when you have to change planes—sometimes, your luggage does not change with you. Usually, such luggage is quickly located and returned. Smart travelers, however, prepare for the worst. Taking valuable items, or necessary items like medication with you in a small carry-on bag eliminates worry if your luggage does go astray. Keeping a list of the contents of your bags in a separate place can help identify the bags if the luggage tags are missing. Put a tag with your last name and destination (place where you will be staying) inside your bag too, so the airline will know where to send the bag when it is recovered.

184. When are travelers most likely to lose their bags?
(A) When they have a non-stop flight
(B) When they have a direct flight
(C) When they have to change planes
(D) When they are frequent flyers

185. What should be carried on the plane, instead of packed in a suitcase?
(A) A change of clothes
(B) A name tag
(C) Anything valuable
(D) A toothbrush

186. Why should travelers keep a list of what is in their bags?
(A) It proves they checked a bag.
(B) It can identify the bag.
(C) They can use it for insurance.
(D) They will know if anything is missing.

Questions 187–189 refer to the following article. p 267

Many visitors to our area remark on the many statues and monuments in our city. They serve as constant reminders of our history. They are also constant collectors of dirt and grime. That is where a special team of city employees comes in. This team is assigned the task of keeping the statues clean. Depending on size and composition, a statue can take one to three days to clean thoroughly. It takes about a year to get through all the statues—and then, it is time to start again. However, the team members claim they never get bored. Each statue has its own personality, and they get to know each one as a friend.

187. What is this article about?
(A) Preserving history
(B) Keeping statues clean
(C) Monuments in the city
(D) Teams in city government

188. How often is each statue cleaned?
(A) Every day
(B) Every three days
(C) Once a month
(D) Once a year

189. Who cleans the statues?
(A) Park rangers
(B) Volunteers
(C) A special team
(D) Artists

Questions 190–192 refer to the following announcement.  p 267

190. Why are there new instructions about parking at the airport?
(A) They needed more room for cars.
(B) There is construction at the terminal.
(C) There was an accident on the runway.
(D) The road is under repair.

191. Where should drivers park if they are leaving their cars overnight?
(A) Where there is hourly parking
(B) Wherever there is a space
(C) In the short-term lot
(D) In the satellite lot

192. How will drivers know where the new lots are?
(A) The lots are easily seen.
(B) Drivers can follow other cars.
(C) There are signs.
(D) Policemen are directing traffic.

> **ATTENTION**
>
> Passengers planning to drive and park at the airport should be aware of several changes due to construction at the terminal. Short-term parking is available in a new parking lot at the south end of the terminal. This lot provides hourly parking for those who are meeting or dropping off passengers. Travelers who plan to park overnight or longer can park in the new satellite lot and board a shuttle bus to the terminal. New signs at the entrance of the airport will direct travelers to the appropriate parking area.

Questions 193–196 refer to the following article. p 268

> If you dine out often, there are things that you can do to make the experience even better. Let the waiter know your expectations for the evening. If you want to linger over your meal, or if you are in a hurry, the waiter can adjust the service to suit your needs. If you have special dietary restrictions, let the restaurant know. Most restaurants are happy to leave salt out of a dish, or steam your fish instead of fry it if you just ask. If there is a problem with the service, speak to the waiter before talking to the manager; the waiter may be able to correct the problem immediately. Above all, be polite.

193. What should diners do if they are in a hurry when eating out?
(A) Tell the waiter
(B) Order something simple
(C) Eat quickly
(D) Pay cash

194. What can the restaurant do if customers do not use salt?
(A) Serve them raw vegetables
(B) Get food from a hospital
(C) Allow them to eat food from home
(D) Leave the salt out of the recipe

195. What should diners do if there is a problem?
(A) Go to another restaurant
(B) Talk to the manager
(C) Discuss it with the waiter
(D) Stay angry all evening

196. What rule should diners always follow?
(A) Be funny
(B) Be polite
(C) Be punctual
(D) Be hungry

Questions 197–200 refer to the following article.  p 268

Coffee, one of the oldest drinks in the world, is still one of the most popular. The fact that its popularity has lasted over the years, is probably due to its versatility. It is frequently used as a flavoring for cookies and baked goods, and is often combined with chocolate to make the mocha flavor of chocolate candies and of dairy products such as ice cream. It even appears in savory recipes, such as traditional red-eye gravy. But coffee is most popular as a drink.

Coffee drinks can be found in almost any country at any time of day or night. These drinks have many forms, depending on the way the beans are roasted and how the coffee is made. Lightly roasted beans, brewed with water, form the lighter style of coffee popular in the United States. Dark-roasted beans are more common in Europe, and more variety is found in preparation. Coffee made primarily with milk is popular for breakfast. Coffees drunk at other times seem to be stronger, from the espresso types made with steam to the thick, strong Turkish brew prepared by boiling crushed coffee beans.

Coffee has also survived because it has been thought to keep well without refrigeration or other special handling. However, this view is beginning to change. Experts say that most of the coffee that is widely available in the world's markets has actually gone stale before it is drunk. Coffee beans, they say, typically remain fresh only about a month after they have been roasted. But the coffee may not even have been sold, much less drunk, within this period. Modern packaging methods help, but coffee is usually purchased in quantity and brewed a little at a time, so the packaging does not help keep the coffee fresh once a consumer has broken its air-tight seal.

Judging from the amount of traditional coffee currently sold, many people are perfectly happy with stale coffee. But some companies are trying to give coffee-drinking consumers an alternative. Gourmet coffee shops, often known as coffee bars, have opened in many urban areas for the purpose of serving and selling coffees at their peak of freshness. They also brew coffee in a variety of styles, so coffee drinkers can have their choice. Such shops, along with a few specialty mail-order businesses, are virtually the only sources for coffee that passes the rigorous tests of the experts.

197. Why is coffee popular?
  (A) It is old.
  (B) It is available.
  (C) It is versatile.
  (D) It is cheap.

198. What do experts say is a problem with most coffee?
  (A) It is stale.
  (B) It is grown in poor soil.
  (C) It is roasted too long.
  (D) It is not stored properly.

199. How long does coffee stay fresh after roasting?
  (A) A few days
  (B) A week
  (C) Two weeks
  (D) A month

200. What is a good source of fresh coffee?
  (A) Coffee farms
  (B) Urban gourmet coffee shops
  (C) Any grocery store
  (D) Expensive restaurants

Stop! This is the end of the test. If you finish before the time is called, you may go back to Parts V, VI, and VII and check your work.

Tapescript

1 Review

Practice: Part I

1.
   (A) He is working at his desk.
   (B) He is asleep.
   (C) He is answering his mail.
   (D) He is talking to someone on the telephone.

2.
   (A) One woman is giving her address.
   (B) They're discussing fashion.
   (C) A woman is addressing the group.
   (D) They are hairdressers.

3.
   (A) A man is buying a book.
   (B) They are talking about the experiment.
   (C) The workers are having lunch.
   (D) A man is pointing to the book.

4.
   (A) They are cleaning the tables.
   (B) They are washing their clothes.
   (C) They are serving dinner.
   (D) They are eating lunch.

5.
   (A) He is repairing his car.
   (B) He is watching the clock.
   (C) He is standing by the door.
   (D) He is wearing a mask.

6.
   (A) The men are carrying pearls.
   (B) Two women are talking.
   (C) The scientists are doing experiments.
   (D) The engineers are on the train.

Practice: Part II

1. Where are you going?
   (A) Yes, we are.
   (B) We're going to lunch.
   (C) It's time to go.

2. Didn't your friends leave late?
   (A) To the meeting.
   (B) No, they ate at noon.
   (C) Yes, but they still arrived on time.

3. Where did you leave the car?
   (A) Sometimes.
   (B) In the parking lot.
   (C) I'm not sure.

4. Have you calculated the ad revenue for this quarter?
   (A) Yes, here is the total.
   (B) No, we need to subtract.
   (C) Because we needed the sum.

5. On what date was the invoice sent?
   (A) My voice is too weak.
   (B) The boys arrived yesterday.
   (C) The tenth.

6. Was it difficult to contact the reservation department?
   (A) A round-trip ticket.
   (B) I don't think so.
   (C) Hardly ever.

7. Did you forget to weigh the shipment?
   (A) No, the weight is listed here.
   (B) I don't know the way.
   (C) It's too long to wait.

8. Could I help you?
   (A) No, thank you.
   (B) Please don't do that.
   (C) Downtown.

9. When will Mr. Yoshimura arrive?
   (A) In two weeks.
   (B) Yes, it's possible.
   (C) Last month.

10. Could you give me your account number please?
   (A) We've counted 150.
   (B) Certainly.
   (C) Yes, I'm pleased.

Practice: Part III

Narrator	Number 1.
Man	Do you have an appointment Wednesday morning?
Woman	No. Why? Do you want to meet about the overseas project?
Man	No, it's about the employees' schedules.
Narrator	Number 2.
Woman A	I'm Sarah Preloh. Ms. Salam is expecting me.
Woman B	Yes, she told me. Please go right in. Her office is down the hall, the first door on the left.
Woman A	Thank you.
Narrator	Number 3.
Woman	Your presentation was very well received.
Man	Thank you. I was worried there would be no interest, but there were more than a dozen questions.
Woman	And you weren't nervous at all!
Narrator	Number 4.
Woman	Have you had any news from Mr. Ling?
Man	He sent a fax this morning. He feels very positive about the deal.
Woman	I certainly hope he's not mistaken.
Narrator	Number 5.
Man	How did your interview with the manager go?
Woman	I'm not sure. Mr. Ruda seemed interested in my production experience, but he didn't ask for my recommendations.
Man	Don't worry. He will. He doesn't hire a production manager without getting recommendations.
Narrator	Number 6.
Woman	Why has your department been so successful?
Man	Probably because we've changed schedules.
Woman	It doesn't hurt to promote new supervisors, either.
Narrator	Number 7.
Woman	They're angry because we didn't reply to their inquiry about vacating the warehouse.
Man	How long has it been?
Woman	Their letter is dated May 25.
Narrator	Number 8.
Woman	We should encourage the passengers to tip the crew at the end of the cruise.
Man	That's a great idea. It would be good for morale.
Woman	But we mustn't offend our guests, though.
Narrator	Number 9.
Woman	Have you discussed the problem with the customer?
Man	Actually I've spoken with him every day for a week.
Woman	I'd like to speak with him next time he calls.
Narrator	Number 10.
Woman	I'm very hungry. I think I'll have an appetizer.
Man	This menu is long. I'm having trouble making a decision!
Woman	Try the mushrooms. They're great!

Practice: Part IV

Questions 1 through 3 refer to the following advertisement.

Your company's computer keyboard, monitor, and mouse could cause problems and injuries. Make some changes in work habits and avoid wrist injuries and other computer-related stresses. Computer Accessories has produced the most up-to-date designs for compatible computer keyboards, monitors, and mouse units.

Call now to receive information and a catalog of products.

Questions 4 and 5 refer to the following advertisement.

Timeshares go on sale at the annual international meeting scheduled for September 28 in Honolulu. Interested buyers can participate in person, by mail, or by fax. Last year, 90 timeshares sold at prices as low as $500US for one week in Rio de Janeiro to $10,000US for two weeks in Hawaii. The sponsors of the event say resales come in at approximately 50% of the original price. Call Timeshares/ Landshares at 01 (800) 345-7866 for an advance copy of the listings.

Practice Test 1
Part I

Sample question:
(A) They're looking out the window.
(B) They're having a meeting.
(C) They're eating in a restaurant.
(D) They're moving the furniture.

1.
    (A) They are looking for books.
    (B) The library is closed today.
    (C) Everything but books is on the shelves.
    (D) The men are writing a story.

2.
    (A) They are taking a nap.
    (B) The light show is very beautiful.
    (C) The trees lose their leaves in winter.
    (D) Some skiers are sitting on the snow.

3.
    (A) All of the chairs are occupied.
    (B) The people are eating lunch.
    (C) The label is long.
    (D) They are having a meeting.

4.
    (A) The rain is coming down quickly.
    (B) The swimmers are in training.
    (C) The bridge crosses the water.
    (D) The plane goes to Cambridge.

5.
    (A) The cooks are preparing the meal.
    (B) The farmers grow vegetables to eat.
    (C) The waiter serves the customer.
    (D) The menu is in French.

6.
    (A) They are playing volleyball.
    (B) Beyond the valley are tall hills.
    (C) The fish are caught in the net.
    (D) The players are looking for a match.

7.
    (A) The sheep are ready for market.
    (B) The ship is being loaded.
    (C) The containers are made of paper.
    (D) The doctor is busy.

8.
    (A) There are everything but machines here.
    (B) The computer store has big windows.
    (C) She is talking on the phone.
    (D) The woman is mailing a letter.

9.
    (A) The door to the plane is closed.
    (B) The men are carrying a box.
    (C) The helicopter is in the air.
    (D) The pilot light is on.

10.
    (A) The keys are on the table.
    (B) The circus posters cover the wall.
    (C) The computer salesroom is open.
    (D) The men are watching the monitors.

11.
    (A) The workers are on strike.
    (B) The artist draws a straight line.
    (C) The men are assembling an engine.
    (D) Everyone wears a coat and tie.

12.
    (A) The windows are cleaned automatically.
    (B) They are washing their car.
    (C) The car is made by hand.
    (D) They are taking a bath.

13.
    (A) The passengers will board the train.
    (B) The man is checking his bags.
    (C) The goods are lifted by crane.
    (D) The conductor is taking tickets.

14.
    (A) He is tied down.
    (B) Let's tell her about the band.
    (C) He is holding a bank card.
    (D) He is taking out the trash.

15.

(A) The men are digging a trench.
(B) The worker fell into a hole.
(C) They are smoking pipes.
(D) The signs are laying in a ditch.

16.

(A) The artist is drawing a picture.
(B) The bird is in a cage.
(C) The couple is admiring the sculpture.
(D) The statue is in the harbor.

17.

(A) The gas station is on the corner.
(B) The containers are being transferred.
(C) The boxes are on the shelf.
(D) The soup cans are in storage.

18.

(A) The pedestrians are crossing the street.
(B) The film was exposed in the light.
(C) The conference room is occupied.
(D) The trade fair is well-attended.

19.

(A) The doctor examines the patient.
(B) The patient is lying down.
(C) The doctor is listening to music.
(D) The man is buttoning his shirt.

20.

(A) They need a loan.
(B) The television is not working.
(C) They are talking on the phone.
(D) The telephones are in the hallway.

Part II

21. Where do you live?
(A) I live on Church Street.
(B) My parents are still alive.
(C) You're in room C.

22. Can we reschedule our meeting for Friday?
(A) Here's the plane schedule.
(B) No, I don't eat meat on Friday.
(C) No, I'm busy then.

23. Who are you sending this memo to?
(A) I'll send both memos.
(B) To the housekeeping staff.
(C) My secretary sent it.

24. What do you think of her idea?
(A) I didn't do it.
(B) He's very clever.
(C) I wasn't impressed.

25. Has this product been tested yet?
(A) It's being tested now.
(B) He failed the class.
(C) She won't pass the exam.

26. When will the weather get warmer?
(A) Not until July.
(B) Her sweater is very warm.
(C) December is not very warm.

27. How long have you been working here?
(A) I'm busy.
(B) Not until five.
(C) For three months now.

28. Would you like more coffee?
(A) No. There isn't any more.
(B) Yes, thank you.
(C) You like coffee.

29. When are you leaving?
(A) At six tonight.
(B) To San Francisco.
(C) By plane.

30. I can return this if it doesn't match, can't I?
(A) You can't play in the rain.
(B) Yes, we have a return policy.
(C) It's not too much.

31. How fast can you read?
(A) I learned in school.
(B) I write fast too.
(C) Only 90 words a minute.

32. Why don't we plan a picnic for Sunday?
(A) I've lost the map.
(B) Use a blanket instead.
(C) Sure. That sounds fun.

33. Does every employee have to fill out this form?
(A) Sign your name here.
(B) Your interview is at one.
(C) Yes. It's required by law.

34. What is good at this restaurant?
    (A) We're ready to order.
    (B) I recommend the grilled fish.
    (C) The check, please.

35. Can you pick up the package when you go?
    (A) I'm sorry. I won't have time.
    (B) It's too heavy for her.
    (C) I'm going to the park soon.

36. Why didn't you call the repair person earlier?
    (A) He couldn't hear me.
    (B) I didn't know there was a problem.
    (C) She's always late.

37. Do you know her?
    (A) Yes, but not well.
    (B) I'll show up on time.
    (C) She won't say no.

38. I think it's a big risk, don't you?
    (A) I ruined the disk.
    (B) It's too small.
    (C) I certainly do.

39. When will the speeches be over?
    (A) The president is speaking.
    (B) Probably about ten o'clock.
    (C) They'll come over after lunch.

40. Why aren't they taking the subway?
    (A) There's a delay on the tracks.
    (B) I took the pictures on the way.
    (C) We should stop for the day.

41. Do you bring lunch from home every day?
    (A) I commute by car.
    (B) No. It's too cold at noon.
    (C) Yes. It's expensive to eat out.

42. May I help you?
    (A) She doesn't know where.
    (B) I'll help you into the car.
    (C) Yes, I'm looking for the shoe department.

43. I can't find my briefcase.
    (A) I like short speeches.
    (B) Did you leave it in the conference room?
    (C) He's doing fine, thank you.

44. Is that coat comfortable?
    (A) Yes, he was able to afford a coat.
    (B) I could do it.
    (C) No, it's tight in the shoulders.

45. Who are they talking about?
    (A) Because they're both cooks.
    (B) His latest game.
    (C) The new assistant manager.

46. How does the camera work?
    (A) Just push the button on top.
    (B) I need to get it fixed.
    (C) She works very quickly.

47. Are you the head of security?
    (A) Yes, she will.
    (B) No, he can't.
    (C) Yes, I am.

48. What's wrong with the fax machine?
    (A) The room was very clean.
    (B) It won't send documents.
    (C) It's too long.

49. Will you be able to attend the reception?
    (A) No, I'll be out of town.
    (B) The reservation clerk is on duty.
    (C) She likes to stay home.

50. Do we have enough time?
    (A) There are always too many limes.
    (B) Stay until six thirty.
    (C) No, we'll have to finish tomorrow.

Part III

Narrator	Number 51.
Woman	Let's meet on Tuesday.
Man	I'm tied up all day Tuesday.
Woman	Then we'll have to make it Wednesday.
Narrator	Number 52.
Woman A	Do you have the latest profit statement?
Woman B	My secretary is typing it now.
Woman A	Please let me know when it is done.
Narrator	Number 53.
Man	Would you like to fill out a card for our store's mailing list?
Woman	What kind of mail would I receive?

Man	You would receive notices about upcoming sales.

Narrator   Number 54.
Woman A   Would you like some coffee and a roll?
Woman B   Just coffee, thanks.
Woman A   Cream and sugar?

Narrator   Number 55.
Woman   Since the presentation ends at eleven thirty, everyone can break for lunch.
Man   Isn't that too early for lunch?
Woman   Yes, but with so many people, we'll need the extra time.

Narrator   Number 56.
Woman   I'm expecting a new client this morning.
Man   Shall I send him up when he arrives?
Woman   No, call me instead. I'll come get him.

Narrator   Number 57.
Man   This tour bus stops at all museums and monuments.
Woman   Will we stop in the market district?
Man   The last stop on the tour is next to the market district.

Narrator   Number 58.
Man   I can get you on the seven o'clock flight.
Woman   Great. I'd like a window seat, please.
Man   I'm sorry. There are only aisle seats left.

Narrator   Number 59.
Man   I'm in the mood for a concert this weekend.
Woman   I'd rather go to a play.
Man   We'll go to the opera. That will suit us both.

Narrator   Number 60.
Man   I can't get the fax machine to work.
Woman   Put each sheet of paper in very slowly.
Man   Oh! Thanks, it's working now.

Narrator   Number 61.
Man   This book is due back in the library in two weeks.
Woman   What happens if I turn it in late?
Man   We charge 25 cents for every day the book is overdue.

Narrator   Number 62.
Woman   Book the conference room for our ten o'clock meeting.
Man   The conference room is being used every morning this week.
Woman   But no other room is large enough for our group.

Narrator   Number 63.
Man   You are reserved for two nights.
Woman   I'll pay by credit card.
Man   Thank you. Here are your card and your room key.

Narrator   Number 64.
Man   Where is the nearest parking garage?
Woman   Around the corner. But you can park your car on the next street.
Man   Thank you. I'll try that first.

Narrator   Number 65.
Man   I commute from the suburbs every morning.
Woman   Doesn't the long ride bother you?
Man   No, I use the time to think about work.

Narrator   Number 66.
Man   I'd like to get this prescription filled.
Woman   We have this medicine in stock. I'll fill it right away.
Man   Thank you. I'll wait.

Narrator   Number 67.
Man   Does the coat in the window come in gray?
Woman   I'm sorry, it only comes in black and brown.
Man   Then I'll try on the black.

Narrator   Number 68.
Man   Shall we get some lunch?
Woman   That sounds good. I've been working on my computer all morning.
Man   Then the break will do you good.

Narrator   Number 69.
Man   Has the mail arrived yet?
Woman   Not yet. Are you expecting something besides bills?
Man   I'm supposed to get an important package.

Narrator	Number 70.
Woman A	Excuse me, ma'am. I'll have to check your bag.
Woman B	Can't I take it on the plane?
Woman A	No, ma'am. It's too big to fit under the seat.
Narrator	Number 71.
Man	Oh, no! It's five o'clock, and I haven't set the tables.
Woman	Don't worry. That clock is fifteen minutes fast.
Man	Good. I still have time to finish then.
Narrator	Number 72.
Woman	Do you need to make copies of that memo?
Man	Yes, but I just found a mistake on line one.
Woman	Then you should fix it before you make copies.
Narrator	Number 73.
Man	What is the fare to the university?
Woman	It's 95 cents, and the driver doesn't make change.
Man	Now what? I only have a dollar bill.
Narrator	Number 74.
Woman	Do you type?
Man	Yes, and I am an expert at word processing.
Woman	What software are you familiar with?
Narrator	Number 75.
Man	It's raining again.
Woman	And I've lost my umbrella.
Man	Take mine. I have another in my car.
Narrator	Number 76.
Man	There will be two hundred people at the banquet.
Woman	We can set up enough tables in the ballroom.
Man	We can't do that because there's dancing afterward.
Narrator	Number 77.
Man	I forgot my glasses, so I can't read anything on this menu.
Woman	Shall I read it to you?
Man	Just the seafood dishes, please.

Narrator	Number 78.
Man	How can I get to the mail room?
Woman	Go straight past the marketing department and turn left at the water fountain.
Man	I can find that. Thanks.
Narrator	Number 79.
Man	Would you like a table inside or on the patio?
Woman	It's such a lovely day. I'll eat on the patio.
Man	Certainly. Right this way, please.
Narrator	Number 80.
Man	These messages came while you were out.
Woman	Thanks. Was there any mail?
Man	It's on your desk.

Part IV

Questions 81 and 82 refer to the following announcement.

We are now boarding Flight three-fifty-seven to Tokyo. Passengers should have their boarding passes ready and approach the gate when their row number is called. First Class passengers may board at their convenience.

Questions 83 and 84 refer to the following announcement.

May I have your attention, please. A fire has been reported in the building. The fire department is on the way. Please exit the building now. Move quickly. Do not stop for personal belongings. Exit using the stairways. Do not use the elevators.

Questions 85 and 86 refer to the following recording.

Thank you for calling the Tour Service Line. If you would like to book a guided tour of the city, press 1. If you would like maps for the walking tour, press 2. If you would like personal tours of the city's museums, press 3. If you would like information about special tours not listed, press 4.

Questions 87 through 89 refer to the following advertisement.

Call Business Printing Services for all your printing needs. We specialize in designs for stationery and brochures for the company that wants a professional image. We offer special low rates for volume orders. Visit us soon at one of our five convenient locations throughout the city.

Questions 90 through 92 refer to the following weather report.

Tonight we expect partly cloudy conditions and colder temperatures with lows around 40 degrees. The wind will be picking up too, with gusts to 25 miles an hour. Tomorrow morning the skies will be mostly cloudy, developing into rain by late afternoon.

Questions 93 through 95 refer to the following explanation.

In the mail room, we sort the incoming mail for employees and deliver it to their office mailboxes. We also help employees with their outgoing mail. We ask them to bring all fragile packages to us for wrapping. We have envelopes, boxes, and special packing materials so nothing will get broken in the mail.

Questions 96 and 97 refer to the following introduction.

Our next speaker is Dr. Anna Yung. Dr. Yung is well known for her research on new techniques for increasing the strength of metals used in industrial machinery. She is here today to bring us up to date on her latest research findings.

Questions 98 through 100 refer to the following news item.

New car sales have risen by nearly 2.2 percent over the same period last year. Economists attribute the rise to the increase in loans available for new car purchases. Auto experts, however, say that the increase is due to the innovative safety features on new car models. These features are the result of consumer demand for safer, more reliable cars.

Practice Test 2
Part I

Sample question:
- (A) They're looking out the window.
- (B) They're having a meeting.
- (C) They're eating in a restaurant.
- (D) They're moving the furniture.

1.
- (A) The mountain climbers are at the summit.
- (B) The family is taking a walk.
- (C) The mother is carrying her child.
- (D) The talk is very familiar.

2.
- (A) The bureau chief is out to lunch.
- (B) The tomato sauce is spicy.
- (C) The chef is holding a basket of tomatoes.
- (D) The cook is chopping vegetables.

3.
- (A) There are flags over the counter.
- (B) The arrival hall is empty.
- (C) The tickets to the fair are free.
- (D) They will pass the port after dinner.

4.
- (A) The players are on the field.
- (B) The man is shooting wild game.
- (C) There is a pool in Bill's yard.
- (D) The woman is watching the man.

5.
- (A) His hobby is collecting stamps.
- (B) The visiting team will rest tonight.
- (C) She guessed the answer.
- (D) The couple are talking in the lobby.

6.
- (A) The doctors are performing an operation.
- (B) The men are playing golf.
- (C) The lazy workers are taking a nap.
- (D) The technicians are discussing the equipment.

7.
- (A) The man points to the book.
- (B) They are sitting in the forest.
- (C) The pharmacist is dispensing medicine.
- (D) They are buying flowers.

8.

   (A) The musicians are practicing.

   (B) The drum is in the window.

   (C) They are listening to music on the radio.

   (D) Prisoners would like freedom.

9.

   (A) He is talking on the phone.

   (B) There is no lamp on the table.

   (C) The journalist is reporting the news.

   (D) The man is reading the paper.

10.

   (A) The bellhop reaches for the bag.

   (B) The couple is driving away.

   (C) They fell down the stairs.

   (D) The car door is locked.

11.

   (A) She is looking through papers.

   (B) She is reading the newspaper.

   (C) She is hanging up her coat.

   (D) She is watching the presentation.

12.

   (A) Everyone is standing up.

   (B) The workers are having lunch.

   (C) The restaurant is closed for repairs.

   (D) There are a lot of windows.

13.

   (A) The shopping cart is empty.

   (B) They are driving on the highway.

   (C) The man is walking behind the car.

   (D) She is explaining the street sign.

14.

   (A) The girls are making tea.

   (B) The students perform an experiment.

   (C) The children play after school.

   (D) The chemist is mixing the solution.

15.

   (A) The button is falling off.

   (B) They stopped writing.

   (C) The number of the house is four.

   (D) Someone is getting on the bus.

16.

   (A) A bicyclist is by the vending machine.

   (B) She can drink several sodas.

   (C) He is watching the time.

   (D) The motor bike is old.

17.

   (A) The customers are buying office furniture.

   (B) People are working at their desks.

   (C) The electrician is repairing the light fixtures.

   (D) The lunchroom is crowded.

18.

   (A) The workers wear hard hats.

   (B) The car is turning around.

   (C) None of the men wear protective glasses.

   (D) The engine needs more oil.

19.

   (A) He enjoys water skiing.

   (B) He's wading in the lake.

   (C) He's drinking cold water.

   (D) He would see better without glasses.

20.

   (A) They are playing checkers.

   (B) The banquet hall is not crowded.

   (C) The woman works behind a glass window.

   (D) The clerk saved the man's life.

Part II

21. May I borrow your dictionary?

   (A) Sure. I never use it.

   (B) I know how to spell that.

   (C) You have too many books.

22. Do you know when she is scheduled to lecture?

   (A) The plane left on schedule.

   (B) I don't like to speak in public.

   (C) No, I haven't seen the agenda.

23. Better staff training would solve the problem, don't you think?

   (A) The train service is really bad here.

   (B) It would certainly help.

   (C) No, I'm afraid I can't.

24. Who opened the window?
    (A) It always stays closed.
    (B) I did; it was stuffy in here.
    (C) No, I'm comfortable, thanks.

25. When will we hear from the client?
    (A) He's fine, thank you.
    (B) By telephone.
    (C) After their board meeting next week.

26. Do you think print advertising reaches the right market?
    (A) It depends which magazines run our ads.
    (B) The fish is always fresh there.
    (C) Yes, turn right at Market Street.

27. Who was on the phone?
    (A) I loaned them my skis.
    (B) She didn't hear it ringing.
    (C) It was our supplier.

28. Did you see the accident happen?
    (A) No. I heard the crash and then looked up.
    (B) No one was hurt.
    (C) Nobody called the police.

29. What did you think of the movie?
    (A) Those movers were very efficient.
    (B) The actors were wonderful.
    (C) We do need more ink.

30. Have you ever been to Paris?
    (A) No, I want a pair of those.
    (B) You always seem to arrive late.
    (C) Actually, we went there on our honeymoon.

31. Is it snowing yet?
    (A) No, he won't be here until four.
    (B) No, but it could start any minute.
    (C) Yes, they finished last week.

32. May I speak to someone in your billing department, please?
    (A) I'll connect you with Ms. Smith.
    (B) We never get letters, just bills.
    (C) I told him to pay it already.

33. Do you know of a way to increase our efficiency?
    (A) Faster computers would be a start.
    (B) We can place an order for more.
    (C) It takes longer to get there.

34. You've worked with this director before, haven't you?
    (A) Yes, I worked overtime yesterday.
    (B) No, I remember him.
    (C) Yes, many years ago.

35. Is someone sitting here?
    (A) We have to stand.
    (B) Yes, I'm sorry.
    (C) The seats are too hard.

36. At what time did the call come in?
    (A) At two-ten exactly.
    (B) Into the lobby.
    (C) It was cold outside.

37. How about working late tonight?
    (A) You always get up early.
    (B) I can't. I have plans.
    (C) I'll go later.

38. Didn't you remind her about her appointment?
    (A) I did, but she forgot.
    (B) She left an hour ago.
    (C) It's on the corner.

39. Do you want pepper on your salad?
    (A) My salary is high.
    (B) The salad is served before the soup.
    (C) Yes, thank you.

40. Do you take the bus?
    (A) Only 75 cents.
    (B) No, the subway.
    (C) I can't find a parking space.

41. Are you going out for lunch?
    (A) They are predicting rain.
    (B) Only long enough to get a sandwich.
    (C) No, a bunch of grapes.

42. When do you open on Sundays?
    (A) Not until one o'clock.
    (B) Be sure to close it tightly.
    (C) I opened the present this morning.

43. Do you know if the order was placed?
    (A) Yes, I placed it myself.
    (B) He's always losing things.
    (C) I'll have the chicken.

44. Whose notebook is this?
    (A) The musicians read sheet music.
    (B) I can't read my handwriting.
    (C) It looks like mine.

45. Can I have her return your call?
    (A) She will be back on Wednesday.
    (B) No, I won't be near a phone.
    (C) Yes, I'd like a refund.

46. Where will you go on your vacation?
    (A) We don't have any vacancies.
    (B) He's leaving next week.
    (C) I'm going to the beach.

47. Can I help you with that report?
    (A) That broadcast has the best reporters.
    (B) Thanks, but I've just finished it.
    (C) I'm too busy right now.

48. The new ship will have more deck space, won't it?
    (A) Yes, that should attract more passengers.
    (B) No, I can't race.
    (C) We need to redecorate.

49. Are the new cabin assignments posted yet?
    (A) Thanks, I already have a cab.
    (B) Yes, they're posting them right now.
    (C) The fence needs to be repaired.

50. How much is the full fare?
    (A) It lasts until five.
    (B) Five hundred dollars each way.
    (C) It's already empty.

Part III

Narrator	Number 51.
Man	What's wrong?
Woman	I can't find my notes from the meeting.
Man	I've got mine. I'll make a copy for you.

Narrator	Number 52.
Man	May I help you?
Woman	I need a birthday present for my brother.
Man	Does he play sports? We have a good selection of exercise wear.

Narrator	Number 53.
Woman	It's so hot in this room I can't concentrate.
Man	The air conditioner broke this morning.
Woman	Again? We should buy a new one.

Narrator	Number 54.
Woman	Why are you so late?
Man	It's the road construction. It slows down traffic.
Woman	It's annoying now, but we'll enjoy the new road when it's finished.

Narrator	Number 55.
Man	I'd like to reserve a room for the third.
Woman	Certainly. A double room, or a single?
Man	A double, please. There will be two of us.

Narrator	Number 56.
Woman	How far away is the courthouse?
Man	Not far. It's just by the police station.
Woman	I know where that is. It's close enough to walk.

Narrator	Number 57.
Man	I'm ready for some dinner.
Woman	Me, too. Where would you like to eat?
Man	Let's go to that seafood place you like.

Narrator	Number 58.
Man	The paper jams in this copier.
Woman	The problem is your paper. The sheets are too thin to go through the rollers.
Man	I'll try this thicker paper then.

Narrator	Number 59.
Man	Now I've spilled coffee all over my jacket!
Woman	It will probably come out if you get it to the cleaner's right away.
Man	I hope so. I don't want to buy another one.

Narrator	Number 60.
Woman	I'm going to the bookstore to buy some books to read on the trip.
Man	Why don't you check some out of the library? It'll be cheaper.
Woman	I'm always afraid I'll lose library books when I travel.

| Narrator | Number 61. |
| Woman | It's raining again. |

Man	Oh, no. And I'd planned a camping trip this weekend.
Woman	I would cancel it if I were you. Even if the rain stops, the ground will be soaking wet.

Narrator	Number 62.
Man	There's no more space in this closet.
Woman	No wonder. It's full of clothes.
Man	I know, but I'm afraid I'll need something if I throw them out.

Narrator	Number 63.
Man	You're seeing that movie again? But I saw it with you last year!
Woman	I see it every year when it plays. It's a classic.
Man	Even so, it seems like it would get boring after a while.

Narrator	Number 64.
Man	Here's a sofa that's in your price range.
Woman	The size is right, and I like the shape. But the fabric won't match my living room.
Man	That's no problem. You can choose any fabric you want from our upholstery catalogue.

Narrator	Number 65.
Man	Excuse me. This fork appears to be dirty.
Woman	I'm so sorry, sir. Here is a new set of silverware.
Man	Thank you. I'm ready to order now.

Narrator	Number 66.
Man	The client needs this document right away. I'll call the messenger service.
Woman	Why don't we just fax it?
Man	The messenger service is actually less expensive when the document is as long as this one.

Narrator	Number 67.
Man	The job description called for twice as much work at the same salary I'm making now.
Woman	So I guess that means you aren't taking the job?
Man	No one will take it unless they offer a higher salary.

Narrator	Number 68.
Woman	That new employee in the mail room is very helpful.
Man	Didn't you know? That's the owner's daughter. She's here to learn the business.
Woman	I guess the owner believes in starting at the bottom.

Narrator	Number 69.
Man	I'd like to make an appointment.
Woman	Of course. Are you having trouble with your filling?
Man	No trouble. I just have my teeth cleaned every six months.

Narrator	Number 70.
Man	That's the most boring seminar I've been to in a long time.
Woman	Well, it wasn't the regular speaker. She got sick at the last minute.
Man	I'm surprised they didn't have a better substitute.

Narrator	Number 71.
Woman	We have to get this out by Wednesday, or the entire project will be delayed.
Man	I can't do it unless I have more help.
Woman	Hire as many temporary workers as you need. This has to get done.

Narrator	Number 72.
Man	Did you hear that Ms. Greene's surgery went well?
Woman	Yes, we should send her a card and some flowers.
Man	Let's order balloons instead. She's allergic to flowers.

Narrator	Number 73.
Man	The subway train is late again.
Woman	The trains are often late during tourist season. The tourists are slow getting on and off at the stops.
Man	Then they ought to wait until after rush hour to take the trains.

Narrator	Number 74.
Man	There's a message on your desk from Mr. Gomez.

Woman	Oh, good. I'll call him before the meeting.
Man	Wait. The message was to tell you that he is away today and tomorrow.

Narrator Number 75.

Man I can't wait for that new restaurant to open.

Woman Yes, we will finally have a place with good food nearby.

Man I'm tired of having the same old thing at the sandwich shop every day.

Narrator Number 76.

Woman I've got my suggestion all ready for the meeting.

Man You should let the moderator know you'll have something important to say.

Woman You're right. That way, he'll be sure to allow time for me.

Narrator Number 77.

Man Will you be at the reception tonight?

Woman Yes, but I can't stay late. I'm leaving at six in the morning for Toronto.

Man That's okay. It won't last long anyway.

Narrator Number 78.

Man Our order for office supplies is late again.

Woman It's the third time. I say we do business with someone else.

Man I agree. Draw up a list of other suppliers, and we'll try someone new.

Narrator Number 79.

Woman Our cost analysis shows we're spending too much on mailing and postage.

Man Does the analysis show why?

Woman Yes. No one sends anything by regular mail anymore. They always use the expensive overnight service.

Narrator Number 80.

Man Could you take this list to the purser's office for me? I've got to set up the stage for the concert tonight.

Woman I'll be glad to. I've got some tickets to take there, anyway.

Man Thanks. Now I can get things ready ahead of time.

Part IV

Questions 81 and 82 refer to the following notice.

For your safety, please exercise caution when using the moving sidewalk. Please stand to the right and hold on to the hand rails. Place your luggage in front of you so it will not obstruct the sidewalk. If you prefer to walk, please use the left-hand side. Do not run, and be careful when stepping off the sidewalk.

Questions 83 and 84 refer to the following announcement.

Welcome to the seminar. Before we begin our presentations, let me say that we welcome questions from the audience. But in the interest of time, we ask that you hold your questions until all speakers have finished their presentations. Then, please step to the microphone in the center of the room so that everyone may hear your question.

Questions 85 and 86 refer to the following advertisement.

This set of everyday cookware is the most convenient thing in your kitchen. Mix your ingredients in the dish and put it directly into the oven. Our cookware is made to withstand even the hottest oven temperatures. When your food is done, take the dish out of the oven and put it on the table. Our cookware is so pretty, you can serve directly from it. Even leftovers are not a problem. Just snap on our convenient plastic lids and refrigerate in the dish for later use. Freezing is not recommended.

Questions 87 through 89 refer to the following talk.

Construction crews are getting ready to start improvement on River Parkway into the city. Because this road is a vital artery into the business district, a series of construction crews will work around the clock for the next four weeks to finish the repairs as quickly as possible. One lane each way will be kept open during the morning and evening rush hours, but motorists are advised to find alternate routes into the city for the next month.

Questions 90 through 92 refer to the following announcement.

One of the most charming houses to visit while in town is Madison House, on Broad Street in the old downtown district. Built in 1780, it is not as large as the newer houses on the tour. But Madison House is far more valuable historically for the care and detail that went into building it. Everything in the house, from the woodwork to the custom furniture, represents the highest quality available at that time. Be sure to notice the intricate carved ceilings throughout the house, specially designed for the house and carved by an unknown artisan.

Questions 93 and 94 refer to the following weather report.

We can expect another unseasonably warm weekend. Usually the beginning of November feels as if it is already winter. But not this weekend. We can look forward to sunny skies both Saturday and Sunday, with the temperature at a very comfortable 70 degrees. It will get chilly after the sun goes down, though, so be sure to carry a light jacket if you plan to be out after dark.

Questions 95 through 97 refer to the following announcement.

Your attention, please. We invite our Vista-Rail passengers to relax with a gourmet meal while enjoying the beautiful countryside from our observation windows. The first seating for dinner will begin at six o'clock. If you have tickets for the first seating, you may take your place in the dining car at that time. Those passengers who hold tickets for the second seating will be served in the dining car at eight thirty. There will be an announcement for the second seating at that time.

Questions 98 through 100 refer to the following report.

Most retailers of electronic goods concentrate on price, and count on bringing customers into their stores by advertising the lowest prices. But our survey shows that potential buyers have some surprising preferences about how they shop.

They acknowledge that price is important, but say it is not the determining factor in their purchases. Equally important is the quality of service they can expect from the store if something goes wrong with their purchase. Consumers also say they appreciate a knowledgeable sales staff, who keeps up with the rapid advances in technology.

Practice Test 3
Part I

Sample question:
(A) They're looking out the window.
(B) They're having a meeting.
(C) They're eating in a restaurant.
(D) They're moving the furniture.

1.
(A) They are having lunch at the table.
(B) The woman is making a point.
(C) They are walking around the table.
(D) The men are listening to the radio.

2.
(A) The train is in the station.
(B) The musicians tune their instruments.
(C) The passenger is in first class.
(D) The pilot is at the controls.

3.
(A) The woman is making the bed.
(B) He is buying a purse.
(C) The nurse tends to the patient.
(D) The report is very thick.

4.
(A) The technician is using a microscope.
(B) They are looking for their glasses.
(C) The mathematicians perform division.
(D) This laboratory is for studying languages.

5.
(A) The palm tree is by the beach.
(B) They are checking in at the hotel.
(C) The man is buying a briefcase.
(D) No one is behind the counter.

217

6.

    (A) The commuters wait for a bus.
    (B) The employees are having tea.
    (C) The service department repairs the equipment.
    (D) There are computers on every desk.

7.

    (A) The mother is holding her children.
    (B) The family doesn't celebrate birthdays.
    (C) There are a lot of candles on the cake.
    (D) The baker is making pastry.

8.

    (A) The men are discussing the brochure.
    (B) The man is opening the door.
    (C) All of the men are dressed alike.
    (D) The prescription is hard to read.

9.

    (A) They are writing for a magazine.
    (B) They are picking cherries.
    (C) They are sitting in the lounge.
    (D) They are brewing coffee.

10.

    (A) They are waving their handkerchiefs.
    (B) The classroom is empty.
    (C) The pupils are raising their hands.
    (D) The speaker is at the lectern.

11.

    (A) All telephone circuits are busy.
    (B) The factory makes bread boards.
    (C) The circus is in town.
    (D) She is holding a circuit board.

12.

    (A) Their clothing protects them from the cold.
    (B) The pipe is full of tobacco.
    (C) The men are shoveling snow.
    (D) They are laying in the sand.

13.

    (A) There are two monitors on the desk.
    (B) The engineer runs the train.
    (C) This play is too long.
    (D) Both windows have screens.

14.

    (A) The children are running.
    (B) The politicians are running for office.
    (C) They are playing in the snow.
    (D) They stopped for a rest.

15.

    (A) The technician services the line.
    (B) She is climbing a tree.
    (C) She is on top of the building.
    (D) The engineer turns on the lights.

16.

    (A) They are standing by the fountain.
    (B) The books are stored in cartons.
    (C) The woman is looking at a magazine.
    (D) The journalist is faxing a story.

17.

    (A) The team is leaving the field.
    (B) The golfer is holding the flag.
    (C) Many players are on the course.
    (D) The man is having tea.

18.

    (A) He is looking at a map.
    (B) He is ordering French fries.
    (C) He is resigning.
    (D) He is taking a nap.

19.

    (A) They are building a tunnel.
    (B) They are paying their bill.
    (C) All three wear glasses.
    (D) The women all wear earrings.

20.

    (A) He is serving drinks.
    (B) The plane is landing.
    (C) The restaurant is full.
    (D) The security agent checks the passengers.

Part II

21. Would you like to see the dessert menu?
    (A) No, thanks. Just the check, please.
    (B) No, I wouldn't go to the Sahara.
    (C) Yes, I saw the men.

22. What are you going to do this weekend?
    (A) He will be back next week.
    (B) We are going hiking.
    (C) The show ended last week.

23. Excuse me, do you know if there's a grocery store close by?
    (A) The stationery store is closed at six.
    (B) You're excused.
    (C) No, there isn't. There are only new offices around here.

24. Can we finish by the end of the month?
    (A) Yes, we can advertise.
    (B) Not and do a good job.
    (C) The fiscal year ended last month.

25. The head of housekeeping checked each room, didn't he?
    (A) No, only the occupied ones.
    (B) Yes, he wrote them a check.
    (C) She checked into the hotel.

26. What time did the client arrive?
    (A) Five more minutes.
    (B) At noon.
    (C) Since ten.

27. Are there any part time positions available?
    (A) Sitting too long can cause back strain.
    (B) I think we can repair the watch.
    (C) Not now, but we'll need help during the holidays.

28. How long will you be with us?
    (A) It's about three inches.
    (B) You will take the short cut with us.
    (C) I'll be here for a week.

29. Where did you put the light bulbs?
    (A) They're on the shelf.
    (B) The light switch is by the door.
    (C) Put it on the shopping list.

30. When will the new ship sail?
    (A) Earlier this week.
    (B) Everything is on sale.
    (C) In three days.

31. Are there any messages for me?
    (A) No one is here.
    (B) Yes, on your desk.
    (C) Your drawers are a mess.

32. Could you connect me with Room Service please?
    (A) The connection is loose.
    (B) Please clean your room.
    (C) Yes, certainly, sir. One moment please.

33. You should let a mechanic take a look at this car.
    (A) I always buy gas here.
    (B) Do you know a good one?
    (C) I looked all over the parking garage for my car.

34. When will you get to town?
    (A) Expect me next Friday.
    (B) I go there often.
    (C) I live downtown.

35. How often does the mail arrive?
    (A) Once a day.
    (B) Two days ago.
    (C) It will be soon.

36. The logo is well designed, don't you think?
    (A) I wasn't well enough to go.
    (B) He resigned last week.
    (C) Yes, the graphics department did a great job.

37. Is anyone on duty in the lobby?
    (A) I don't have a hobby.
    (B) Yes, the assistant manager is there.
    (C) The duty-free shop is in the lobby.

38. How long will it take to get to the airport?
    (A) The flight lasts two hours.
    (B) You can take the bus to the airport.
    (C) About 40 minutes.

39. Can I get your opinion on this letter?
    (A) Of course. Let me see it.
    (B) I wouldn't ask him.
    (C) No, it's opposite the post office.

40. Which way is the art museum?
    (A) I'm painting the hallway white.
    (B) Take a left at the next corner, then a right.
    (C) No, I didn't see them.

41. What is your favorite food?
    (A) I really hate fish.
    (B) It's an excellent restaurant.
    (C) I like anything with tomatoes.

42. What's wrong with your foot?
    (A) I hurt my ankle on the stairs.
    (B) I corrected the errors.
    (C) You have to make a right turn.

43. Do you have any non-smoking rooms?
    (A) No, I don't smoke.
    (B) You can smoke in the lobby.
    (C) Yes, most rooms are smoke-free.

44. Shall we send the fax to your cabin?
    (A) Yes, please. As soon as it comes.
    (B) I don't have all the facts.
    (C) No, send it by cab.

45. Could you show me how to use this software program?
    (A) I used to go every day.
    (B) I prefer a firm pillow myself.
    (C) Of course. It's really easy.

46. Why couldn't she come?
    (A) It should be fun.
    (B) Her daughter is sick.
    (C) He doesn't like the work.

47. Do you have an apartment?
    (A) Yes, I put it back together.
    (B) Yes, she lives in the city.
    (C) No, I have a house.

48. Which sports do you prefer?
    (A) I prefer to stay at resorts.
    (B) I like both football and golf.
    (C) I always wear tennis shoes.

49. Have you decided which candidate to hire?
    (A) The last applicant is my choice.
    (B) I hope he didn't get hurt.
    (C) I can't come on that date.

50. When does the plane from Tokyo come in?
    (A) The flight is about twelve hours.
    (B) It arrives in 45 minutes.
    (C) I live close to the airport.

Part III

Narrator	Number 51.
Man	We're about to have lunch. Won't you join us?
Woman	I wish I could, but I have to finish this report.
Man	Oh, well. Some other time then.
Narrator	Number 52.
Man A	Would you like starch in your shirts, sir?
Man B	Just light starch, thank you.
Man A	And would you like them folded, or on hangers?
Narrator	Number 53.
Woman	Waiter, may we move to another table? The sun is shining in our eyes.
Man	Of course, ma'am. Just let me draw the curtains.
Woman	That took care of the problem. We'll stay here.
Narrator	Number 54.
Man	I'm sorry. We have no rooms available for that weekend.
Woman	Could you recommend another hotel in town?
Man	Yes, but there is a big convention this weekend. The other hotels are probably full, too.
Narrator	Number 55.
Man	This chart is too big to fit on one page.
Woman	You can use this button to reduce the size of the copy.
Man	That's great! It fits on one page, and the print is still large enough to read.
Narrator	Number 56.
Man A	What seems to be the problem with your car?
Man B	There is a knocking sound when I put on the brakes.
Man A	That could be serious. I'll take a look and give you a call this afternoon.
Narrator	Number 57.
Man	Have you given your suggestion to the director yet?

Woman	I've tried, but he's always busy with something else.
Man	I hate to say it, but that's typical. He never makes time for his staff.

Narrator   Number 58.

Man	I'm very sorry that this sweater has a hole in it. We can replace the sweater, or give you a refund.
Woman	I really like this sweater. I'll take another if it's in good condition.
Man	Here's one. I'll double check the stitching for you.

Narrator   Number 59.

Man	It's really crowded in here. People can't work comfortably.
Woman	I sure hope we find more office space soon.
Man	Especially since we need to hire two more people!

Narrator   Number 60.

Woman	I could never stand commuting an hour to work.
Man	I don't mind it at all. I'm comfortable in my car. I listen to news and music on the radio.
Woman	I prefer to watch the news in the comfort of my living room.

Narrator   Number 61.

Man	We'll need a couple of hours to do this. How about tomorrow afternoon?
Woman	I can't. I'm seeing a client. Can we meet on Thursday?
Man	I have a doctor's appointment in the morning, but I'm free in the afternoon.

Narrator   Number 62.

Man	It's getting late. Let's get something to eat before we go home.
Woman	Sure. What kind of food are you in the mood for?
Man	Something unusual and spicy that I can't make myself.

Narrator   Number 63.

Woman	Hi! How was your trip?
Man	It was great! The mountain air was fresh, and the hiking trails were spectacular. The fishing was good, too.
Woman	You make it sound wonderful. It makes me want to take a vacation!

Narrator   Number 64.

Man	This coffee is delicious. It's not our usual brand, is it?
Woman	No, it isn't. I bought it at that new gourmet coffee shop.
Man	I've heard they are expensive. But if the coffee is this good, they're worth it.

Narrator   Number 65.

Woman	Are you ready to go?
Man	Not quite. I've got to wait for this document to finish printing.
Woman	I hope it's only a few more pages. We really should be on our way.

Narrator   Number 66.

Man	What do you do?
Woman	I'm a conference planner. I arrange hotel rooms, conference space, and sightseeing activities for conventions in the city.
Man	Wow! You must have a good grasp of detail.

Narrator   Number 67.

Woman	Excuse me. I couldn't help noticing your suitcase. Is it really as convenient as it looks?
Man	Yes, it's wonderful. It's much easier to roll a suitcase than to carry one. The long handle makes it comfortable to pull.
Woman	I must get one. I'm tired of carrying this heavy bag every trip.

Narrator   Number 68.

Woman	What's wrong with your hand?
Man	I hurt it yesterday. It's swollen, and it hurts to move my fingers.
Woman	You should get someone to look at it. It sounds serious to me.

Narrator   Number 69.

Man	I'm used to large cities with museums and concerts. In a small town like this, what do you do for fun?
Woman	People entertain at home a lot.

Everyone invites friends for dinner and for holidays.

Man   It sounds as if I need to buy a big house and learn to cook!

Narrator   Number 70.

Man   You look terrible! Are you okay?

Woman   I've been up all night watching the test run of our new computer program.

Man   If you've worked all night, you should take the day off. You need some rest.

Narrator   Number 71.

Man   Where did you learn to cook so well?

Man   The only way to learn is to practice. Cooking is really just a matter of experience.

Man   Maybe that's why I'm no good. I've never spent any time at it.

Narrator   Number 72.

Man   I'm so disgusted with newspapers. They never report anything good.

Woman   Good news doesn't sell papers. People want to know about the things that go wrong.

Man   But if no one writes about the solutions, we can never learn to solve those problems.

Narrator   Number 73.

Man   I'd like you to go to the project site next Tuesday and Wednesday.

Woman   Isn't it a little early for me to be giving advice? I'm not familiar with the project yet.

Man   That's why I'm sending you. You'll catch on faster if you can see it for yourself.

Narrator   Number 74.

Man   Did you read the research report?

Woman   Yes, but it wasn't well written. I sent it back to the department with some editorial suggestions.

Man   Good. I couldn't understand it either, but I thought it was just me!

Narrator   Number 75.

Man   Oh, no. I can't find my guidebook.

Woman   That's okay. We'll get another at the Tourist Center.

Man   But mine had all my notes on the historic homes.

Narrator   Number 76.

Man   The melons are terrible this year.

Woman   Yes. There were floods in that region during the growing season.

Man   That explains why they are tasteless and soggy.

Narrator   Number 77.

Woman   Did you get the details on their latest bid?

Man   I've got them right here. Shall I mail them?

Woman   I need them now. Fax them instead.

Narrator   Number 78.

Woman   Have you finished packing for your business trip?

Man   Yes. I'm taking my blue suit and my tan jacket.

Woman   But those are wool! They'll be much too hot where you're going.

Narrator   Number 79.

Man   When is the receptionist scheduled to start?

Woman   Not for another week. Why?

Man   I just discovered a package that was delivered 3 days ago, and a visitor without a name tag in the hall.

Narrator   Number 80.

Woman   I'm sorry we're late for the art tour. The map shows you are located on Hollywood Avenue.

Man   That's just our business office. The museum entrance is on Garden Street.

Woman   Now, we've missed the most important galleries.

Part IV

Questions 81 and 82 refer to the following announcement.

May I have your attention, please. The track number for the five o'clock train from New York has been changed. It is now scheduled to arrive on Track 7. I repeat, the Chicago train will not arrive on Track 4. Please meet the Chicago train at Track 7.

Questions 83 and 84 refer to the following correction.

We here on this broadcast would like to take a moment to correct an error on yesterday's show. We mistakenly identified Sam Williams, the man who rescued a young mother from the bus accident, as a police officer. Mr. Williams is actually a firefighter for the city. We apologize for the error.

Questions 85 and 86 refer to the following weather announcement.

A winter weather advisory is in effect for the next eight hours. A storm front is moving in, and could dump heavy snow in our area. High winds are also expected, which could cause drifts of up to twelve feet. People are advised to prepare for hazardous driving conditions in tomorrow's rush hour.

Questions 87 through 89 refer to the following recorded message.

Thank you for calling the New-View cable television service. If you would like to order cable television service for your home, please press 1 now. If you would like to make changes to your current cable television service, press 2 now. If you have a complaint or a repair request concerning your current cable service, press 3 now. Otherwise, please stay on the line and a representative will be with you shortly.

Questions 90 through 92 refer to the following public service announcement.

If you are wondering what to do with all of those fallen leaves in your yard, the county government would like to help. The county will provide, free of charge, special biodegradable paper bags that you can use to collect your leaves. Filled bags will be collected by the county on the same day as your regular trash pick-up. These bags allow the leaves to be turned into organic fertilizer for your garden. This fertilizer will be available without cost to county residents next spring.

Questions 93 through 95 refer to the following announcement.

Summer picnics are fun for everyone, but you should be sure to handle food safely to keep it, and your family, free of contaminants. Avoid particularly perishable items such as eggs and egg products. Instead, choose items that do not spoil easily, such as breads and fruits. Make sure you have a good cooler to carry ice and food. Freeze containers the night before and place in the cooler the next day to help keep food cold. Don't let food sit on the picnic table for more than two hours. For even greater safety, place containers back in the cooler immediately after serving.

Questions 96 through 98 refer to the following boarding announcement.

Thank you for your patience during this long delay. Your aircraft has been repaired and maintenance crews are leaving the plane. We would like to board as quickly as possible, so we will board the plane in zones, rather than in rows. First, we will board all zone 1 passengers, with window seats A or E. Next, we will board all zone 2 passengers, with center seats B, and aisle seats D. Finally, we will board all zone 3 passengers, with aisle seats C. This will facilitate faster boarding and a faster departure time.

Questions 99 and 100 refer to the following announcement.

Good morning, commuters. I am pleased to say that the disabled train has been removed from the tracks and that regular service will resume immediately. The first few trains at this platform will be filled with passengers from earlier stations. Please do not crowd these trains. We do have empty trains reserved for this station, and will get them to you as soon as possible.

Answer Key

1 Review

Part I

Skill 1: Looking for the Main Idea

1. (A)
2. (C)
3. (A)
4. (C)
5. (D)

Skill 2: Distinguishing Similar Sounds

1. pipe
2. high
3. show
4. smokes
5. trunk
6. glib
7. cost
8. choose
9. bin
10. cut

Skill 3: Making Assumptions

1. **(B)** If the sky is cloudy, it probably means it is going to rain. Choice (A) is incorrect because it could be cloudy for days. Choice (C) is incorrect because a cloudy sky does not mean that stars will come out. Choice (D) is incorrect because it confuses the similar sound *cloud in the sky* with *cloudy sky*.

2. **(C)** If the cars are in a traffic jam, the cars wouldn't be able to move forward, and people might be late. Choice (A) is the opposite situation to a traffic jam. Choice (B) is incorrect because drivers may not be patient in a traffic jam. Choice (D) is incorrect because *no one is driving slowly* means everyone is driving fast.

3. **(A)** If they are lined up at an airport gate, they are probably boarding a plane. Choice (B) is incorrect because the picture suggests that their flight is ready now. Choice (C) is incorrect because some passengers may be beginning trips, not ending trips. Choice (D) might be true, but it is an assumption that cannot be made from the description of the photograph.

4. **(C)** Since the housekeeper is entering a messy room, the housekeeper is probably going to clean it. Choice (A) is incorrect because a housekeeper cleans hotel rooms, not checks into them. Choice (B) is incorrect because housekeepers would receive tips, not give tips. Choice (D) is incorrect; since the room is messy, the housekeeper is probably going to clean it, not sleep in it.

5. **(B)** Since the person is carrying a package, he is probably going to take it somewhere. Choice (A) is incorrect because he may open the package, but he needs to put it down or deliver it first. Choice (C) is incorrect because he is holding the package and there is no way of telling if he will drop it. Choice (D) might be true, but cannot be determined from the description of the photo.

Practice: Part I

1. **(D)** The man is holding the telephone receiver and probably having a conversation with a person on the other end. Choice (A) is incorrect because the man may be working, but he is not sitting at his desk. Choice (B) is incorrect because the man is lying down, but there are no other signs that he is sleeping. Choice (C) is incorrect because the man is talking on the phone, not answering his mail.

2. **(C)** *A woman is addressing the group* is the statement that gives the main idea. Be aware of the meaning of the verb *to address*. Choice (A) is incorrect because it confuses the verb *address* with the noun *address* (a home address or a business address). Choice (B) is incorrect because it confuses the similar sound *address* with *dress*, or the idea of fashion. Choice (D) is incorrect because it

confuses the similar sound *address* with *hairdressers*.

3. **(B)** One man is pointing with a pencil at a machine; they seem to be discussing the equipment. Choice (A) incorrectly identifies the action. The man is *holding* a book. Choice (C) is not represented in the picture. Choice (D) incorrectly identifies what the man is pointing to.

4. **(A)** Two workers are wiping the tables. Choice (B) uses the related word *washing*. Choice C uses the related words *serving* and *dinner*. Choice (D) also uses the related words *eating* and *lunch*.

5. **(D)** The man is wearing protective clothing: a mask, gloves, suit, and boots. Choice (A) incorrectly identifies the action. Choice (B) incorrectly identifies what he is watching. Choice (C) incorrectly identifies the action; he is kneeling on the floor.

6. **(B)** *Two women are talking* is the statement that gives the main idea. Choice (A) confuses the sounds *women wearing* and *men carrying*; the picture shows women wearing pearls, not men carrying pearls. Choice (C) confuses the related word *science* with *scientists* doing experiments. Choice (D) confuses the related word *technical engineers* with *train engineers*.

Part II

Skill 1: Distinguishing Wh- and Yes/No Questions

1. Wh-
2. Yes/No
3. Wh-
4. Yes/No
5. Wh-

Skill 2: Identifying Homophones

1. **(A)** The homophones are *where* and *wear*. A second pair of homophones is *meet* and *meat*.

2. **(B)** The homophones are *hire* and *higher* (related word *lower*).

3. **(A)** The homophones are *sum* and *some* (related word *any*).

4. **(A)** The homophones are *fare* and *fair*. A second pair of homophones is *raise* and *raze*.

5. **(C)** The homophones are *aisle* and *I'll*.

Skill 3: Recognizing Negative Meaning

1. (B)
2. (A)
3. (A)
4. (B)
5. (A)

Practice: Part II

1. **(B)** *We're going to lunch* is the only response that answers the question *where*. Choice (A) is incorrect because it answers the question *Are you going to lunch?* Choice (C) is incorrect because it answers *when*.

2. **(C)** This is the only response that logically answers the Yes/No question. Choice (A) is incorrect because it answers the Wh- question *where*. Choice (B) confuses the similar sound *ate* with *late*.

3. **(B)** This is the only response that answers with a specific location. Choice (A) is not a logical response. Choice (C) is incorrect because it does not answer the question *where*.

4. **(A)** *Yes, here is the total* answers the Yes/No question by offering the total of the ad revenue. Choice (B) is incorrect because although it answers a Yes/No question, it confuses the related word *subtract* with the incorrect homophone *add*. Choice (C) is incorrect because it confuses the related word *sum* with the incorrect homophone *add*; it also answers the Wh- question *why*, not a Yes/No question.

5. **(C)** *The tenth* is the only response that gives a specific date. Choice (A) confuses the similar sound *weak* with *week*. Choice (B) is incorrect because the question asks *when the invoice was sent*, not *when the boys arrived*.

6. **(B)** *I don't think so* is the best response to the question. Choice (A) is incorrect because it confuses the related word *reservation* with *round-trip ticket*. Choice (C) would answer a

habitual tense question, not a past tense question.

7. **(A)** *No, the weight is listed here* is the only Yes/No response to this Yes/No question. Choice (B) is incorrect because it confuses the similar sound *way* with *weigh*. Choice (C) is incorrect because is confuses the similar sound *wait* with *weight*.

8. **(A)** *No, thank you* is a polite response to the question. Choice (B) confuses *please don't do that* with *please help me*. Choice (C) is incorrect because it gives a location.

9. **(A)** *In two weeks* answers *when will*. Choice (B) is incorrect because the question is not a Yes/No question. Choice (C) is incorrect because it refers to the past tense.

10. **(B)** *Certainly* is a polite answer to the question. Choice (A) confuses the related words *count(ed)* and *account*. Choice (C) is incorrect because it answers a Yes/No question and confuses *pleased* with *please*.

Part III

Skill 1: Listening for the Main Idea

1. (B) Main idea: check a late order.
2. (A) Main idea: making a presentation.
3. (A) Main idea: offer her a job.
4. (B) Main idea: negotiating a contract.
5. (A) Main idea: finding exercise facilities.

Skill 2: Understanding Wh- Questions

1. (B)   4. (B)
2. (A)   5. (B)
3. (A)

Skill 3: Understanding Modal Verbs

1. (C)   4. (D)
2. (B)   5. (A)
3. (C)

Practice: Part III

1. **(A)** A future meeting is the main idea. It is in the present continuous tense. Choice (B) is incorrect because you hear Wednesday when the man asks about the woman's availability, but the woman doesn't agree right away. Choice (C) is incorrect because you hear *overseas* when the woman refers to an overseas project, but not a meeting. Choice (D) is incorrect because the question asks what the man and woman are generally discussing, not about the specifics of the meeting.

2. **(B)** *At a receptionist's desk* is the main idea. Choice (A) is incorrect because you hear directions to an office, and you hear the word *down*, but there is no other clue about an elevator. Choice (C) is incorrect because the first woman's introduction is often heard on the telephone, but other clues help you understand this is not a telephone conversation. Choice (D) is not possible.

3. **(C)** *Approximately twelve* provides a specific number and twelve means the same as a dozen. Choice (A) is incorrect because *more than a dozen* means more than twelve questions. Choice (B) is incorrect because it confuses the phrase *no interest* with *none*. Choice (D) is incorrect because the conversation states that a dozen questions were asked, not five.

4. **(C)** *He's confident* provides specific information. Choice (A) is incorrect because it confuses the negative *not mistaken* for a negative meaning. Choice (B) is incorrect because you hear the positive form *certainly*. Choice (D) is incorrect because there is no indication that the man is not correct.

5. **(D)** *Production manager* provides specific information. Choice (A) is incorrect because the conversation mentions production duties, but not secretarial duties. Choice (B) is incorrect because you hear general vocabulary about an office, but the position of office worker isn't mentioned. Choice (C) is incorrect because it confuses the similar sound *receptionist* with *receptive*.

6. **(D)** *His department is successful* is the main idea. Choice (A) is incorrect because the woman's opinion is the opposite. Choice (B) is

incorrect because you hear *hurt* in the woman's last sentence, but it is negative, *It doesn't hurt*. Choice (C) is incorrect because you hear about changing schedules, but not as advice.

7. **(A)** *A problem* is the main idea. Choice (B) is incorrect because you hear a date, May 25, but it is a detail of the conversation. Choice (C) is incorrect because it confuses the related words *vacation* and *vacating*. Choice (D) is incorrect because it confuses the meaning of *vacating* with *taking a holiday*.

8. **(C)** *Reward the employees* is the main idea. Choice (A), *Hand out paychecks*, is not correct. Choice (B) is incorrect because it confuses the similar sound *deserve* with *dessert*. Choice (D) is incorrect because it confuses the similar sound *morale* with *morals*.

9. **(C)** *Discuss the problem with the customer* is the correct answer. The question asks for an assumption. Choice (A) is incorrect because it confuses the man's action with the woman's plan. Choice (B) is incorrect because she will talk to the customer when he calls next time. Choice (D) is incorrect because the customer will make the telephone call, not the woman.

10. **(D)** *He doesn't know what to order* is the man's problem. Choice (A) is incorrect because it confuses the related words *long* and *tall*. Choice (B) is incorrect because it confuses the similar sound *appetite* with *appetizer*. Choice (C) is incorrect because it confuses the similar sound *room* with *mushrooms*.

Part IV

Skill 1: Listening for Answers to Wh- Questions

1. (A)   4. (C)
2. (D)   5. (C)
3. (A)

Skill 2: Following the Questions Chronologically

1. (A)   4. (D)
2. (B)   5. (B)
3. (C)

Skill 3: Making Assumptions

1. (A)   4. (A)
2. (B)   5. (B)
3. (A)

Practice: Part IV

1. **(A)** The fact is heard in the second sentence, … *avoid wrist injuries* … Choice (B) confuses *injuries to the mouse* with *injuries to the wrist*. Choice (C) confuses *keyboard injuries* with *wrist injuries*. Choice (D) is not mentioned.

2. **(C)** The fact is heard in the third sentence, *Computer Accessories has produced* … Choice (A) confuses *computer operators* with *computer accessories*. Choices (B) and (D) are not mentioned.

3. **(A)** We don't hear this in the advertisement, but the vocabulary *computer, keyboard, mouse, monitor, products* should help you make the correct assumption that the advertisement is meant for people who use computers. Choices (B), (C), and (D) are not necessarily people who would face these problems.

4. **(B)** This fact is heard in the first sentence, … *scheduled for September 28* …. Choice (A) is incorrect because it answers *where*, not *when*. Choice (C) is incorrect because the question asks *when will*, not *when did*. Choice (D) is incorrect because it gives a duration of time.

5. **(B)** This fact is heard in the third sentence, … *ninety timeshares sold at prices* … Choice (A) is incorrect because it confuses the resale price of the timeshares. Choice (C) is last year's lowest price of timeshares. Choice (D) is the price of timeshares for two weeks in Hawaii.

Part V

Skill 1: Understanding Prefixes

1. anti-, contra-, counter-, dis-, il-, in-, ir-, mal-, mis-
2. bene-, pro-
3. bi-, multi-, hyper-, hypo-, poly-
4. after-, ante-, post-, pre-

Skill 2: Understanding Suffixes

1. -ance, -ancy, -ency, -hood, -ity, -ment, -ness, -ship
2. -al, -ary, -ic, -ous
3. -ly
4. -ate, -en, -fy, -ize

Skill 3: Recognizing Time Markers

1. (B)   4. (B)
2. (A)   5. (A)
3. (A)

Skill 4: Understanding the Passive Voice

1. (A)   4. (B)
2. (B)   5. (A)
3. (A)

Skill 5: Identifying the Correct Prepositions

1. in (at)   4. until
2. in   5. since
3. at

Skill 6: Using Relative Pronouns

1. (A)   4. (B)
2. (B)   5. (B)
3. (A)

Practice: Part V

1. **(D)** The sentence should read, *The restaurant that has just opened has a famous chef.* The sentence requires a relative pronoun to refer to *the restaurant.* The relative pronoun *that* can refer to things, so it is the correct answer. Choice (A) can refer to things, but it indicates possession. Choice (B) refers to people. Choice (C) is not a relative pronoun.

2. **(B)** The sentence should read, *Negotiations will take place in London.* Notice that you need a preposition to introduce a phrase showing place (*London*). Choice (A), *at,* is not used with cities. Choice (C), *by,* is not used with cities. Choice (D), *to,* can be used with the meaning of destination.

3. **(C)** The sentence should read, *We were in agreement with our supplier.* Notice the preposition *in.* You need to follow the preposition with a noun. Choice (A) is incorrect because *agree* is the verb form. Choice (B) is incorrect because *agreeing* is the present participle. Choice (D) is incorrect because *agreed* is the past verb form.

4. **(A)** The sentence should read, *Mrs. Dubois is a confident supervisor.* You need an adjective to modify the noun *supervisor.* Choice (B) is incorrect because *confidence* is a noun form. Choice (C) is incorrect because *confidentially* is an adverbial form; notice the suffix -*ly.* Choice (D) is incorrect because *confidently* is also an adverbial form.

5. **(D)** The sentence should read, *Our store gets more business in our new location.* Choice (A) is incorrect because *of* suggests possession. Choice (B) is incorrect because *to* is used with destinations. Choice (C) is incorrect because *from* means *direction away.*

6. **(C)** The sentence should read, *The proposal is delivered by messenger.* The preposition *by* introduces the agent in a passive voice construction. This lets you know to choose a passive verb form. Choices (A), (B), and (D) are all incorrect because they are active verb forms.

7. **(C)** The sentence should read, *On what date did you receive the shipment?* Use your knowledge of prefixes to choose the best answer. Choice (A) is incorrect because *per-* means *through.* Choice (B) is incorrect because *de-* means *away from.* Choice (D) is incorrect because *recede* has a different root, and therefore, a different meaning.

8. **(C)** The sentence should read, *Two weeks ago, Mr. Uto made his reservations*. Notice the doer of the action is important. So, you need to use the active voice. Notice also the tense marker *ago*, which indicates the past tense. Choice (A) is incorrect because *makes* is present tense. Choice (B) is incorrect because *was made* is the passive voice. Choice (D) is incorrect because *has made* is not a correct passive form.

9. **(D)** The sentence should read, *All the members have arrived except Mr. Sampson*. Notice that you need a preposition in this sentence. Choice (A) is incorrect because it confuses the similar sounding words *accept* and *except*. Choice (B) is incorrect because *without* has the wrong meaning for this sentence. Choice (C) is incorrect because *not* is not a preposition.

10. **(C)** The sentence should read, *She expressed her appreciation*. The sentence requires a noun to be the object of *expressed*. Choice (A) is incorrect because *appreciate* is the verb form. Choice (B) is incorrect because *appreciative* is the adjectival form. Choice (D) is incorrect because *appreciated* is the past participle or the past tense and cannot stand alone in this sentence.

11. **(C)** The sentence should read, *Eliza Donato will be promoted to Vice President in January*. Notice that Eliza Donato is the receiver of the action. So, you need to use the passive voice. Choices (A), (B), and (D) are all incorrect because they are active voice.

12. **(D)** The sentence should read, *Mr. Yung sent a reminder to customers who didn't pay their bills*. You need a relative pronoun that can refer to people. Choice (A) is incorrect because *what* is not a relative pronoun. Choice (B) is incorrect because *whom* is a relative pronoun that is used as an object. Choice (C) is incorrect because *which* is a relative pronoun used to modify things.

13. **(D)** The sentence should read, *Mr. Weber hired a new assistant*. You need a noun that

means a person. Choice (A) is incorrect because *assist* is a verb form. Choice (B) is incorrect because *assistance* is a noun form, but the suffix -*ance* means *the state or quality of assisting*. Choice (C) is incorrect because *assisted* is the past verb form.

14. **(B)** The sentence should read, *Send a fax to verify the prices*. You need a verb; notice the infinitive signal, *to*, which is followed by the base form of the verb. Choice (A) is incorrect because *verily* is an adverbial form with a different meaning. Choice (C) is incorrect because *verifying* is the present participle. Choice (D) is incorrect because *verified* is the past verb form.

15. **(A)** The sentence should read, *That product wasn't invented until recently*. Someone else invented the product, so you need to use the passive voice. Choices (B), (C), and (D) are all incorrect because they are active voice.

16. **(D)** The sentence should read, *We're sending Mary Sula to participate in the seminar*. Choice (A) is incorrect because *at* indicates location. Choice (B) is incorrect because *to* indicates destination. Choice (C) is incorrect because *from* means *direction away*.

17. **(C)** The sentence should read, *The employees are asked by the director to give suggestions*. Notice the *by* phrase signals the passive form. So, you need to use the passive voice. Choice (A) is incorrect because *are asking* is active voice. Choice (B) is incorrect because *asking* is the present participle, and cannot stand alone here. Choice (D) is incorrect because *be asked* is the base form of the passive voice.

18. **(D)** The sentence should read, *Mr. Caputo usually travels with a translator*. Notice the tense marker, *usually*, which indicates the present tense. Choice (A) is incorrect because *is traveled* is passive voice. Choice (B) is incorrect because *travel* is the plural, and cannot agree with a singular subject. Choice (C) is incorrect because *is traveling*

is the present continuous, and cannot be used with the tense marker, *usually*.

19. **(D)** The sentence should read, *Her previous employer gave her a good recommendation. Previous* means the one before. All choices have the prefix *pre-*, so you must pay attention to the root. Choice (A) means appears often. Choice (B) means to keep from happening. Choice (C) means to look at something before (someone else does).

20. **(B)** The sentence should read, *Flight 201 will be arriving at Gate 7B on time.* Notice that you need a preposition to introduce a phrase of time, with the meaning of being punctual. Choice (A) is incorrect because *by* is not used in phrases of time. Choice (C) is incorrect because *at* is used with specific hours, but not with unspecified time. Choice (D) is incorrect because *within* is not used with phrase of time.

Part VI

Skill 1: Recognizing Subject and Verb Agreement

1. To match the plural subject *files*, the verb should be *are*.

2. To match the plural subject *police*, the verb should be *arrive*.

3. To match the plural subject *man and woman*, the verb should be *were*.

4. To match the plural subject *eyeglasses*, the verb should be *were broken*.

5. To match the plural subject *parents*, the verb should be *live*.

Skill 2: Using the Correct Verb Tense

1. (A) The verb *slept* should be *was sleeping*.

2. (C) The verb *has worked* should be *will have worked*.

3. (B) The verb *had been* should be *has been*.

4. (B) The verb *will have called* should be *called*.

5. (A) The verb *am having* should be *have*.

Skill 3: Maintaining Correct Adjective Placement

1. An *inexpensive Italian* restaurant has opened on the corner.

2. The *long boring* speech made everyone *restless*.

3. The *new white* paint makes the office seem brighter.

4. An *old American* movie is on television tonight.

5. This *new conference* table is better than the *old square* one.

Skill 4: Recognizing Questions in Longer Sentences

1. Do you know *when the deadline is?*

2. I would like to know *why we don't have reservations.*

3. In the program it should say *what the name of the playwright is.*

4. I hope *the letter has arrived.*

5. The committee will have to vote on *who the next chairman will be.*

Skill 5: Identifying Pronouns

1. our
2. us
3. She
4. you
5. their, they

Skill 6: Understanding Conjunctions

1. *While* should be replaced with *because* or *so that*.

2. *Either* and *nor* are the conjunctions. They form an incorrect pair. The correct pairs would be *either … or* and *neither … nor*. The sentence should read, *I will see **either** the play **or** the movie this weekend* or *I will see **neither** the play **nor** the movie this weekend.*

3. *Until* should be replaced with *when*.

4. *Or is* should be replaced with *but*.

5. *Though* should be replaced with *Because*.

Practice: Part VI

1. **(A)** The sentence should read, *Ms. Cescu had paid her registration fee when she discovered that she would not be able to attend the*

convention. The verb *discovered* is in the past tense. The first action happened before, so it should be in the past perfect tense, *had paid.* Choice (B) is a correct pronoun referring to Ms. Cescu. Choice (C) is the correct word to make a verb negative, *would not be able to.* Choice (D) is a correct noun phrase, an article followed by a noun.

2. **(B)** The sentence should read, *The director thought that both the blue invitations and the green ones were appropriate for the seminar.* The words in paired conjunctions cannot be changed. Since the word *and* cannot be changed, you should use the pair *both … and.* Choice (A) is a correct past tense verb. Choice (C) is a correct adjective modifying *invitations.* Choice (D) is a correct noun phrase.

3. **(C)** The sentence should read, *By the time the final report is due, the technicians will have resolved their problem.* The final report has not been due yet, so the future perfect tense is needed to indicate an action in the future that will be completed before another future action. Choice (A) is a correct preposition used with a specific indication of time. Choice (B) is a correct adjective modifying *report.* Choice (D), *their,* is a correct pronoun referring to *technicians.*

4. **(D)** The sentence should read, *I asked the department secretary, but she did not know when the managers would take a break from their meeting.* Choice (A) is a correct past tense verb. Choice (B) is a correct conjunction showing a contrast between events. Choice (C) is a correct pronoun referring to (a female) secretary.

5. **(B)** The sentence should read, *Ms. Morisot lost her wallet while she was walking in the park at lunchtime.* A female third person pronoun is required to refer to Ms. Morisot. Choice (A) is a female third person pronoun and correctly refers to Ms. Morisot. Choice (C) is the correct form of a past continuous verb. Choice (D) is a correct preposition used to refer to a location.

6. **(B)** The sentence should read, *The shipment of machine parts was delayed by the workmen's sudden strike.* A singular verb *was* is needed to refer to the singular subject *shipment* to form the correct passive *The shipment was delayed.* Choice (A) is a correct preposition indicating possession. Choice (C) is the correct proposition for indicating the object (agent) in a passive sentence. Choice (D) is a correct adjective modifying *strike.*

7. **(A)** The sentence should read, *The first fast train leaves for the city at 8:00 every weekday morning.* Numerical adjectives come before other descriptive adjectives in a sentence. Choice (B) is a correct present tense verb indicating habitual action. Choice (C) is a correct preposition for use with a specific time. Choice (D) is a correct adjective modifying *morning.*

8. **(C)** The sentence should read, *Ms. Arnet asked the manager how late the store would be open tonight. How late will the store be open tonight* is a question within a longer sentence, so the subject must come before the verb in statement order. Choice (A) is a correct noun phrase, an article followed by a noun. Choice (B) is a correct question word. Choice (D) is a correct noun indicating time.

9. **(A)** The sentence should read, *Even though he comes into the office on weekends, Mr. Fortescue never gets enough work done.* The two clauses do not have a cause and effect relationship. *Even though* indicates that the relationship between the two events is unexpected. *Although* could also be used. Choice (B) is a correct male third person pronoun referring to Mr. Fortescue. Choice (C) is a correct preposition referring to days of the week. Choice (D) is a correct negative word indicating time.

10. **(C)** The sentence should read, *Although the article is clearly written, it contains factual information that is inaccurate.* An article is a thing. A neuter third person pronoun, *it,* is required to refer to things. Choice (A) is a

correct conjunction indicating an unexpected result. Choice (B) is a correct adverb describing how the article was written. Choice (D) is a correct present tense verb indicating current time.

Part VII

Skill 1: Recognizing the Main Idea

1. (C)   4. (B)
2. (A)   5. (C)
3. (D)

Skill 2: Understanding the Facts

1. (B) and (E)   4. (D) and (F)
2. (C) and (H)   5. (G) and (J)
3. (A) and (I)

Skill 3: Predicting Inferences

1. (B)   4. (A)
2. (A)   5. (B)
3. (C)

Skill 4: Understanding the Purpose

1. (D)   4. (A)
2. (C)   5. (B)
3. (C)

Practice: Part VII

1. **(A)** The calendar is marked with times and events. Choice (B) is incorrect because what you read are not ideas, but appointments. Choice (C) is incorrect because it is the opposite of making appointments. Choice (D) is incorrect because you usually don't take notes on a calendar.

2. **(C)** Since *golf course* is written after John Ling's name, it is safe to assume that is where they will meet. Choice (A) is incorrect because it answers *when* and confuses 7:30 *P.M.* with 7:30 *A.M.* Choices (B) and (D) are incorrect because they answer *when*.

3. **(B)** On Friday there is a 10:00 A.M. staff meeting followed by an 11:00 A.M. meeting with Mr. Gonsalves; therefore, we can assume the staff meeting will be over before

the next meeting is scheduled, which is an hour later. Choice (A) is incorrect because it confuses *tennis with T. Kral* with *teleconference* and *Tuesday* with *Thursday*. Choice (C) is incorrect because it confuses *Thursday* with *Tuesday*. Choice (D) is incorrect because this information is not given on the calendar.

4. **(D)** The calendar shows a schedule for Monday through Sunday. Choice (A) is incorrect because a work week is Monday through Friday, and does not include the weekend. Choice (B) is incorrect because the calendar dates from March 28 to April 3. Choice (C) is incorrect because the calendar shows both the week and the weekend.

5. **(C)** *Noon* means the same as *12:00 P.M.* Choice (A) is incorrect because, although the meeting is on Wednesday, it confuses *12:00 P.M.* with *midnight*. Choice (B) incorrectly answers *where*. Choice (D) answers *where* correctly, but *when* incorrectly.

6. **(B)** The first part of the form specifies that the form is for reserving accommodations for next year. Choices (A), (C), and (D) are not indicated, although they might use similar looking forms.

7. **(D)** *Rec'd by* is found under the heading *reserved for office use* on the form. Choices (A), (B), and (C) are items to be filled in by the person reserving the accommodations.

8. **(B)** There is no space given for credit card information, so you can assume that you cannot pay by credit card. Choices (A), (C), and (D) are options of payment given on the form.

9. **(B)** The article is about increases in tourist taxes in Washington, D.C. Choice (A) is incorrect because the article mentions the survey, but that is not the main idea of the article. Choice (C) is incorrect because the article is about tourist taxes in Washington, D.C., not about Washington, D.C. in general. Choice (D) is incorrect because the article is about more than just taxes in restaurants.

10. **(B)** Hotel taxes in Washington, D.C. will increase from 11 to 13 percent, which is a 2 percent increase. Choice (A) confuses the location of the organization that conducted the survey (San Francisco) with the city that is raising hotel tax rates (Washington, D.C.). Choice (C) confuses restaurant tax increases of 1 percent with hotel increases of 2 percent. Choice (D) is incorrect: the article mentions the average tourist taxes in the 50 most-visited cities, but does not mention how much the taxes have increased.

11. **(D)** The article states that the increase gives Washington the highest restaurant taxes in the country, although New York has higher hotel taxes than Washington. Choices (A), (B), and (C) are all true.

12. **(A)** The reason that tourists are easy to tax is stated in the last sentence. Choice (B) confuses *tourists are easily found* with *tourists are the easiest target to tax*. Choice (C) is incorrect because it assumes that tourists don't mind paying high taxes for their holidays. Choice (D) is incorrect because it makes an assumption that cannot be made from the article.

13. **(A)** Mr. Keng had telephoned. Choice (B) is incorrect because the call was made *to* Mr. Ramen, not *by* Mr. Ramen. Choice (C) is incorrect because Ms. Murohisa is the operator, the person who took the call and the message. Choice (D) is incorrect because the call was made by Mr. Keng who works for the Hotel Service Corporation.

14. **(C)** Ms. Murohisa, the operator, is the person who took the message. Choice (A) is the person who called and left the message. Choice (B) is the person for whom the message was taken. Choice (D) is the organization for which Mr. Keng works.

15. **(A)** The message on the form states that Mr. Keng cannot make the meeting. Choice (B) is incorrect because Mr. Keng is canceling the meeting, not verifying it.

Choice (C) is incorrect because it does not answer *why* he left a message. Choice (D) is incorrect because *telephoned* and *please call* are checked on the form, but *returned your call* is not checked.

16. **(C)** The message indicates that Mr. Keng wants Mr. Ramen to call him. Choice (A) is incorrect because *please call* is checked, but *will call* is not. Choice (B) is incorrect because there may not be a meeting on Monday; Mr. Ramen has not confirmed it. Choice (D) confuses the *operator* and the *recipient* of the message.

17. **(B)** The form is self-addressed to CompuSys Conference and contains conference registration fees. Choice (A) confuses the fact that the form is to be returned to a foreign country with it being a customs declaration. Choice (C) is incorrect because the form is for conference reservations, not hotel reservations. Choice (D) confuses the conference reservation rates with dollar amounts that could be found on a duty-free voucher.

18. **(D)** The answer is in the last column of the Opening Ceremony row. Choice (A) is the cost for members registering in advance. Choice (B) is the cost for members registering on site. Choice (C) is the cost for non-members registering in advance.

19. **(D)** Since the form is to be sent to Brazil, the conference is probably to take place there. Choices (A) and (B) are not mentioned or indicated by this form. Choice (C) is the location of the bank branch where conference payments should be sent.

20. **(A)** If you pay by July 10, you pay advance registration fees, which are less expensive than on-site fees. Choices (B), (C), and (D) are the dates of the conference.

21. **(B)** The purpose of the faxed letter, *to confirm his suite reservation*, is stated in the second paragraph. Choice (A) is incorrect because there is a reference to the hotel, but hotel promotion is not the purpose of the letter.

Choice (C) is incorrect because Mr. Dubois works for a law firm, but the letter does not concern legal advice. Choice (D) is incorrect because there is no mention of a change in the arrival date.

22. **(D)** The first paragraph states that the letter was addressed to Ms. Wong. Choice (A) is incorrect because it confuses *Mr. Leger* with *Dubois and Leger, L.L.P.* Choice (B) is incorrect because he originally wrote to the *Assistant Sales Manager*, not the *General Manager*. Choice (C) is incorrect because Mr. Dubois originally wrote to Ms. Wong; Mr. Ashton responded on behalf of Ms. Wong.

23. **(A)** Since the letter mentions that his *usual* suite may be unavailable, he is probably a frequent guest of the hotel. Choice (B) is incorrect because he has asked for a non-smoking room. Choice (C) is incorrect because the reservations are from January 20 to January 28, a total of eight nights; therefore, he does stay more than two nights. Choice (D) is incorrect because he has asked NOT to be near the waiter area.

24. **(B)** *Inclusive* means the same as *included in.* Choice (A) is incorrect because Value Added Tax is *excluded* from the daily rate. Choices (C) and (D) are not mentioned.

25. **(C)** A *suitable alternative* means the same as a *comparable suite.* Choice (A) confuses *a refund of £500* with the daily rate for the accommodation. Choice (B) is not mentioned, but you assume that the room would be cleaned regardless. Choice (D) confuses *an extra bed* with Mr. Dubois' request for a king-sized bed with bed boards.

26. **(C)** The announcement is about the public transportation available in the city. Choice (A) is incorrect because although hotels are mentioned, and are certainly places that visitors stay, they are not the main idea of the passage. Choice (B) is incorrect because visitors are the audience for the announcement, not the subject. Choice

(D) is incorrect because tourist attractions are mentioned, but not described or enumerated.

27. **(B)** The announcement clearly states that the use of private cars is discouraged. This means that visitors should not drive their cars in the city. Choice (A) is not logical; hotels are mentioned and presumably visitors would stay overnight in the city. Choice (C) may or may not be a good idea, but it is not discussed in the announcement. Choice (D) is incorrect because the hours at which visitors might travel are not discussed.

28. **(B)** The announcement gives the hours of subway service as 6:00 in the morning until 12 midnight. Choice (A) is incorrect because the announcement states that buses run 24 hours a day, which means that they operate after midnight. Choice (C) is incorrect because the hours for tour service are not discussed in the announcement. Choice (D) is incorrect because taxi service is not mentioned as a way to get around the city and its hours are not discussed.

29. **(A)** The announcement says that buses may appeal to people who want to sneak in extra sightseeing en route. This suggests they will see more of the city. Choice (B) is incorrect because speed is not mentioned in connection with the bus service. Choice (C) is incorrect because the cost of the buses is not mentioned, but the article does say that the subway is inexpensive. This could mean that the subway is less expensive than the buses. Choice (D) is incorrect because the convenience of the routes for different forms of transportation is not discussed and cannot be determined from the announcement.

30. **(D)** The article states that visitor's passes for all forms of public transportation are sold at most hotels. *Visitor's passes* means the same as *tickets.* Choice (A) is incorrect because the existence of special stands for

purchasing tickets is not mentioned in the article. Choice (B) is incorrect because the announcement states that subway tickets can be purchased at subway stops, but does not say that bus tickets may be purchased on buses. Choice (C) is incorrect because although the different forms of public transportation make stops at tourists attractions, there is no indication that tickets may be purchased there.

Practice Test 1

Part I

1. **(A)** The people are in a bookstore looking at books. Choice (B) confuses the word *library* with *bookstore*. Choice (C) is incorrect because there are *only* books on the shelves. Choice (D) confuses the word *writing* with *reading* and uses the related word *story*.

2. **(D)** The people are surrounded by skis and poles and are wearing ski clothes. They are probably skiers. Some are sitting on the snow. Choice (A) incorrectly identifies the action of the skiers; they are *resting*, not *sleeping*. Choice (B) confuses the similar sound *light snow* with *light show*. Choice (C) is a correct statement for deciduous trees, but these trees are not shown in the picture.

3. **(D)** The people seem to be discussing something. They are probably having a meeting. Choice (A) is incorrect because only four of the chairs are occupied. Choice (B) is incorrect because the people are reading, talking, or discussing, but not eating. Choice (C) confuses the similar sound *label* with *table*.

4. **(C)** A train is on the bridge going over the water. Choice (A) confuses the similar sound *rain* with *train*; the train is moving quickly, not the rain. Choice (B) is incorrect because it confuses *train* with *swimmers in training*. Choice (D) confuses the similar sounds *plane* with *train* and *Cambridge* with *bridge*.

5. **(A)** The two men are preparing food. They are probably chefs. Choice (B) incorrectly identifies the activity of the people; they are preparing vegetables, not growing them. Choice (C) uses words related to a restaurant but describes an incorrect action. Choice (D) uses other related words *menu* and *French*, but there is no menu in the picture.

6. **(A)** They are playing volleyball. Choice (B) confuses the similar sounds *valley* with *volley* and *tall* with *ball*. Choice (C) confuses *fishing net* with *volleyball net*. Choice (D) incorrectly identifies the action; the players are playing a *match* (game), not looking for a *match* (to light a cigarette) or (game).

7. **(B)** A ship is at a loading dock. Choice (A) confuses the similar sound *sheep* with *ship* and contains the related word *market*. Choice (C) is incorrect because the containers are made of metal, not paper. Choice (D) confuses the similar sound *doctor* with *dock*.

8. **(C)** The woman is in her office, talking on the phone and looking at her computer monitor. Choice (A) is incorrect because there are many machines in the office. Choice (B) incorrectly identifies the location; there are big windows and a computer on the desk, but it is an office, not a computer store. Choice (D) incorrectly describes the action; she seems to be touching a key on her keyboard, so she may be typing a letter, but she is not mailing one.

9. **(B)** Two men wearing hard hats are loading a box onto a helicopter. Choice (A) is incorrect because the door to the aircraft is open, not closed; Choice (A) also confuses the related word *plane* with *helicopter*. Choice (C) incorrectly identifies the location of the helicopter, which is on the landing pad, not in the air. Choice (D) confuses *pilot light* (flame on a stove) with *pilot* (person who flies aircraft).

10. **(D)** The men are working on their computers. Choice (A) confuses the word *keys* with *keyboard*. Choice (B) confuses the similar

sound *circus* with *circuits*. Choice (C) incorrectly identifies the location; the men are in a control room, not a salesroom.

11. **(C)** The men are assembling engines at a factory. Choice (A) incorrectly identifies the action; the men are working, not striking. Choice (B) incorrectly identifies the actors and action and confuses the similar sound *line* with *assembly line.* Choice (D) is incorrect because *no one* in the picture is wearing a coat and tie.

12. **(B)** They are washing their car. Choice (A) is incorrect because the people are *manually* washing the car; Choice (A) uses the related words *windows* and *cleaned.* Choice (C) identifies an incorrect action; the car is *cleaned* by hand, not *made* by hand. Choice (D) incorrectly describes the action and uses the related words *taking a bath.*

13. **(A)** The train is in the station and people are on the platform. The man carrying his baggage is probably boarding the train. Choice (B) is incorrect because the man is carrying his bags, not checking them. Choice (C) confuses the similar sound *crane* with *train.* Choice (D) is incorrect and uses the related words *tickets* and *conductor.*

14. **(C)** You can assume the man is holding a bank card because he is at a cash machine. Choice (A) confuses the similar sound *tie* (n) with *tie* (v); the man is wearing a tie, but is not tied down. Choice (B) confuses the similar sounds *tell her* with *teller* and *band* with *bank.* Choice (D) incorrectly describes the action and confuses the similar sound *trash* with *cash.*

15. **(A)** The men wearing hard hats have shovels; they are digging a hole. Choice (B) could be true, but is not what you see in the picture. Choice (C) uses the related word *pipe,* but is incorrect because the men are *laying pipes,* not *smoking pipes.* Choice (D) confuses the similar sound of the related word *mine* (as in a tunnel in the earth) with *sign.*

16. **(C)** The people are looking at a sculpture of a bird. Choice (A) uses the related word *artist,* but an artist is not in the picture. Choice (B) uses the related word *bird* but the bird is not in a cage. Choice (D) identifies the incorrect location of the statue; it is in the park, not the harbor.

17. **(B)** The man is standing among containers and there is a lorry (truck) behind him. He is probably loading the containers on the lorry to be transferred. Choice (A) uses the related word *gas,* but incorrectly identifies the picture. Choice (C) uses the similar words *boxes,* but incorrectly describes the location of the containers, they are not on a shelf. Choice (D) is incorrect because it confuses *soup cans* with *storage (oil) containers.*

18. **(D)** There are many people and many exhibits on display; this is probably a trade fair. Choice (A) uses the related word *pedestrians,* but incorrectly identifies the action. Choice (B) confuses the similar sounds *film* with *firm* and *exposed* with *exposition.* Choice (C) confuses the similar word *conference room* with *conference.*

19. **(A)** The doctor is taking a patient's blood pressure. Choice (B) is incorrect because the patient is sitting up, not lying down. Choice (C) is an action that is unable to be determined by looking at the picture; the doctor is listening to the patient's heart rhythm, not a radio. Choice (D) confuses the similar ideas *he is buttoning his shirt* and *the man's shirt is unbuttoned.*

20. **(C)** The people are talking on public telephones. Choice (A) confuses the similar sound *loan* with *phone.* Choice (B) confuses the similar word *television* with *telephone.* Choice (D) incorrectly identifies the location of the telephones; they are on the street, not in the hallway.

Part II

21. **(A)** *I live on Church Street* answers the question *where* do you live. Choice (B) is incorrect because it confuses the similar sound *alive* with *live*. Choice (C) confuses the similar sounds *you're* and *you* but is incorrect because, although it answers *where*, it is given in a different context.

22. **(C)** *No, I'm busy then* is a logical response. Choice (A) confuses the related word *schedule* (n) with *reschedule* (v). Choice (B) confuses the similar sound *meat* with *meeting*.

23. **(B)** *To the housekeeping staff* answers the question *to whom*. Choice (A) confuses the similar sound *to* with *two* (both) and confuses the verb tense *will send* with *are sending*. Choice (C) uses the related word *secretary*, and incorrectly answers the question *who* sent it, not *to whom* it is being sent.

24. **(C)** *I wasn't impressed* is a logical answer. Choice (A) confuses the similar sound *I didn't* with *idea* and confuses the verb tense *didn't do* (past) with *do* (present). Choice (B) confuses the pronoun *he* with *her*.

25. **(A)** This statement indicates that the product (*it*) is currently being tested. Choice (B) confuses the related word *class* with *test*. Choice (C) is incorrect because the question asks if the product *has been tested*, not if the girl *passed the exam*.

26. **(A)** *Not until July* answers the question *when*. Choice (B) confuses the related words *warm(er)* with *her*, *worn* with *warm*, and *sweater* with *weather*. Choice (C) repeats the word *warm* but confuses the similar sound Dec(*ember*) with *warmer*.

27. **(C)** This statement uses *for* to show duration and is the best response. Choice (A) confuses the related word *busy* with *work*. Choice (B) is incorrect because the response is given in a different tense than the question requires.

28. **(B)** *Yes, thank you* is a polite response to the question. Choice (A) is an incorrect response to a polite offer. Choice (C) repeats the word *you*, but does not answer the question.

29. **(A)** This statement uses *at* to express a time and answers the question *when*. Choice (B) does not answer *when*, but *where*. Choice (C) does not answer *when*, but *how*.

30. **(B)** This statement answers the question *can't I* and mentions that there is a *return policy*. Choice (A) confuses *play* with *match* (game). Choice (C) confuses similar sounds *match* and *much*.

31. **(C)** The question asks for speed which is usually given in numerical terms; (C) gives a numerical response. Choice (A) incorrectly responds with a location, but not speed. Choice (B) confuses the related word *write* with *read*.

32. **(C)** *Sure. That sounds fun* is the best response to *why don't we*. Choice (A) confuses the related word *map* with *plan*. Choice (B) confuses the related word *blanket* with *picnic*.

33. **(C)** This is the only choice that responds to the question *does*. Choice (A) confuses the related word *sign* with *form*. Choice (B) confuses the related word *interview* with *employee*.

34. **(B)** From the question you can assume the person is asking for a recommendation for what to order; (B) is the only question that proposes a dish. Choice (A) uses the related word *order*. Choice (C) has the related word *check*.

35. **(A)** *I'm sorry. I won't have time* is the best response to *can you*. Choice (B) confuses the related word *heavy* with *package*. Choice (C) confuses the similar sound *park* with *package* and does not answer the question *when*.

36. **(B)** *I didn't know there was a problem* gives a reason for not calling the repair person.

Choice (A) confuses the related word *call* (v) with *telephone* (n). Choice (C) is incorrect because it confuses *arriving late* with *calling earlier*.

37. **(A)** *I* is the understood subject; *I don't know her well* is the best response to the question. Choice (B) confuses the similar sound *show* with *know*. Choice (C) confuses the similar sound *no* with *know*.

38. **(C)** *I certainly do* is the best response to the question. Choice (A) confuses the similar sounds *disk* and *risk*. Choicc (B) confuses the antonym *small* with *big*.

39. **(B)** *Probably about ten o'clock* answers the question *when will the speeches be over*. Choice (A) confuses the related word *speaking* with *speeches*. Choice (C) is incorrect because the question asks when the *speeches* will be over, not when *they* (people) are coming over.

40. **(A)** *A delay on the tracks* is a possible reason for not taking the subway. Choice (B) confuses *taking pictures* with *taking the subway*. Choice (C) confuses the similar sound *day* with *subway*.

41. **(C)** *Yes. It's expensive to eat out* answers the question and gives a reason. Choice (A) incorrectly relates *from home every day* with *commute*. Choice (B) confuses the related word *noon* with *lunch*.

42. **(C)** *Yes, I'm looking for the shoe department* is the only possible response to *may I help you*. Choice (A) is an illogical response. Choice (B) repeats the word *help* but does not logically answer the question.

43. **(B)** This statement offers a suggestion about where the briefcase might be. Choice (A) confuses the related word *short* with *brief*(case). Choice (C) confuses the similar sound *fine* with *find*.

44. **(C)** If it is tight in the shoulders, we can assume *it* refers to the coat, and that it is not comfortable. Choice (A) confuses the related word *spend* with *comfort* and the

similar sounds *able* and comfort(*able*). Choice (B) confuses the similar sound *could* with *coat* and *confident* with *comfortable*.

45. **(C)** *The new assistant manager* answers the question *who*. Choice (A) is incorrect because it does not answer *who*, but *why*. Choice (B) is incorrect because it does not answer *who*, but *what*.

46. **(A)** This statement provides instructions for using the camera. Choice (B) could be correct if the question was *why* doesn't the camera work, but that is not the question asked. Choice (C) confuses the related *works* with *work* and *she* with *it*.

47. **(C)** The question asks about *you* and requires an *I* response. Choice (A) answers in the incorrect pronoun and tense. Choice (B) uses an incorrect pronoun.

48. **(B)** *It won't send documents* tells *what's wrong*. Choice (A) confuses the similar sound *clean* with *machine*. Choice (C) confuses the similar sound *long* with *wrong*.

49. **(A)** This statement gives an answer and an excuse. Choice (B) confuses the related word *reservation* with *reception*. Choice (C) uses *she* which is the incorrect subject/pronoun for the response.

50. **(C)** *No, we'll have to finish tomorrow* is the best response to the question. Choice (A) confuses the similar sound *limes* with *time*. Choice (B) gives the time, *six thirty*, but does not answer the question.

Part III

51. **(C)** The woman suggests they *meet* on Tuesday. Choices (A), (B), and (D) are not mentioned.

52. **(B)** The secretary *is typing it now*. Choices (A) and (C) are not mentioned. Choice (D) confuses the similar sounds *late* and *latest*.

53. **(D)** She would receive *notices about upcoming*

sales. Choice (A) confuses the similar sounds *bill* and *fill* and has the related word *purchase.* Choice (B) has the related word *credit card.* Choice (C) confuses *price list* and *mailing list.*

54. **(A)** She'll have *coffee.* Choice (B) can be added to coffee. Choice (C) is contradicted by *just coffee.* Choice (D) is not mentioned.

55. **(B)** They need *extra time.* Choice (A) is not mentioned. Choice (C) is incorrect because there are many people, but not *too* many. Choice (D) is not mentioned.

56. **(C)** The woman asks him to *call.* Choice (A) confuses the related words *wait* and *expect.* Choice (B) is contradicted by *no ... instead.* Choice (D) confuses the similar sounds *inside* and *instead.*

57. **(C)** Since the last stop is *next to the market district,* she can go at the end of the tour. Choices (A) and (B) are contradicted by *last stop is next to the market district.* Choice (D) is incorrect because other tours are not mentioned.

58. **(A)** She requests a *window seat.* Choice (B) is the only kind of seat available. Choices (C) and (D) are not mentioned.

59. **(D)** He suggests an *opera.* Choice (A) is his first suggestion. Choice (B) is what the woman would like to see. Choice (C) is not mentioned.

60. **(A)** If putting the paper in slowly makes it work, he was probably *putting the paper in too fast.* Choices (B), (C), and (D) would not be solved by putting the paper in slowly.

61. **(B)** If they charge *25 cents a day for overdue books,* they are charging a *fine.* Choices (A), (C), and (D) are not mentioned.

62. **(C)** The woman says *no other room is large enough.* Choice (A) is contradicted by *our 10:00 meeting.* Choices (B) and (D) are not mentioned.

63. **(D)** *Reserved for two nights* and *room key*

indicate a *hotel.* Choice (A) has the related word *airport.* Choice (B) makes reservations but doesn't provide keys. Choice (C) confuses the similar sounds *car* and *card.*

64. **(A)** He asks for a *parking garage.* Choice (B) confuses *parking garage* and *garage* (for fixing cars). Choice (C) confuses *park* (v) and *park* (n). Choice (D) has related word *map.*

65. **(C)** He uses the time to *think about work.* Choice (A) confuses similar sounds *subway* and *suburbs.* Choice (B) confuses the similar sounds *bother* and *brother.* Choice (D) confuses the similar sounds *computer* and *commute.*

66. **(B)** A *pharmacist* fills prescriptions. Choices (A), (C), and (D) do not fill prescriptions.

67. **(D)** He is *shopping for a coat.* Choice (A) confuses *(store) window* with *open a window.* Choice (B) suggests the related word *black,* as in *black coffee.* Choice (C): he is trying on a *coat,* not *shoes.*

68. **(B)** He thinks *the break will do her good.* Choice (A) is contradicted by *get some lunch.* Choice (C) confuses the words *good* with *has a nice voice.* Choice (D) confuses past tense *broke* (v) with *break* (n).

69. **(A)** He is supposed to get a *package.* Choice (B) has the related word *letter.* Choice (C) confuses the similar sound *pills* with *bills.* Choice (D) is not mentioned.

70. **(C)** The woman must *check the bag.* Choices (A) and (B) are contradicted by *it's too big to fit under the seat.* Choice (D) is not mentioned.

71. **(D)** The clock is *15 minutes fast.* Choice (A) is contradicted by *I still have time to finish.* Choices (B) and (C) are not mentioned.

72. **(B)** She advises him to *fix it.* Choice (A) is contradicted by *fix it before you make copies.* Choice (C) confuses *line* (of text) and *telephone line.* Choice (D) confuses *fix the mistake* and *fix the copier.*

73. **(A)** The driver *can't give him change* for his dollar bill. Choice (B) confuses *change* (v) and *change* (coins). Choice (C) confuses *bill* (payment notice) and *bill* (paper money). Choice (D) has the related word *class* (university) but is not mentioned.

74. **(D)** He is *applying for a job*. Choice (A) has the related phrase *type a letter*. Choice (B) is not mentioned. Choice (C) has the related word *computer*.

75. **(C)** He has *another umbrella in his car*. Choices (A), (B), and (D) are not mentioned.

76. **(B)** They probably work at a *hotel*. Choices (A), (C), and (D) do not have ballrooms.

77. **(A)** He *forgot his glasses*. Choice (B) is not a reason for his needing her help. Choice (C) is contradicted by *I forgot my glasses, so I can't read*. Choice (D) confuses *glasses* (eyeglasses) and *dishes* (ways of preparing food) with *tableware* (glasses, dishes, spoons, etc.).

78. **(C)** He's looking for the *mail room*. Choices (A) and (B) are mentioned but are not his destination. Choice (D) is not mentioned.

79. **(D)** She'll eat *on the patio*. Choice (A) is contradicted by *on the patio*. Choice (B) is incorrect because she's in a restaurant. Choice (C) is not mentioned.

80. **(A)** A *secretary* takes messages and handles mail for the boss. Choices (B), (C), and (D) are contradicted by the information given.

Part IV

81. **(D)** They should approach when *their row number is called*. Choices (A) and (C) are not mentioned. Choice (B) is contradicted by *when their row number is called*.

82. **(C)** *At their convenience* means *any time*. Choices (A), (B), and (D) are contradicted by *at their convenience*.

83. **(A)** It says *do NOT stop for personal belongings*. Choice (B) is contradicted by *move quickly*. Choice (C) is contradicted by *the fire*

department is on the way. Choice (D) is not mentioned—the announcement notifies everyone.

84. **(B)** It says *exit using the stairways*. Choice (A) is contradicted by *do not use the elevators*. Choices (C) and (D) are not mentioned.

85. **(C)** A Tour Service Line has information about *tours*. Choices (A), (B), and (D) are not mentioned.

86. **(B)** A *candlelight tour* is not mentioned. Choices (A), (C), and (D) are types of tours that are explicitly mentioned.

87. **(D)** *Printing services* are advertised. Choices (A), (B), and (C) are not consistent with the information in the advertisement.

88. **(A)** They offer *special low rates for volume orders*. Choices (B), (C), and (D) are contradicted by *special low rates*.

89. **(C)** They have *five convenient locations throughout the city*. Choices (A), (B), and (D) imply that they have only one location.

90. **(B)** They expect it to be *partly cloudy tonight* and *mostly cloudy tomorrow*. Choice (A) is contradicted by *cloudy*. Choices (C) and (D) are contradicted by *colder temperatures*.

91. **(A)** The *wind will pick up*. Choice (B) is contradicted by *pick up*. Choice (C) is not mentioned. Choice (D) is contradicted by *gusts to 25 miles an hour*.

92. **(D)** Rain is expected *late tomorrow afternoon*. Choices (A), (B), and (C) are all contradicted by *late tomorrow afternoon*.

93. **(B)** *Employees* and *office mailboxes* suggest a large company. Choices (A), (C), and (D) are not consistent with the information given.

94. **(C)** *Selling stamps* is not mentioned. Choices (A), (B), and (D) are all explicitly mentioned.

95. **(A)** Employees should bring *fragile* packages to the mail room. Choices (B), (C), and (D) are not mentioned.

96. **(A)** She is probably a *scientist*. Choices (B), (C), and (D) would not research the strength of industrial metals.

97. **(D)** It is probably given *at a conference*. Choices (A), (B), and (C) are not consistent with the information given.

98. **(C)** It discusses *new car sales*. Choices (A) and (B) are not mentioned. Choice (D) confuses the similar sounds *export* and *expert*.

99. **(B)** Economists attribute it to the increase in *loans* for new car purchases. Choices (A), (C), and (D) are not mentioned.

100. **(D)** The new safety features are the result of *consumer demand*. Choices (A), (B), and (C) are not mentioned.

Part V

101. **(B)** *People* requires a plural verb. Choice (A) is the singular form. Choice (C) is the simple form. Choice (D) is the gerund or present participle form.

102. **(D)** Superlative comparisons require *the* and the superlative form of the adjective. Choice (A) has the simple form of the adjective. Choice (B) requires *the*. Choice (C) is the comparative form.

103. **(C)** The noun *advice* means *recommendations*. Choices (A) and (B) are verbs. Choice (D) is a noun, but means *exciting experience*.

104. **(A)** The main verb *is completed* requires a future or present tense verb as the secondary verb. Choice (B) is the past tense. Choice (C) is the present perfect. Choice (D) is the gerund or the present participle form.

105. **(A)** *During* is a preposition and is followed by a noun phrase. Choices (B), (C), and (D) are conjunctions that introduce a clause.

106. **(B)** An adjective or restrictive clause referring to a person begins with *who*. Choice (A) is a relative pronoun but refers to things.

Choice (C) is a relative pronoun but indicates possession. Choice (D) is not a relative pronoun.

107. **(B)** The future tense in a real condition requires the present tense in the *if* clause. Choice (A) is the future tense. Choice (C) is the past tense. Choice (D) is the present tense, but for a plural subject.

108. **(C)** *And* is a coordinating conjunction used to join items. Choice (A) excludes all items. Choice (B) contrasts items. Choice (D) indicates a choice among items.

109. **(D)** Causative *need* requires the infinitive. Choice (A) is the gerund or the present participle form. Choice (B) is the past tense. Choice (C) is the present tense.

110. **(C)** *On* is a preposition that can be used with days of the week. Choice (A) indicates possession. Choice (B) indicates location. Choice (D) indicates time.

111. **(A)** An adverb of indefinite frequency may come before the verb. Choice (B) incorrectly places *carefully* before the verb it modifies. Choices (C) and (D) have *always* after the verb.

112. **(C)** Items linked by *and* must have the same form. In this case, the second verb must be the participle form to match *worrying*. Choice (A) is the present tense. Choice (B) is the past tense. Choice (D) is an infinitive.

113. **(B)** *Reports* is a plural noun that is the subject of the sentence and that agrees with the plural adjective *both*. Choice (A) is a noun, but a person is not likely to be placed on a desk. Choice (C) is the gerund or the present participle form. Choice (D) is a singular noun.

114. **(D)** *Despite* is logical and can be followed by a noun phrase. Choice (A) is not logical. Choices (B) and (C) are usually followed by a clause.

115. **(A)** Subject *offices* requires a plural verb. Choices (B), (C), and (D) are singular.

116. **(C)** The participants are affected by the meeting. They are bored. Therefore, the past participle is required. Choice (A) is the present participle. Choice (B) is the present tense. Choice (D) is the present continuous.

117. **(B)** An adverb of definite frequency can appear at the end of a sentence. Choices (A), (C), and (D) are adverbs of indefinite frequency and appear within the sentence.

118. **(A)** A noun that is specified usually requires *the*. Choices (B) and (C) are indefinite articles. Choice (D) is a pronoun.

119. **(B)** Equal comparisons require *as* on both sides of the adverb. Choices (A) and (C) use *as* only once. Choice (D) is the comparative form.

120. **(D)** A past action that occurs before another past action requires the past perfect. Choice (A) is the present perfect. Choice (B) is the present tense. Choice (C) is the past tense.

121. **(B)** *That* can introduce relative clauses referring to things. Choice (A) is not a relative pronoun. Choice (C) is a possessive relative pronoun. Choice (D) is a relative pronoun that refers to people.

122. **(C)** *To* indicates direction toward a place. Choices (A) and (D) indicate location. Choice (B) indicates possession.

123. **(A)** *Suggest* requires the simple form (subjunctive form) when it indicates that someone else will do something. Choice (B) is the past tense. Choice (C) is the infinitive. Choice (D) is a gerund or the present participle form.

124. **(C)** When *the argument* is the cause (not the effect), use the present participle *convincing*. Choice (A) is the past tense. Choice (B) is the present tense. Choice (D) is the infinitive.

125. **(B)** The sentence requires a singular noun. Choice (A) is a plural noun. Choice (C) is an adjective. Choice (D) is a verb.

126. **(C)** If you need a count noun, add a countable term (such as *sheet*) to a non-count noun (such as *paper*) to use it in a countable sense. Choice (A) is non-count. Choice (B) is only possible when it means kinds of paper. Choice (D) is not plural (*three sheets*).

127. **(D)** The preposition *in* indicates location within a place. Choice (A) indicates location outside of a place. Choice (B) indicates possession. Choice (C) indicates direction toward a place.

128. **(C)** Since *and* connects two similar items and since *research* is a noun, you need the noun *development*. Choice (A) is the past tense or the past participle form. Choice (B) is the gerund or the present participle form. Choice (D) is the present tense.

129. **(A)** *Both* is often paired with *and*. Choices (B), (C), and (D) are not paired with *both*.

130. **(B)** A comparison between two things requires the comparative form. Choice (A) is an incorrect equal comparison. Choice (C) is an incorrect comparative. Choice (D) is the superlative.

131. **(C)** *Or* indicates a choice between two items: a *room* or a *suite*. Choice (A) indicates a contrast. Choice (B) joins the items. Choice (D) eliminates both items.

132. **(D)** *Devise* is a verb meaning to develop or invent a method of doing something. Choice (A) is a verb meaning to dedicate. Choice (B) is a verb meaning to want something. Choice (C) is a noun meaning machine (usually a small one).

133. **(B)** Non-restrictive relative clauses referring to things are introduced by *which*. Choice (A) is a relative pronoun referring to things, but cannot be used in a non-restrictive clause. Choice (C) is not a relative pronoun. Choice (D) is a relative pronoun indicating possession.

134. **(D)** A future tense verb in the main clause of an *if* sentence requires a simple present

tense verb in the *if* clause. Choice (A) is the past perfect. Choice (B) is the future perfect. Choice (C) is a continuous verb form that must be used with a form of *be*.

135. **(C)** The causative verb *urge* followed by a noun clause requires the simple verb form. Choice (A) is a participle form. Choice (B) is the infinitive. Choice (D) is the future.

136. **(A)** Since *the highways* are affected by the crowds (they are made crowded), use the past participle. Choice (B) is the present participle. Choices (C) and (D) are the present tense or nouns.

137. **(C)** In this context, only *waited* is the appropriate past tense verb. Choices (A), (B), and (D) are not logical.

138. **(C)** The present tense in the *if* clause of a real condition requires a present or future form in the remaining clause. Choice (A) is the present perfect. Choice (B) is the past perfect. Choice (D) is the past continuous.

139. **(B)** The causative verb *make* requires the simple form of the verb. Choice (A) is the gerund or present participle form. Choice (C) is the infinitive. Choice (D) is a noun.

140. **(D)** The preposition *at* indicates a specific time. Choice (A) indicates location. Choice (B) indicates the day of the week. Choice (C) indicates a duration of time.

Part VI

141. **(D)** Items joined by *and* must have the same grammatical form; *quality, service,* and *value*. Choice (A) is a correct noun. Choice (B) is a correct relative pronoun. Choice (C) is a correct verb.

142. **(B)** Clauses referring to people begin with *who*. Choice (A) is a correct article. Choice (C) is a correct infinitive. Choice (D) is a correct preposition.

143. **(B)** In this context the verb *allow* requires the

infinitive *to make*. Choice (A) is a correct past participle. Choices (C) and (D) are correct conjunctions.

144. **(C)** *Affect* is a verb; use the noun *effect*. Choice (A) is a correct pronoun. Choice (B) is a correct conjunction. Choice (D) is a correct verb.

145. **(D)** *Since* must be followed by reference to a single point in time; use prepositions *in* or *during*. Choice (A) is a correct noun. Choice (B) is a correct superlative. Choice (C) is a correct verb.

146. **(C)** Adverbs of definite frequency cannot appear after the verb; move to the end of the sentence; *reports are printed out on the first Monday of every month*. Choice (A) is a correct article. Choice (B) is a correct verb. Choice (D) is a correct preposition.

147. **(A)** *The* is used in a superlative comparison: *The best treatment*. Choices (B) and (D) are correct prepositions. Choice (C) is a correct verb.

148. **(A)** In this context, the verb *insist* is followed by a secondary verb in the simple form: *The company insists that security guards meet … and walk*. Choice (B) is a correct preposition. Choice (C) is a correct conjunction. Choice (D) is a correct preposition.

149. **(D)** Someone else invited the guests; therefore, you should use the past participle *invited guests*. Choice (A) is a correct superlative. Choice (B) is a correct preposition. Choice (C) is a correct verb.

150. **(B)** Present perfect continuous requires *have*: *have been advertising*. Choice (A) is a correct conjunction. Choice (C) is a correct preposition. Choice (D) is a correct verb.

151. **(B)** Plural subject *members* requires a plural verb *have*. Choice (A) is a correct preposition. Choice (C) is a correct infinitive. Choice (D) is a correct article.

152. **(A)** The coordinating conjunction that introduces the clause should show cause and effect, not contrast; use *Because*. Choice (B) is a correct adverb. Choice (C) is a correct verb. Choice (D) is a correct preposition.

153. **(C)** *Software* is a non-count noun and does not use *a*; use *the software* to refer to specific software. Choice (A) is a correct conjunction. Choices (B) and (D) are correct verbs.

154. **(B)** *Either … or* is a paired conjunction; *either her assistant or the division manager.* Choices (A) and (D) are correct prepositions. Choice (C) is a correct article.

155. **(A)** Use *for* to express duration; *for six months.* Choice (B) is a correct conjunction. Choice (C) is a correct infinitive. Choice (D) is a correct noun.

156. **(D)** *Had already been published* is a previous past action; use a more recent past for the more recent action *was discovered.* Choice (A) is a correct article. Choice (B) is a correct adverb. Choice (C) is a correct preposition.

157. **(A)** In this context, *fish* is a generic noun and does not require an article. Choice (B) is a correct adjective. Choice (C) is a correct preposition. Choice (D) is a correct adverb.

158. **(B)** The plural subject *waiters* requires a plural verb *have*. Choices (A) and (D) are correct prepositions. Choice (C) is a correct gerund.

159. **(A)** You know which company you are talking about if you refer to it by its name; use *the.* Choice (B) is a correct verb. Choice (C) is a correct article. Choice (D) is a correct preposition.

160. **(C)** Adverbs of indefinite frequency appear before the main verb of the clause: *he rarely stays.* Choice (A) is a correct subordinating conjunction. Choice (B) is a

correct infinitive. Choice (D) is a correct comparative.

Part VII

161. **(C)** Businesses are doing well. Choice (A) is contradicted by *increases in employment.* Choices (B) and (D) are not mentioned.

162. **(D)** Research is not mentioned. Choices (A), (B), and (C) are explicitly mentioned.

163. **(A)** The subscription is for season tickets to plays. Choices (B), (C), and (D) are not mentioned.

164. **(B)** The price is determined by the day you attend. Choice (A) is incorrect because all plays are at the same theater. Choice (C) is incorrect because the tickets are for six plays. Choice (D) is incorrect because the type of play is not mentioned.

165. **(D)** The memo is about saving cab costs. Choices (A), (B), and (C) are not mentioned.

166. **(A)** The memo is to all employees. Choices (B) and (D) would not see the company's memo. Choice (C) is incorrect because the accounting department is the source of the memo.

167. **(C)** The driver should turn the meter on after you are in the cab. Choices (A), (B), and (D) are contradicted by *after you sit down in the cab.*

168. **(B)** The receipt verifies the trip. Choices (A) and (D) are part of the receipt. Choice (C) is not the purpose of the receipt.

169. **(A)** They have a meeting known as the power breakfast. Choices (B), (C), and (D) are not mentioned.

170. **(D)** People who consider themselves too busy to meet any other time started the power breakfast. Choices (A), (B), and (C) are not mentioned.

171. **(B)** Some restaurants require reservations before 9:00 A.M. Choices (A) and (C) are

possible but not mentioned. Choice (D) is not mentioned.

172. **(C)** Companies must look for a match between needs and resources. Choice (A) may not be appropriate for every company. Choices (B) and (D) are not mentioned.

173. **(B)** Tax advantages are not mentioned. Choices (A), (C), and (D) are mentioned.

174. **(D)** A pro-business attitude is essential. Choices (A), (B), and (C) are not essential for every company.

175. **(C)** The peak is in December. Choices (A), (B), (D) reflect lower spending than in December.

176. **(A)** February and August show the lowest sales. Choices (B), (C), and (D) have at least one month with higher sales.

177. **(C)** The purpose of the letter is to return a purchase. Choices (A), (B), and (D) are not consistent with the information given.

178. **(A)** It was made by credit card. Choices (B), (C), and (D) are not consistent with the information given.

179. **(D)** She requests that they credit her credit card. Choices (A), (B), and (C) are not consistent with the information given.

180. **(B)** The article recommends fruits and vegetables to stay healthy. Choices (A) and (C) contain dietary fat, which should be reduced. Choice (D) is not mentioned.

181. **(C)** Experts think that the compounds may fight disease. Choices (A) and (D) may be true but are not mentioned. Choice (B) is not mentioned.

182. **(B)** People should eat five servings a day. Choices (A), (C), and (D) are contradicted by *five servings a day*.

183. **(A)** People should reduce dietary fat. Choices (B) and (D) may be true, but are not mentioned. Choice (C) is contradicted by *reduction in dietary fat*.

184. **(D)** It describes a festival. Choices (A), (B),

and (C) are not consistent with the information given.

185. **(A)** The children can learn folk dances. Choices (B), (C), and (D) are not mentioned.

186. **(D)** The advertisement assumes that people will drive their cars since it is far to the fairgrounds and parking is available at no extra charge. Choice (A) is unlikely considering the distance. Choices (B) and (C) are not mentioned.

187. **(C)** The admissions fee is donated to the Preserve Our History Fund. Choices (A), (B), and (D) are not mentioned.

188. **(D)** The article encourages people to pay more attention to their pens. Choice (A) is incorrect because it tells people what to write with, not how to write. Choice (B) is incorrect because the article tells how to purchase pens, not printers. Choice (C) is incorrect because although the article mentions that few things are written by hand, it does not encourage people to write more.

189. **(A)** The most important characteristic for determining comfort is thickness. Choice (B) is mentioned, but is not as important as thickness. Choice (C) is not mentioned. Choice (D) is incorrect because size is a combination of thickness, length, and weight.

190. **(B)** An irregular flow of ink may cause skips or gaps. Choice (A) is not mentioned. Choice (C) is the result of failure of the pen to seal off the flow of ink. Choice (D) is not mentioned.

191. **(C)** The advantage of fine-line pens is that they may compensate for bad handwriting. Choice (A) is not mentioned. Choice (B) and (D) refer to pens that make a bold, dark line.

192. **(B)** *Executives* belong to ORE. Choices (A), (C), and (D) are not consistent with the information given.

193. **(A)** The purpose of ORE is to provide responsible solutions. Choices (B), (C), and (D) are not mentioned.

194. **(D)** It has been operating for five years. Choices (A), (B), and (C) are contradicted by *five years ago*.

195. **(C)** ORE *has grown fast*. Choices (A), (B), and (D) are not mentioned.

196. **(C)** It concerns *help for flood victims*. Choices (A), (B), and (D) are not consistent with the information given.

197. **(A)** *Medical supplies* are not mentioned. Choices (B), (C), and (D) are mentioned.

198. **(D)** *Volunteers* are needed. Choices (A), (B), and (C) are not consistent with the information given.

199. **(C)** They will *replace all parts that fail due to defective workmanship*. Choices (A), (B), and (D) are not consistent with the information given.

200. **(B)** It does not cover damage by the consumer. Choices (A), (C), and (D) are all examples of poor workmanship.

Practice Test 2
Part I

1. **(B)** The people are walking together in the park and a woman is holding a child's hand. The group is probably a family. Choice (A) is incorrect because the people are on level ground, not at a summit. Choice (C) is incorrect because the mother is holding the child's hand, not carrying him. Choice (D) confuses the similar sounds *familiar* with *family* and *talk* with *walk*.

2. **(C)** The man wearing a tall, white hat and white uniform is holding a basket of tomatoes; he is probably a chef. Choice (A) uses the related word *lunch* and confuses the similar sounds *chief* and *chef*. Choice (B) confuses the related word *tomato sauce* with *tomatoes*. Choice (D) describes an incorrect action;

the man is *showing*, not *chopping* the vegetables.

3. **(A)** The people are at an airport check-in counter. There are flags above the counter. Choice (B) is incorrect because the counter is a departure area, not an arrival hall; you do not need to visit the counter when your flight arrives; Choice (B) is also incorrect because the area is not empty. Choice (C) confuses the similar sound *tickets to the fair* with *air tickets*. Choice (D) confuses the similar sound *pass the port* with *passport*.

4. **(D)** The woman is watching the man shoot the billiard ball. Choice (A) incorrectly identifies the location; they are in a billiard hall, not on the field. Choice (B) confuses the definition of *shooting* (hunting) with *shooting* (billiards) and the definition of *game* (animal) with *game* (sport). Choice (C) confuses the related word *swimming pool* with the game *pool* and the similar sound *Bill's yard* with *billiards*.

5. **(D)** A man and woman are talking in the hotel lobby while a bellhop takes a bag to the reception desk. Choice (A) confuses the similar sound *hobby* with *lobby*. Choice (B) confuses the related word *visiting* (adj) with *visitors* (n) and uses the related words *rest* and to(*night*). Choice (C) confuses the similar sound *guess* with *guest*.

6. **(D)** The men dressed in white laboratory coats looking at the machinery are probably technicians. Choice (A) incorrectly assumes the men wearing white coats are doctors. Choice (B) incorrectly identifies the scenery and the action. Choice (C) confuses the similar sound *lazy* with *laser* and incorrectly identifies the action.

7. **(A)** The man is pointing to the book the woman is showing him. Choice (B) incorrectly identifies the location; they are in an office with a palm tree behind them, not in the forest. Choice (C) is incorrect because although the man may be a pharmacist, he is not dispensing medicine. Choice (D) identifies an incorrect action; they are not

buying flowers.

8. **(A)** The men have musical instruments. Choice (B) incorrectly identifies the location of the drum; the drum is on the man's knee, not in the window. Choice (C) is incorrect because they are playing live music, so they probably would not be listening to music on the radio. Choice (D) confuses the similar sound *freedom* with *drum*.

9. **(D)** The man is reading a newspaper. Choice (A) identifies an incorrect action; he is reading a paper, not talking on the phone. Choice (B) is incorrect because there is a lamp on the table. Choice (C) is incorrect because although the man may be a journalist, he is not reporting.

10. **(A)** People are getting out of a car and handing a bag to the bellhop. Choice (B) is incorrect because the couple just arrived and are staying, not driving away. Choice (C) is incorrect because the couple are *going up* the stairs, not *falling down* them. Choice (D) is incorrect because the car door is *open*, not *closed*.

11. **(A)** The woman is sorting through the papers on her desk. Choice (B) confuses the related word *newspaper* with *paper*. Choice (C) is incorrect because although there are coats in the picture, she is not hanging hers. Choice (D) confuses the action *watching* with *looking through*.

12. **(B)** The people are in a crowded cafeteria eating lunch. Choice (A) is incorrect because only *one* person is standing, not *everyone*. Choice (C) uses the similar word *restaurant*, but the cafeteria is in use, not closed and repair persons are not shown. Choice (D) is incorrect because there are no windows.

13. **(C)** The man is walking towards the car outside of a shop in a Spanish-speaking area. Choice (A) confuses the similar sound *shopping cart* with *shop*. Choice (B) uses the related word *drive* but incorrectly identifies the location and the action. Choice (D)

confuses the similar sound *explain* with *Spain*.

14. **(B)** You can assume from the context that the woman is a teacher and the children are students doing an experiment. Choice (A) uses the related word *girls*, but is incorrect because they are doing a science experiment, not making tea. Choice (C) uses the related word *children*, but is incorrect because the children are in school and you cannot tell from the picture what they will do after school. Choice (D) uses the related words *solution* and *mixing*, but incorrectly identifies the actor.

15. **(D)** People are standing at a bus stop and one person is getting on the bus. Choice (A) confuses the similar sounds *button* with *bus* and *falling off* with *getting off*. Choice (B) confuses the similar sounds *stop* with *bus stop* and *writing* with *riding*. Choice (C) is incorrect because the number of the bus, not the house, is four.

16. **(A)** A young man on his bike is by a vending machine. Choice (B) confuses the similar sound *can* (modal) with *cans* (n) and uses the related words *drink* and *sodas*. Choice (C) identifies an incorrect action; he is *wearing a watch* but not *watching the time*. Choice (D) confuses the similar sound *old* with *cold*.

17. **(B)** The people are in the office working. Choice (A) is incorrect because although there are many desks, the picture shows people *working* at their desks, not customers *shopping*. Choice (C) identifies light fixtures, which can be seen in the picture, but there is no repair person present. Choice (D) incorrectly identifies the location; the room is crowded, but it is an *office*, not a *lunchroom*.

18. **(A)** The men wearing hard hats are working on an oil rig. Two are drilling; the other two are looking at a clipboard. Choice (B) confuses the similar sound *turning around* with *turning the drill*. Choice (C) is incorrect because they are all wearing

protective glasses. Choice (D) uses the related word *oil* but is not identified in the picture.

19. **(A)** The person is waterskiing. Choice (B) uses the related words *wading* and *lake* but incorrectly identifies the action. Choice (C) is incorrect because the person is waterskiing, not drinking water. Choice (D) confuses the similar sound *would see* with *waterski*.

20. **(C)** The man is writing a check to give to the bank teller. Choice (A) confuses the similar sound *playing checkers* with *paying the check*. Choice (B) confuses the similar sound *banquet* with *bank*. Choice (D) confuses the similar word *saved* (v) with *savings* (n).

Part II

21. **(A)** *Sure. I never use it* is a proper response. Choice (B) confuses the related word *spell* with *dictionary*. Choice (C) confuses the related words *books* and *dictionary*.

22. **(C)** The agenda would include a schedule of presentations. Choice (A) confuses *plane schedule* and *lecture schedule*. Choice (B) confuses the related words *speak* and *lecture*.

23. **(B)** This statement suggests training would help the problem. Choice (A) confuses the related word *bad* with *problem* and the similar sound *train* (n) with *train* (v). Choice (C) confuses *I can't* with *it wouldn't*.

24. **(B)** *I did* answers *who*. Choice (A) confuses *open* with *closed*. Choice (C) answers the question *shall* I open the window.

25. **(C)** *After their board meeting* answers *when*. Choice (A) answers *how* is the client. Choice (B) confuses the related words *telephone* and *hear* and answers *how*.

26. **(A)** *It depends which magazines run our ads* is the best response to the question. Choice (B) confuses *fish market* with *market*. Choice (C) confuses *right* (direction) with *right* (correct).

27. **(C)** *It was our supplier* answers *who*. Choice (A) confuses the similar sound *loan* with *phone*. Choice (B) confuses the related words *ring* and *phone*.

28. **(A)** *No. I heard the crash and then looked up* is the best response to the question. Choice (B) confuses the related words *hurt* and *accident*. Choice (C) confuses the related words *police* and *accident*.

29. **(B)** This statement offers a critique of the acting in the film. Choice (A) confuses the related words *movers* and *movie*. Choice (C) confuses the similar sounds *ink* and *think*.

30. **(C)** *Actually, we went there on our honeymoon* is the best response to the question. Choice (A) confuses the similar sound *pair of those* with *Paris*. Choice (B) uses the incorrect pronoun.

31. **(B)** The question requires a time; Choice (B) suggests it could start snowing any minute. Choice (A) uses a time marker, but confuses the subject *he* with *snow*. Choice (C) uses the incorrect tense.

32. **(A)** This statement offers to connect the caller with a woman in the billing department. Choice (B) confuses the related word *bill* with *billing*. Choice (C) confuses the related word *pay* with *bill*.

33. **(A)** *Faster computers* would increase efficiency. Choice (B) confuses the related words *more* and *to increase*. Choice (C) confuses *longer way* with *a way*.

34. **(C)** *Many years ago* answers the question *have you worked with the director in the past*. Choice (A) is incorrect because it refers to working longer than an eight hour day, while the statement implies the woman has worked with the director over a period of time. Choice (B) does not answer the question.

35. **(B)** *Yes, I'm sorry* is a polite response to the question. Choice (A) confuses the related word *stand* with *sitting*. Choice (C) confuses the related word *seats* with *sitting*.

36. **(A)** This choice is the only response that gives a time. Choice (B) answers *where* and not *when*. Choice (C) confuses the similar sounds *cold* and *call* and answers *what*.

37. **(B)** *I can't. I have plans* is the best response to the question. Choice (A) confuses *early* and *late*. Choice (C) confuses the related word *later* with *late*.

38. **(A)** This statement uses the correct pronoun *I* and gives a possible explanation for the woman being late for the appointment. Choice (B) answers *when*. Choice (C) answers *where*.

39. **(C)** *Yes, thank you* is a polite answer to the question. Choice (A) confuses the similar sound *salary* with *salad*. Choice (B) answers *when* the salad is served.

40. **(B)** *No, the subway* answers the question *do you take the bus*. Choice (A) answers *how much* the bus costs. Choice (C) answers the question *why*.

41. **(B)** *Only long enough to get a sandwich* answers the question *are you going out for lunch*. Choice (A) is an incorrect response because the question does not ask about the weather. Choice (C) confuses the similar sound *bunch* with *lunch*.

42. **(A)** *Not until one o'clock* is the best response to the question. Choice (B) confuses *close* with *open*. Choice (C) answers *when* but confuses *open the present* with *open the store*.

43. **(A)** Since the woman placed the order herself, she knows it was placed. Choice (B) confuses the related words *misplaced* and *placed*. Choice (C) contains the related words *restaurant* and *chicken*, but does not answer the question.

44. **(C)** *It looks like mine* answers the question *whose*. Choice (A) confuses the related word *music* with *notes*. Choice (B) confuses the related word *handwriting* with *notebook*.

45. **(B)** *No, I won't be near a phone* is the best response to the question. Choice (A) answers *when* not *can*. Choice (C) confuses the similar sound *refund* with *return*.

46. **(C)** *To the beach* correctly answers the question *where*. Choice (A) confuses the similar sounds *vacancies* and *vacation*. Choice (B) answers *when* but not *where*.

47. **(B)** *Thanks, but I've just finished it* is a polite response to the question. Choice (A) confuses the similar sounds *report* and *reporters*. Choice (C) does not answer the question *can I help you*.

48. **(A)** More deck space will attract more passengers. Choice (B) confuses the similar sound *race* with *space*. Choice (C) confuses the similar sound *redecorate* with *renovate*.

49. **(B)** *Yes, they're posting them right now* correctly rephrases and answers the question. Choice (A) confuses the similar sound *cab* with *cabin*. Choice (C) confuses the related word *fence* with *post*.

50. **(B)** *Five hundred dollars each way* is the amount of the fare. Choice (A) answers *when*. Choice (C) confuses *empty* with *full*.

Part III

51. **(B)** The man says he will *make a copy* (of his notes) for the woman. Choice (A) is a common expression with *notes*. Choice (C) is incorrect because the meeting they mention is in the past. Choice (D) is contradicted by *I'll make a copy*.

52. **(D)** The clerk mentions *sports* and *exercise wear*, so he is suggesting clothes for physical activity. Choice (A) confuses a selection of exercise wear and a selection of sweets. Choice (B) confuses the similar sounds *sports* and *shorts*. Choice (C) confuses *exercise* (physical activity) with *exercise* (practice in English).

53. **(C)** She says they should *buy a new one*. Choices (A) and (D) are not mentioned. Choice (B) is contradicted by *buy a new one*.

54. **(A)** The man mentions *road construction*; the woman implies the construction is for a *new*

road. Choice (B) is not mentioned. Choice (C) confuses *new road being constructed* with *trying a new road.* Choice (D) confuses the similar sounds *annoying* and *noise.*

55. **(B)** The customer requested a *double room.* Choice (A) is contradicted by *double room.* Choices (C) and (D) are not mentioned.

56. **(C)** She asks for directions to the *courthouse.* Choice (A) confuses the related words *walk* and *park.* Choice (B) is located *next to the courthouse.* Choice (D) confuses the similar words *courthouse* and *home.*

57. **(D)** He suggests *seafood.* Choices (A) and (B) are contradicted by *ready for some dinner.* Choice (C) confuses the similar sounds *salad* and *seafood.*

58. **(C)** The paper is *too thin to go through the rollers*; he will try *thicker paper.* Choice (A) confuses the similar words *roll* and *rollers.* Choice (B) confuses *jam* (for toast) with *jam* (a clog). Choice (D) is contradicted by *too thin.*

59. **(A)** She says the coffee stain *will probably come out.* Choice (B) is not mentioned. Choice (C) is contradicted by *not wanting to buy a new one.* Choice (D) is incorrect because the cleaners will *clean* it, not *ruin* it.

60. **(B)** She is afraid she will lose them when she travels. Choice (A) is not mentioned. Choice (C) is true but not the reason. Choice (D) is contradicted by *going to buy some books.*

61. **(D)** She says that the ground will be *soaking wet.* Choice (A) confuses the similar sounds *damp* and *camp.* Choice (B) confuses the similar sounds *town* and *ground.* Choice (C) confuses the similar sounds *hassle* and *cancel.*

62. **(A)** His closet is full with too many clothes. Choice (B) confuses *not wearing the right clothes* with *having too many clothes.* Choice (C) is incorrect because if the closet were too wide, he wouldn't have a space problem. Choice (D) might be true but you cannot determine if the clothes are out-of-date by the conversation.

63. **(C)** She sees it *every year when it plays.* Choice (A) is contradicted by *seeing that movie again.* Choice (B) is incorrect because she saw it last year, as well as other times. Choice (D) confuses *after a while* with *once in a while.*

64. **(D)** She can choose a different fabric from the upholstery catalogue. Choice (A) is not mentioned. Choice (B) is incorrect because she likes the size and shape of this sofa. Choice (C) is not mentioned.

65. **(B)** *Ready to order now* suggests a restaurant. Choices (A), (C), and (D) are not consistent with the conversation.

66. **(B)** *Less expensive* means cheaper. Choice (A) is incorrect because both methods are fast. Choices (C) and (D) are not mentioned.

67. **(A)** The man will not take the job because the salary is too low. Choices (B) and (C) are not mentioned. Choice (D) is incorrect because the work was different; the salary was the same.

68. **(C)** She is working *in the mail room.* Choice (A) confuses the related words *school* and *learn.* Choice (B) confuses *basement* with the expression *start at the bottom.* Choice (D) confuses the related words *mail* and *post office.*

69. **(D)** Dentists clean teeth. Choice (A) confuses *trouble* and *filling* with *mechanic.* Choices (B) and (C) are not mentioned.

70. **(C)** There was a *substitute speaker.* Choices (A) and (B) are incorrect because the speaker got sick and couldn't give her presentation. Choice (D) is contradicted by *didn't have a better speaker.*

71. **(A)** She says to *hire as many temporary workers as you need.* Choices (B) and (C) are outcomes they are trying to avoid. Choice (D) is not mentioned.

72. **(C)** They will *order balloons*. Choice (A) is incorrect since they can't send flowers because she is allergic. Choice (B) is incorrect because a card might accompany balloons or flowers, but is not the focus here. Choice (D) is incorrect because they do not decide to call her.

73. **(B)** The man thinks tourists should *wait until after rush hour* to use the subway. Choices (A) and (D) are alternatives to the subway but are not mentioned. Choice (C) is not mentioned.

74. **(D)** Mr. Gomez is *out of town*. Choice (A) does not prevent her from returning the call. Choice (B) is unlikely, since he left a message. Choice (C) is not mentioned.

75. **(B)** The restaurant will provide *good food nearby*. Choices (A) and (C) are not mentioned. Choice (D) is incorrect because they can get sandwiches now.

76. **(C)** She should *let the moderator know she'll have something important to say*. Choice (A) is incorrect because she is attending the meeting; the question asks what she should do before the meeting. Choice (B) is not mentioned; she already has her suggestion ready. Choice (D) is what she will do at the meeting.

77. **(A)** The woman *can't stay late*. Choice (B) confuses related phrases *be late* and *stay late*. Choice (C) is incorrect because it is when her plane leaves the next morning. Choice (D) is incorrect because it is where she is going.

78. **(A)** *Do business with someone else* means change suppliers. Choices (B) and (C) are not mentioned. Choice (D) is incorrect because it is a step involved in changing suppliers.

79. **(C)** Employees use the *expensive overnight service*. Choices (A), (B), and (D) are not mentioned.

80. **(D)** The woman agrees to *take a list to the purser's office*. Choice (A) confuses going to a concert and setting up for a concert.

Choice B is not mentioned. Choice (C) confuses the related word *check*.

Part IV

81. **(B)** It is described as a *moving sidewalk*. Choices (A), (C), and (D) are not mentioned.

82. **(D)** References to *luggage* suggest an airport. Choices (A), (B), and (C) are not consistent with the information given.

83. **(C)** People should wait until *all the speakers have finished*. Choices (A), (B), and (D) are not consistent with the information given.

84. **(D)** People are asked to *use the microphone*. Choice (A) is not mentioned. Choices (B) and (C) are contradicted by *the microphone in the center of the room*.

85. **(A)** The ad is for *dishes*. Choices (B), (C), and (D) are not consistent with the information given.

86. **(C)** You cannot *freeze food in them*. Choices (A), (B), and (D) are explicitly mentioned.

87. **(D)** The road *leads to the business district*. Choice (A) is contradicted by *construction crews are working*. Choice (B) is not mentioned. Choice (C) is not as explicit as *business district*.

88. **(C)** Repairs will take *four weeks* (one month). Choice (A) is confused with *crews will work around the clock*. Choices (B) and (D) are contradicted by *four weeks*.

89. **(A)** They should *find alternate routes*. Choices (B), (C), and (D) are not mentioned.

90. **(B)** Madison House is *older and smaller*. Choice (A) describes the other houses on the tour. Choices (C) and (D) are not mentioned.

91. **(D)** It represents the *highest quality available at that time*. Choices (A), (B), and (C) are not mentioned.

92. **(C)** Attention is drawn to the *carved ceilings*. Choices (A), (B), and (D) are not mentioned.

93. **(B)** People can look forward to *good weather*. Choices (A), (C), and (D) are not mentioned.

94. **(A)** It will get colder *at night*. Choices (B) and (C) may be true, but are not the focus here. Choice (D) is when it gets warmer.

95. **(C)** You would hear it *on a train*. Choices (A), (B), and (D) are not consistent with the information given.

96. **(D)** The information is about *seatings for dinner*. Choices (A) and (C) are not mentioned. Choice (B) is not the focus of the announcement.

97. **(C)** There are *two seatings*. Choices (A), (B), and (D) are not consistent with the information given.

98. **(B)** It discusses *survey results*. Choice (A) is the opposite of the information in the survey. Choices (C) and (D) are not consistent with the information given.

99. **(D)** Their ads are usually based on *price*. Choices (A), (B), and (C) are contradicted by *concentrate on price*.

100. **(A)** Consumers want *good repair service*. Choices (B), (C), and (D) are not mentioned.

Part V

101. **(B)** *Uniform* begins with a consonant sound and requires *a*. Choice (A) is used before a vowel sound. Choice (C) is the definite article. Choice (D) expresses quantity.

102. **(C)** An action that begins in the past and continues in the present requires the present perfect. Choice (A) is a gerund or a participle form. Choice (B) is the past perfect. Choice (D) is the future perfect.

103. **(A)** The *document* is affected; it does not do the enclosing; use the past participle. Choice (B) is the simple form of the verb. Choice (C) is the present participle. Choice (D) is the infinitive.

104. **(D)** *Accept* means to receive. Choice (A) means to exclude. Choice (B) means something that is excluded. Choice (C) means to alter.

105. **(B)** A relative clause indicating possession begins with *whose*. Choice (A) is not a relative pronoun. Choice (C) does not indicate possession. Choice (D) is not used with people except in restrictive clauses.

106. **(D)** The verb *requires*, in this context, should be followed by a gerund or present participle form. Choice (A) is a noun. Choice (B) is the simple form of the verb. Choice (C) is the infinitive.

107. **(A)** An action that occurs before a past action requires the past perfect. Choice (B) is the present perfect. Choice (C) is the future tense. Choice (D) is conditional.

108. **(C)** *Sensible* means *makes sense*. Choice (A) means *able to detect small differences*. Choice (B) means *to perceive*. Choice (D) refers to senses of touch, sight, etc., which humans use to perceive.

109. **(D)** The preposition *at* indicates location when used with the verb phrase *to be held*. Choice (A) is used with days of the week. Choice (B) is used for a position within something. Choice (C) indicates possession.

110. **(C)** The present tense in the *if* clause of a real condition uses a present, imperative, or future form in the remaining clause. Choice (A) is the past tense. Choice (B) is the present continuous, but is singular. Choice (D) is the past perfect.

111. **(B)** *People* requires a plural verb. Choice (A) is singular. Choice (C) is the infinitive. Choice (D) is the gerund or the present participle form.

112. **(D)** *But* indicates a contrast between items and is used as a conjunction to introduce a clause. Choice (A) is not a conjunction. Choice (B) indicates a choice between

items. Choice (C) eliminates both items.

113. **(A)** Adverbs of definite frequency, such as *every day*, can occur at the end of a sentence. Choices (B), (C), and (D) are adverbs of indefinite frequency.

114. **(C)** A relative clause indicating possession begins with *whose*. Choice (A) is a relative pronoun but it does not indicate possession. Choices (B) and (D) are not relative pronouns.

115. **(B)** *Because* indicates a cause and effect and is used as a conjunction to introduce a clause. Choice (A) indicates possibility. Choice (C) indicates unexpected result. Choice (D) indicates location.

116. **(A)** Non-count nouns do not use an indefinite article. Choice (B) uses the indefinite article. Choice (C) uses the definite article, which is not appropriate here. Choice (D) uses an expression of quantity.

117. **(C)** Comparisons of more than two things require *the* and the superlative form. Choice (A) is the simple form of the adjective. Choice (B) is an equal comparison. Choice (D) is the comparative form.

118. **(B)** Items joined by *and* must have the same form; both *learning* and *improving* are gerunds. Choices (A), (C), and (D) do not match *learning*.

119. **(C)** Relative clauses referring to people begin with *who*. Choices (A) and (B) are not relative pronouns. Choice (D) is used when the objective case of the relative pronoun is required.

120. **(A)** The *statement* is affecting the members; use the present participle. Choice (B) is the past participle. Choice (C) is the simple form of the verb. Choice (D) is the past perfect.

121. **(D)** The comparison of two things requires the comparative form and *than*. Choice (A) uses the superlative *most*. Choices (B) and (C) are incorrect equal comparisons.

122. **(B)** An action that begins in the past and continues in the present requires the present perfect. Choice (A) is the present tense and is plural in number. Choice (C) is the past perfect. Choice (D) is the present continuous.

123. **(A)** Equal comparisons require *as* on both sides of the adjective. Choices (B) and (C) are incorrect comparative forms. Choice (D) is an incorrect superlative form.

124. **(D)** An action that interrupts a past continuous action requires the past tense. Choice (A) is the present tense. Choice (B) is the past perfect. Choice (C) is the present continuous.

125. **(C)** *Production* is the required noun form. Choice (A) is the simple form of the verb. Choice (B) is the gerund or present participle form. Choice (D) is an adjective.

126. **(A)** The causative verb *suggest* is followed by the gerund. Choice (B) is the infinitive. Choice (C) is the future. Choice (D) is a future form with *going to*.

127. **(B)** A continuous action that starts in the past and continues in the present requires the present perfect continuous. Choice (A) is the present continuous. Choice (C) is the future. Choice (D) is the past perfect.

128. **(D)** The causative verb *forced* is followed by the infinitive. Choice (A) is the gerund or present participle form. Choice (B) is the simple form of the verb. Choice (C) is the present tense.

129. **(C)** The preposition *with* indicates association with something. Choice (A) means in place of or on behalf of. Choice (B) indicates direction toward a place. Choice (D) indicates representation by someone.

130. **(A)** The future tense in a real condition requires the present tense in the *if* clause. Choice (B) is the past tense. Choice (C) is the future tense. Choice (D) is the present perfect.

131. **(D)** An action that happens before a future action requires the future perfect. Choice (A) is the present tense. Choice (B) is the past tense. Choice (C) is the present perfect.

132. **(B)** The subject *bags* requires a plural verb. Choices (A), (C), and (D) are singular.

133. **(C)** *In spite of* indicates an unexpected result. Choices (A), (B), and (D) indicate cause and effect.

134. **(A)** A comparison between two things requires the comparative form and *than*. Choices (B) and (C) are not logical in this context. Choice (D) is an incorrect superlative comparison.

135. **(B)** *While* means *during the time when*. Choices (A) and (C) are prepositions and cannot be followed by a clause. Choice (D) is not logical.

136. **(A)** *Not only … but also* is a paired conjunction. Choices (B), (C), and (D) are not the proper form for the second element in the pair.

137. **(C)** *Damaged* refers to things. Choices (A), (B), and (D) refer to people.

138. **(A)** *Is* is in the present tense and, along with *whenever*, suggests habitual action. The present tense *ask* conveys habitual action. Choice (B) is the present tense, but is third person and cannot be used with *I*. Choice (C) is the simple past tense. Choice (D) is the past perfect.

139. **(A)** *And* joins items. Choice (B) contrasts items. Choice (C) offers a choice between items. Choice (D) eliminates both items.

140. **(B)** Adverbs of definite frequency can appear at the beginning of the sentence. Choices (A), (C), and (D) are adverbs of indefinite frequency and appear in the middle of the sentence.

Part VI

141. **(A)** *The store's annual* should be followed by the noun *sale*. Choice (B) is a correct article. Choice (C) is a correct preposition. Choice (D) is a correct adverb.

142. **(B)** The *survey* affected the results; use *unexpected*. Choice (A) is a correct conjunction. Choice (C) is a correct article. Choice (D) is a correct infinitive.

143. **(C)** *The* should be followed by a noun; in this case *simplicity*. Choice (A) is a correct article. Choice (B) is a correct verb. Choice (D) is a correct preposition.

144. **(B)** Action beginning in the past and continuing in the present requires the present perfect *has been located*. Choice (A) is a correct possessive form. Choices (C) and (D) are correct prepositions.

145. **(D)** Items joined by *and* should have the same grammatical form: *quiet and peaceful*. Choice (A) is a correct preposition. Choice (B) is a correct article. Choice (C) is a correct verb.

146. **(A)** *New* begins with a consonant; use *a*; *A new account representative*. Choice (B) is a correct relative pronoun. Choices (C) and (D) are correct verbs.

147. **(D)** Relative clauses referring to people begin with *who*: *who should get the promotion*. Choice (A) is a correct conjunction. Choice (B) is a correct adjective. Choice (C) is a correct infinitive.

148. **(C)** Equal comparisons require *as* on both sides of the adjective: *twice as large as*. Choice (A) is a correct article. Choice (B) is a correct verb. Choice (D) is a correct preposition.

149. **(B)** Adverbs of indefinite frequency can appear between the auxiliary and the main verb: *has rarely made*. Choice (A) is a correct auxiliary. Choices (C) and (D) are correct prepositions.

150. **(C)** The subject *sales representatives* requires a plural verb: *have received*. Choice (A) is a correct article. Choice (B) is a correct preposition. Choice (D) is a correct superlative.

151. **(D)** The infinitive is formed with the simple form of the verb *to reward*. Choice (A) is a correct conjunction. Choice (B) is a correct article. Choice (C) is a correct verb.

152. **(A)** Relative clauses expressing possession begin with *whose*: *That building, whose architect*. Choices (B) and (C) are correct verbs. Choice (D) is a correct preposition.

153. **(B)** Adverbs of indefinite frequency may appear after a form of *be*: *There are never any tables*. Choice (A) is a correct verb. Choice (C) is a correct conjunction. Choice (D) is a correct preposition.

154. **(B)** Food is usually considered non-countable; no article is necessary: *decided to order lamb*. Choice (A) is a correct infinitive. Choice (C) is a correct conjunction. Choice (D) is a correct verb.

155. **(B)** The causative verb *suggest* is followed by the simple form when it causes someone else to do something: *the client suggested that we get*. Choice (A) is a correct adjective. Choice (C) is a correct conjunction. Choice (D) is a correct verb.

156. **(A)** *Police* is considered plural and requires a plural verb: *The police are closing*. Choice (B) is a correct conjunction. Choice (C) is a correct verb. Choice (D) is a correct adjective.

157. **(C)** The causative verb *forbids* is followed by the infinitive *to go*. Choice (A) is a correct non-count noun. Choice (B) is a correct article. Choice (D) is a correct preposition.

158. **(B)** *As* implies that the receptionist pretended to be Ms. Goa; use *for* meaning *in place of*: *took a message for Ms. Goa*. Choice (A) is a correct verb. Choice (C) is a correct pronoun. Choice (D) is a correct preposition.

159. **(A)** Since you know specifically which company you are talking about, use *the*: *The company*. Choice (B) is a correct relative pronoun. Choice (C) is a correct verb. Choice (D) is a correct preposition.

160. **(C)** The conjunction *while* should introduce a clause; use the preposition *during*. Choice (A) is a correct conjunction. Choice (B) is a correct adjective. Choice (D) is a correct present participle.

Part VII

161. **(D)** It warns that items may sell quickly. Choices (A), (B), and (C) are not mentioned.

162. **(A)** They should shop early, so previous customers will not buy what they want. Choices (B), (C), and (D) are not consistent with the information given.

163. **(B)** The bottle has a child-resistant cap. Choices (A), (C), and (D) are contradicted by *child-resistant*.

164. **(C)** The instructions say to press down. Choices (A) and (B) are not mentioned. Choice (D) is the opposite of *press downward*.

165. **(C)** The letter acknowledges conference registration. Choices (A), (B), and (D) are not mentioned.

166. **(B)** A brochure is enclosed. Choices (A) and (D) are not logical if she has already registered for the conference. Choice (C) is not mentioned.

167. **(A)** The letter says to contact the conference coordinator. Choice (B) wrote the letter. Choice (C) is where Le Ziaolie works. Choice (D) is not mentioned.

168. **(D)** It offers a range of shopper services. Choices (A), (B), and (C) are not mentioned.

169. **(B)** It is located by the Gourmet Food Shop.

Choices (A), (C), and (D) may have concierge desks of their own, but are not mentioned.

170. **(D)** There are direct phone lines to the Concierge Desk at the directory maps in the mall. Choices (A), (B), and (C) are not mentioned.

171. **(C)** It discusses the paperless office. Choices (A) and (D) are mentioned but are not the focus of the article. Choice (B) is not mentioned.

172. **(A)** It was predicted when offices began to use computers. Choices (B), (C), and (D) are not mentioned.

173. **(C)** Documents are easy to prepare on a computer, so people print more. Choice (A) is a result, not a reason. Choice (B) is not mentioned. Choice (D) may be true but is not mentioned.

174. **(D)** People prefer paper, so there will probably always be paper in offices. Choices (A), (B), and (C) are not mentioned.

175. **(A)** Commuter flights have decreased. Choices (B), (C), and (D) are not mentioned.

176. **(B)** Commuter flights have been absorbed into the regular schedule. Choices (A), (C), and (D) are not mentioned.

177. **(D)** Larger planes can now fly into these airports. Choice (A) is not mentioned. Choice (B) may be true but is not mentioned. Choice (C) is not mentioned.

178. **(A)** It is more economical to fly one plane with more passengers. Choices (B), (C), and (D) are not mentioned.

179. **(B)** The article gives reasons why commuter flights have changed. Choices (A), (C), and (D) are not mentioned.

180. **(C)** They are returned because they do not fit. Choice (A) is not the most common reason. Choices (B) and (D) are not mentioned.

181. **(C)** Twenty-five percent of people do not like their gifts. Choices (A), (B), and (D) are contradicted by *25%*.

182. **(B)** Only 5% of items are returned because they are damaged. Choices (A), (C), and (D) are not mentioned.

183. **(C)** The ad encourages people to stay in the District. Choices (A), (B), and (D) are related ideas but not the focus of the ad.

184. **(D)** The houses and gardens create a relaxing atmosphere. Choices (A), (B), and (C) are not mentioned.

185. **(B)** Business travelers can get downtown easily. Choice (A) is one way to get downtown. Choice (C) is contradicted by *houses and gardens*. Choice (D) is not mentioned.

186. **(A)** They can call for a visitor's guide. Choices (B) and (C) are not logical. Choice (D) is not mentioned.

187. **(D)** Construction industry figures dropped. Choices (A), (B), and (C) are not mentioned.

188. **(C)** The government produced the report. Choices (A), (B), and (D) are contradicted by *according to a government report*.

189. **(D)** New construction accounted for most of the decrease. Choices (A), (B), and (C) are not mentioned.

190. **(A)** They are offering a publication. Choices (B), (C), and (D) are not mentioned.

191. **(C)** Insurance is not mentioned. Choices (A), (B), and (D) are explicitly mentioned.

192. **(D)** The minimum order is 50 copies. Choices (A), (B), and (C) are contradicted by *50 copies*.

193. **(C)** People are concerned about their pets' diets. Choices (A), (B), and (D) are not the focus of the article.

194. **(B)** At gourmet food stores. Choices (A), (C), and (D) are not mentioned.

195. **(A)** They are supposed to be healthier. Choices (B), (C), and (D) are not mentioned.

196. **(D)** Vegetarian foods are not mentioned. Choices (A), (B), and (C) are explicitly mentioned.

197. **(B)** The article discusses moveable partitions. Choices (A), (C), and (D) are not mentioned.

198. **(C)** You can create space by moving the partitions. Choices (A), (B), and (D) are not mentioned.

199. **(D)** You can change the space for different office projects. Choices (A) and (C) are not mentioned. Choice (B) may be true but is not a reason.

200. **(A)** They provide privacy by absorbing sound. Choices (B), (C), and (D) describe the look of the partitions, which is not discussed in the article.

Practice Test 3

Part I

1. **(B)** There are people seated around a table and the woman's gesture indicates that she is talking; they are probably having a meeting. Choice (A) is incorrect because they are at a table, but are not eating. Choice (C) is incorrect because they are sitting, not walking. Choice (D) is incorrect because the men are listening to the woman, not a radio.

2. **(D)** The cockpit and the woman's uniform indicate that she is a pilot. Choice (A) confuses the similar sound *train* with *plane* and the related word *station* with *airport*. Choice (B) confuses the similar sound *instruments* with *instrument panel*. Choice (C) uses the related words *passenger* and *first class*, but incorrectly identifies the actor and her location.

3. **(C)** The nurse is injecting the patient lying in the bed. Choice (A) is incorrect because the nurse is injecting the patient, not making the bed. Choice (B) confuses the similar sound *purse* with *nurse*. Choice (D) confuses the similar sound *thick* with *sick*.

4. **(A)** The men are using microscopes. Choice (B) is incorrect because they are looking at specimens, not looking for glasses. Choice (C) confuses the similar sounds *mathematician* with *technician* and *division* with *vision*. Choice (D) is incorrect because this laboratory is for scientific research, not studying languages.

5. **(B)** The people are in a hotel lobby; the couple at the reception desk is probably checking in. Choice (A) incorrectly identifies the location of the palm tree; the tree is in the lobby, not by the beach. Choice (C) is incorrect because the man is carrying, not buying, a briefcase. Choice (D) is incorrect because there is one person behind the counter.

6. **(D)** The people are sitting at their desks working on their computers. Choice (A) confuses the similar sound *commuters* with *computers*. Choice (B) identifies an incorrect action; the employees are working, not having tea. Choice (C) uses the related word *equipment*, but there is no repair person or repair work shown in the picture.

7. **(C)** The man's hugging the girl and holding the baby indicate that the man is probably the children's father. There is a birthday cake with many candles on the table in front of them. Choice (A) confuses the similar word *mother* (female) with *father* (male). Choice (B) is incorrect because the presence of the cake indicates that they *do* celebrate birthdays. Choice (D) uses the related words *baker* and *pastry*, but incorrectly identifies the actor and the action.

8. **(A)** A man is pointing to an open brochure while talking to the man next to him. The medication, scale, and the fact that one of the men is wearing a white lab coat indicate that they are probably in a pharmacy. Choice (B) confuses the similar sound *door*

with *drawer.* Choice (C) is incorrect because one of the men is wearing a suit. Choice (D) uses the related word *prescription,* but a prescription cannot be identified in the picture.

9. **(C)** The people are sitting in a lounge. Choice (A) confuses the similar sound *writing for* with *waiting for* and incorrectly describes the action; some are *reading,* not *writing* magazines. Choice (B) confuses the similar sound *cherries* with *chairs.* Choice (D) is incorrect because some are *drinking,* not *brewing* coffee.

10. **(C)** You can assume from the context that the children raising their hands are students. Choice (A) is incorrect because they are *raising their hands,* not *waving handkerchiefs.* Choice (B) is incorrect because the classroom is *full,* not *empty.* Choice (D) uses the related words *lectern* and *lecture hall;* the sentence may be true, but a speaker cannot be seen in the picture.

11. **(D)** The woman is holding up a circuit board. Choice (A) uses the related word *circuit,* but incorrectly identifies the picture. Choice (B) is incorrect because the factory makes *circuit boards,* not *bread boards.* Choice (C) confuses the similar sound *circus* with *circuits.*

12. **(A)** You can assume from the context that they are wearing clothing to protect them from the cold. Choice (B) confuses the related word *pipe* with *pipeline.* Choice (C) incorrectly describes the action; the men are *laying pipe,* not *shoveling snow.* Choice (D) confuses *laying in the sand* with *laying pipe in the snow.*

13. **(A)** The man is looking at two computer monitors. Choice (B) assumes the man working with data is an engineer, but the sentence implies a *train* engineer. Choice (C) confuses the similar sounds *this play* with *display* and *too* with *two.* Choice (D) confuses *window screens* with *computer screens.*

14. **(A)** The children are running through the woods. Choice (B) uses a different definition of *running.* Choice (C) incorrectly identifies the scenery. Choice (D) incorrectly identifies the action of the children and confuses the similar sound *rest* with *forest.*

15. **(A)** The woman is repairing a telephone or an electric line. Choice (B) is incorrect because she is climbing a *pole,* not a *tree.* Choice (C) incorrectly identifies her location; she is at the top of a pole, not on top of a building. Choice (D) uses the related word *engineer;* she may be working to repair the electricity, but, since there is no light switch shown, she is not turning on the lights.

16. **(C)** People are browsing at a magazine shop. One woman is looking through a magazine. Choice (A) incorrectly identifies the location; they are standing, but not by a fountain. Choice (B) confuses the similar sounds *books* with *look* and *cartons* with *cartoons;* Choice (B) is incorrect because although there are books on the floor, they are not in cartons. Choice (D) uses the related word *story,* but confuses the similar sound *journalist* with *journal.*

17. **(B)** The putting green and the man holding a club and a flag above a hole indicate that he is a golfer. Choice (A) is incorrect because the word *team* signifies a number of people, but there is *only one* man on the green, and he is staying, not leaving. Choice (C) incorrectly identifies the number of people shown in the picture. Choice (D) confuses the similar sound *tea* with *tee.*

18. **(A)** The man is looking at a map (plan of the city or Metro) on the building. Choice (B) uses the related word *French,* but incorrectly identifies the action. Choice (C) confuses the similar sound *resign* with *sign.* Choice (D) confuses the similar sound *nap* with *map.*

19. **(D)** Three women are talking on a moving stairway. Choice (A) is incorrect because

they are in a tunnel, not building a tunnel. Choice (B) incorrectly describes the action. Choice (C) is incorrect because *only one* of the women is wearing glasses.

20. **(A)** The man is serving drinks on an airplane. Choice (B) is incorrect because if the plane was landing, the drink cart would not be permitted in the aisle. Choice (C) incorrectly identifies the location; this is a plane, not a restaurant. Choice (D) uses the related action *checking the passengers*, but the man is a *flight attendant*, not a *security agent*.

Part II

21. **(A)** *No, thanks* is a polite answer to the question. Choice (B) confuses the similar sound *desert* with *dessert*. Choice (C) confuses the similar sound *men* with *menu*.

22. **(B)** *We are going hiking* answers *what are you going to do*. Choice (A) answers *when*. Choice (C) uses an incorrect verb tense and confuses the similar sounds *weekend* and *ended last week*.

23. **(C)** *No, there isn't* is the best response to the question. Choice (A) confuses the related word *stationery store* with *grocery store*. Choice (B) confuses *you're excused* with *excuse me* and is an inappropriate response.

24. **(B)** This statement provides a logical *yes/no* response. Choice (A) repeats the word *can* and gives a *yes/no* response, but the question does not ask about advertising. Choice (C) confuses the related word *ended* (v) and *end* (n) and the similar sounds *fiscal* and *finish*.

25. **(A)** This statement is the only logical *yes/no* response. Choice (B) confuses the related words *check* (n) and *check* (v). Choice (C) uses the related word *room* and confuses the related word *hotel* with *housekeeping*.

26. **(B)** *At* signifies a specific time. Choice (A) gives a response in the future tense. Choice (C) gives a duration of time.

27. **(C)** *Not now ...* is the best response to the question. Choice (A) confuses *sitting posture* with *position*. (B) confuses *watch* with part *time*.

28. **(C)** This is the only response that gives a duration of time. Choice (A) confuses *inches* with *length* (of time). Choice (B) confuses *short cut* with *length* (of time).

29. **(A)** This is the only response that logically answers with a location. Choice (B) confuses the related word *light switch* with *light bulb* and answers *where* but in the wrong context. Choice (C) confuses *it* (singular) with *light bulbs* (plural) and *put it on* (write) and *put*.

30. **(C)** *When will* requires a future tense answer. Choice (A) is a past tense response. Choice (B) confuses the similar sound *sale* with *sail*.

31. **(B)** *Yes, on your desk* is a logical *yes/no* response. Choice (A) confuses the similar sound *no one* with *there are none*. Choice (C) confuses the similar sound *mess* with *messages*.

32. **(C)** *Yes, certainly* is a polite response to the question *could you*. Choice (A) confuses the related word *connection* (n) with *connect* (v). Choice (B) confuses *clean your room* with *connect me with Room Service*.

33. **(B)** *One* refers to a *mechanic*. Choice (A) confuses the related word *gas* with *car*. Choice (C) confuses *look at* with *look for* and *parking garage* with *mechanic*.

34. **(A)** *Expect me next Friday* answers *when*. Choice (B) gives an incorrect habitual response to a question in the future tense. Choice (C) confuses *live downtown* with *get to town*.

35. **(A)** *Once a day* is a habitual answer to *how often*. Choice (B) incorrectly answers in the past tense. Choice (C) incorrectly answers in the future tense.

36. **(C)** This is the only answer that gives a *yes/no* response. Choice (A) confuses *well*

(designed) with *well* (health). Choice (B) confuses the similar sound *resigned* with *designed*.

37. **(B)** The assistant manager is in the lobby. Choice (A) confuses the similar sound *hobby* with *lobby*. Choice (C) confuses *duty-free* (tax-free) with *on duty*.

38. **(C)** *About* signifies a duration of time and answers *how long* (time). Choice (A) confuses how long the flight takes with how long the ride to the airport takes. Choice (B) uses the related word *airport*, but answers *how* not *how long*.

39. **(A)** *Of course* is a polite response to the question. Choice (B) is incorrect because the question asks can *you*, not could *he*, look at it. Choice (C) confuses the related words *post office* and *letter* and the similar sound *opposite* with *opinion*.

40. **(B)** This choice gives directions to the art museum. Choice (A) has the related word *painting* but confuses *white* with *which* and *which way* with *hallway*. Choice (C) confuses the similar sound *see them* with *museum*.

41. **(C)** This choice mentions the liking for a particular type of food. Choice (A) confuses the antonym *hate* with *like*. Choice (B) uses the related word *restaurant*, but the question does not ask about restaurants.

42. **(A)** If you hurt your ankle, you would probably be walking differently. Choice (B) confuses *correct errors* with *wrong*. Choice (C) confuses the antonyms *right* and *wrong*.

43. **(C)** *Smoke-free* is the same as *non-smoking*. Choice (A) does not answer the question. Choice (B) is incorrect because the person wants a non-smoking room, and therefore, probably does not smoke.

44. **(A)** As soon as the fax comes, send it to the cabin. Choice (B) confuses the similar sound *facts* with *fax*. Choice (C) confuses *cab* (taxi) with *cabin*.

45. **(C)** *Of course* is a polite response to the question. Choice (A) confuses the related words *used to* and *use*. Choice (B) confuses *firm* with *software*.

46. **(B)** This choice gives a reason for her not coming. Choice (A) does not answer the question *why*. Choice (C) confuses the subject *he* with *she*.

47. **(C)** *No, I have a house* is a logical answer to the question *do you have*. Choice (A) confuses the related word *put back* with *apart*(ment). Choice (B) is incorrect because the question asks about *you*, not *her*, and confuses *lives* with *have*.

48. **(B)** *Like* means the same as *prefer*. Football and golf are sports. Choice (A) confuses the similar sound *resorts* with *sports*. Choice (C) has the related word *tennis shoes*, but does not answer the question posed.

49. **(A)** *Candidate* has the same meaning as *applicant*. Choice (B) confuses *hurt* with *hire*. Choice (C) confuses the similar sounds *can't … date* and *candidate*.

50. **(B)** This choice gives a specific arrival time. Choice (A) has the related word *flight*, but is incorrect because the question does not ask about the length of the flight. Choice (C) has the related word *airport*, but is not a logical response.

Part III

51. **(C)** *Some other time* is the same as *another time*. Choice (A) is not mentioned. Choice (B) prevents her from going today. Choice (D) indicates a place, not a time.

52. **(A)** Shirts are usually starched at the cleaners. Choices (B) is not a logical location. Choice (C) confuses the related word *clothing* with *shirts*. Choice (D) confuses the related word *hangars* (for planes) with *hangers* (for shirts).

53. **(D)** The waiter closed the curtains. Choice (A) has the related word *lights*. Choice (B) is not mentioned. Choice (C) is the woman's

original request.

54. **(B)** The clerk warns that all hotels are probably full. Choice (A) is not mentioned. Choice (C) confuses the words *convenient* and *convention*. Choice (D) is contradicted by *the other hotels*.

55. **(A)** He doesn't know about the reduce button on the copier. Choice (B) is incorrect because if he knows it won't fit on one page, he must have made a copy already. Choice (C) is a possible result, but not the problem. Choice (D) is contradicted by *the print is still large enough to read*.

56. **(B)** The mechanic will give the man a call. Choices (A) and (C) are not mentioned. Choice (D) is a possible result of calling but not the intent.

57. **(D)** *Never makes time for his staff* means rarely available. Choices (A) and (B) are not mentioned. Choice (C) is a possible result of not being available.

58. **(C)** The store replaces the bad sweater with a good one, so the woman is exchanging the sweater. Choice (A) is not mentioned. Choice (B) is incorrect because she has already bought the sweater. Choice (D) has the related word *make*.

59. **(B)** A crowded office is probably too small. Choice (A) is not mentioned. Choice (C) is not a problem. Choice (D) confuses *chairs aren't comfortable* with *can't work comfortably*.

60. **(C)** She doesn't like commuting. Choice (A) confuses *stand up* with *cannot stand* (dislike). Choice (B) is possible but not mentioned. Choice (D) is incorrect because she does watch the news.

61. **(D)** They are trying to set up a meeting. Choice (A) is incorrect because the man has a doctor's appointment Thursday. Choice (B) is incorrect because the woman is meeting a client the next day. Choice (C) is not mentioned.

62. **(A)** The man wants to get something to eat.

Choice (B) is contradicted by his wanting something he can't make himself. Choice (C) is incorrect because he wants to eat before he goes home. Choice (D) is incorrect because it is already late.

63. **(B)** They are discussing his vacation. Choices (A), (C), and (D) are incorrect because they are all parts of his vacation.

64. **(D)** The best description is probably *good*. Choice (A) refers to the shop where the coffee was purchased. Choice (B) doesn't matter since the coffee tastes good. Choice (C) refers to the change from the coffee they usually have.

65. **(A)** She thinks they should be on their way. Choice (B) is not mentioned. Choice (C) is incorrect because she hopes there are NOT many pages. Choice (D) is incorrect because she does not want to wait.

66. **(C)** *Good grasp of detail* means *the ability to handle details*. Choice (A) confuses *eyesight* and *sightseeing*. Choice (B) confuses *good grasp* with *firm handshake*. Choice (D) confuses *confidence* and *conference*.

67. **(D)** A suitcase is a piece of luggage. Choice (A) confuses the similar sounds *carrier* and *carry*. Choice (B) confuses the weight of her suitcase with the man's weight. Choice (C) is not mentioned.

68. **(B)** *Someone to look at it* implies a doctor. Choice (A) has the related word *gloves* but is not mentioned. Choice (C) is *how* he hurt his hand. Choice (D) is not mentioned.

69. **(A)** *Entertain at home* means have parties or guests. Choices (B) and (C) are not possible in a small town. Choice (D) is what the man jokes he will have to do.

70. **(C)** She should get some rest. Choice (A) is contradicted by *take the day off*. Choice (B) is what she did during the night. Choice (D) confuses the meanings of *run*.

71. **(B)** *To practice* means *to do something a lot*. Choices (A), (C), and (D) are not

261

mentioned.

72. **(A)** He thinks writing about solutions will help people solve problems. Choice (B) is contradicted by *good news doesn't sell papers*. Choices (C) and (D) are not mentioned.

73. **(D)** She is going so she will catch on faster. Choice (A) is contradicted by *a little early for me to be giving advice*. Choice (B) confuses the many time references with *schedule*. Choice (C) confuses the related words *speed up* and *faster*.

74. **(D)** Editorial suggestions are suggestions for improving writing. Choice (A) is contradicted by *I couldn't understand it either*. Choices (B) and (C) are not mentioned.

75. **(C)** The man cannot find his guidebook. Choice (A) is incorrect because he can still tour the homes, but without his notes. Choice (B) is incorrect because guidebooks are available at the center. Choice (D) is incorrect because he might go to the Tourist Center.

76. **(A)** *Floods* suggests there was too much rain. Choice (B) is contradicted by *floods*. Choices (C) and (D) are not mentioned.

77. **(B)** She wants them faxed now. Choice (A) is contradicted by *I need them now*. Choices (C) and (D) are not mentioned.

78. **(C)** He hasn't left yet, so he can repack. Choice (A) would not solve the problem. Choices (C) and (D) are not mentioned.

79. **(B)** A receptionist works at the front desk. Choice (A) is incorrect because they do not have a receptionist, so she cannot be late. Choice (C) confuses the related phrase *delivery service*. Choice (D) is not mentioned.

80. **(D)** Words like *art tour, museum entrance*, and *galleries* indicate the place might be a museum. Choice (A) confuses the related words *shopping center* with *galleries* and *business*. Choice (B) confuses the related

phrase *office complex* with *business office*. Choice (C) confuses the related word *movie studio* with *Hollywood*.

Part IV

81. **(C)** You would hear the announcement at a train station. Choices (A), (B), and (D) are not consistent with the information given.

82. **(A)** The purpose was to report the change of track. Choices (B), (C), and (D) are not consistent with the information given.

83. **(D)** They reported that he was a police officer, but he was a firefighter. Choices (A), (B), and (C) are not named in this statement.

84. **(B)** They wanted to correct an error. Choice (A) is incorrect because the accident had been reported the day before. Choices (C) and (D) are not consistent with the information given.

85. **(B)** The advisory is for snow. Choices (A), (C), and (D) are not mentioned.

86. **(C)** They should prepare for bad driving conditions. Choices (A), (B), and (D) are not mentioned.

87. **(D)** The person is calling a cable TV service. Choices (A), (B), and (C) are not mentioned.

88. **(B)** No choice is mentioned for billing inquiries. Choices (A), (C), and (D) are all explicitly mentioned.

89. **(C)** If you stay on the line, a representative will answer. Choice (A) is not given as an option. Choices (B) and (D) refer to calling another company.

90. **(B)** The county is offering bags for leaf collection. Choice (A) is what people do with leaves before they put them in bags. Choice (C) is already a county service. Choice (D) is not mentioned.

91. **(D)** The leaves are turned into fertilizer. Choices (A), (B), and (C) are not consistent with the information given.

92. **(C)** Fertilizer is available to county residents. Choices (A), (B), and (D) are not consistent with the information given.

93. **(A)** The topic is food safety. Choice (B) is an example of where food must be kept safe. Choice (C) refers to picnics. Choice (D) is mentioned as a way to keep food safe.

94. **(D)** People should avoid eggs and other food that spoils easily. Choices (A), (B), and (C) are not mentioned.

95. **(B)** You should keep food cool by carrying it in a cooler. Choices (A), (C), and (D) will carry food but will not keep it safe.

96. **(A)** The announcement says the plane has been repaired. Choices (B), (C), and (D) are not mentioned.

97. **(C)** They will board by zone. Choices (A) and (B) are not mentioned. Choice (D) is the typical method of boarding.

98. **(D)** Zone boarding is faster. Choices (A), (B), and (C) are not mentioned.

99. **(A)** *Immediately* means *right away*. Choice (B) is incorrect because the track has just been cleared. Choices (C) and (D) are not consistent with the information given.

100. **(B)** The trains will be filled with passengers from earlier stations. Choices (A), (C), and (D) are not mentioned.

Part V

101. **(A)** You usually read a manual before operating any equipment. *Before* is a logical conjunction. Choices (B), (C), and (D) are grammatically possible, but they are not logical.

102. **(D)** *Police* is considered plural and requires the plural verb *patrol*. Choice (A) is the infinitive. Choice (B) is the gerund or the present participle form. Choice (C) is the singular form.

103. **(B)** *Even though* joins the contrasting ideas *I am tired* and *I will work late*. Choice (A) indicates a contrast between items. Choice

(C) indicates a cause and effect relationship. Choice (D) indicates cause and effect or result.

104. **(C)** A past action interrupted by another past action requires the past continuous form. Choice (A) is the simple past tense. Choice (B) is the plural form of the past continuous. Choice (D) is the present perfect.

105. **(B)** There is an indirect object *assistant* to whom something was told. The verb *told* does not need a preposition. Choice (A) would be followed by what is said, not the person it is said to: *The boss said there would be changes.* Choices (C) and (D) require a prepositional phrase to express the person told: *said to his assistant, explained to his assistant.*

106. **(D)** The preposition *in* indicates location within. Choice (A) indicates a specific time. Choice (B) indicates possession. Choice (C) indicates a location outside of.

107. **(A)** The causative verb *demand* requires the simple form of the verb. Choice (B) is the future. Choice (C) is the infinitive. Choice (D) is the gerund or the present participle form.

108. **(C)** *Neither ... nor* is a paired conjunction. Choices (A), (B), and (D) are not correct for the second member of the pair.

109. **(B)** Adverbs of definite frequency such as *twice a month* can appear at the end of the sentence. Choices (A), (C), and (D) are adverbs of indefinite frequency which do not appear at the end of a sentence.

110. **(A)** A past action that occurs before a previous past action requires the past perfect. Choice (B) is present perfect. Choice (C) is the past tense. Choice (D) is the present tense.

111. **(D)** Comparisons among more than two things require *the* and the superlative form of the adjective. Choice (A) is an equal comparison. Choice (B) is a comparative form.

Choice (C) is an incorrect superlative.

112. **(B)** The conjunction *but* contrasts the two items *poured water but forgot menus*. The waiter did one thing, but did not do another. Choice (A) joins items. Choice (C) offers a choice between items. Choice (D) eliminates both items.

113. **(C)** The plural subject *customers* requires the plural verb *like*. Choice (A) is the singular form of the present perfect. Choice (B) is the gerund or present participle form. Choice (D) is the singular present tense.

114. **(A)** Equal comparisons require *as* on both sides of the adverb. Choice (B) uses only one *as*. Choices (C) and (D) are incorrect comparative forms.

115. **(D)** The second clause needs a subject which is the noun form *entertainment*. Choices (A) and (B) are verbs. Choice (C) is the gerund or the present participle form.

116. **(C)** The causative verb *need* is followed by the infinitive. Choice (A) is the present tense. Choice (B) is the future. Choice (D) is the simple form of the verb.

117. **(B)** Someone else finished the draft; use the past participle *completed*. Choice (A) means *participated in a contest*. Choice (C) means *capable*. Choice (D) means *expressed dissatisfaction*.

118. **(A)** The preposition *during* means the same as the conjunction *while*. Choices (B) and (C) are conjunctions and must introduce clauses, rather than precede nouns. Choice (D) is not logical.

119. **(C)** The conjunction *or* offers a choice between the two items. Stamps are available at either the post office or a vending machine. Choices (A) and (D) eliminate both items. Choice (B) contrasts items.

120. **(D)** An action that continues to a point in the future requires the future perfect continuous. Choice (A) is the future tense. Choice (B) is the present perfect. Choice

(C) is the present perfect continuous.

121. **(C)** The blank requires a verb. Since the subject is unstated *you*, you should use the imperative form. Choice (A) is the past tense. Choice (B) is the present tense. Choice (D) is the future tense.

122. **(B)** *On* is used with days of the week. Choice (A) indicates location. Choice (C) indicates a position on top of something and is not used with days of the week. Choice (D) indicates association.

123. **(A)** A present tense in the *if* clause of a real condition requires the present, future, or imperative in the remaining clause. Choice (B) is the past tense. Choice (C) is the present perfect. Choice (D) is the past perfect.

124. **(D)** The newspaper article caused the confusion; therefore you should use the present participle as an adjective. Choice (A) is the simple form of the verb. Choice (B) is the infinitive. Choice (C) is the past participle.

125. **(C)** A past action that is interrupted by another past action requires the past perfect. Choice (A) is the past tense. Choice (B) is the present perfect. Choice (D) is the present.

126. **(B)** The preposition *to* indicates the direction toward a place. Choice (A) means concerning. Choice (C) means beneath. Choice (D) indicates possession.

127. **(A)** The sentence has a subject but no verb. The blank requires the simple present tense. Choice (B) is the gerund or the present participle form. Choice (C) is an adjective. Choice (D) is a noun.

128. **(C)** A *check* is a note of payment. Choice (A) is what one pays. Choice (B) refers to the money paid. Choice (D) means the amount required to make the figures agree.

129. **(D)** The present perfect in the remaining clause of an unreal condition requires the

past perfect in the *if* clause. Choice (A) is the present perfect. Choice (B) is the past. Choice (C) is the future.

130. **(A)** *Preserve* means *keep* or *continue*. Choice (B) means to establish in advance. Choice (C) means to be worthy of. Choice (D) means to persist.

131. **(B)** *Unless* indicates an exception or contrast. Choices (A), (C), and (D) are not logical in the sentence.

132. **(C)** Relative clauses referring to people begin with *who*. Choices (A) and (B) are not relative pronouns. Choice (D) does not refer to people.

133. **(D)** *Borrow* means to temporarily use something belonging to someone else. Choices (A) and (C) mean to let someone borrow something. Choice (B) is the past participle of *send*.

134. **(B)** The verb *suggest* is followed by the gerund or present participle form. Choice (A) is the simple form of the verb. Choice (C) is the infinitive. Choice (D) is the future.

135. **(D)** Adverbs of definite frequency may appear at the beginning of the sentence. Choices (A), (B), and (C) are adverbs of indefinite frequency and do not appear at the beginning or end of a sentence.

136. **(A)** An action that starts in the past and continues in the present requires the present perfect *has answered*. Choices (B), (C), and (D) are not logical in the sentence.

137. **(C)** Comparisons of more than two things require *the* and the superlative form. Choice (A) is the comparative form. Choice (B) is an incorrect superlative. Choice (D) is an equal comparison.

138. **(B)** Non-restrictive relative clauses referring to things are introduced by *which*. Choice (A) is not used with non-restrictive relative clauses. Choice (C) is not a relative pronoun. Choice (D) is possessive.

139. **(A)** *And* joins items in a list. Choice (B) eliminates all items. Choice (C) offers a choice between items. Choice (D) contrasts items.

140. **(D)** The verb *encourage* requires the infinitive. Choice (A) is the singular present tense. Choice (B) is the gerund or the present participle form. Choice (C) is the simple form of the verb.

Part VI

141. **(B)** Items joined by *and* must have the same grammatical form: *checked and verified*. Choice (A) is a correct gerund. Choices (C) and (D) are correct prepositions.

142. **(B)** The noun form *conclusion* is the object of the preposition *to*. Choice (A) is a correct article. Choice (C) is a correct relative pronoun. Choice (D) is a correct verb.

143. **(C)** Comparisons among more than two things require *the* and the superlative: *the most comprehensive*. Choices (A) and (D) are correct prepositions. Choice (B) is a correct conjunction.

144. **(A)** Adverbs of indefinite frequency can appear between the auxiliary and main verb: *Ms. Mandia had scarcely gotten*. Choice (B) is a correct preposition. Choice (C) is a correct conjunction. Choice (D) is a correct verb.

145. **(D)** *Both ... and* is a paired conjunction. Choice (A) is a correct article. Choice (B) is a correct noun. Choice (C) is a correct verb.

146. **(B)** Adverbs of indefinite frequency can appear after a form of *be*: *There is still time*. Choice (A) is a correct verb. Choice (C) is a correct conjunction. Choice (D) is a correct verb.

147. **(C)** The verb *consider* requires a following gerund: *seeking*. Choice (A) is a correct relative pronoun. Choice (B) is a correct preposition. Choice (D) is a correct noun.

148. **(A)** The plural subject *people* requires a plural verb *are*. Choice (B) is a correct adverb. Choice (C) is a correct gerund. Choice (D) is a correct preposition.

149. **(A)** A noun follows the article *the*; use the word *rise*. Choice (B) is a correct noun. Choice (C) is a correct adverb. Choice (D) is a correct infinitive.

150. **(C)** Food is considered non-count so no article is necessary; use *fish*. Choice (A) is a correct adverb. Choice (B) is a correct verb. Choice (D) is a correct noun.

151. **(D)** The applicant may or may not get the job; use *whether* or *if*. Choice (A) is a correct article. Choices (B) and (C) are correct verbs.

152. **(A)** Relative clauses referring to things begin with *which* or *that*. Choice (B) is a correct adverb. Choice (C) is a correct verb. Choice (D) is a correct past participle.

153. **(A)** The verb *urge* is followed by the infinitive: *urged city officials to approve*. Choices (B) and (C) are correct nouns. Choice (D) is a correct article.

154. **(B)** The conjunction must show contrast. He did work hard, but he did not get a promotion; use *although* or *even though*. Choices (A) and (C) are correct verbs. Choice (D) is a correct preposition.

155. **(A)** The financial report caused the stockholders to feel reassured; use the present participle *the reassuring financial report*. Choice (B) is a correct adverb. Choice (C) is a correct comparison: *happier than*. Choice (D) is a correct verb.

156. **(A)** You know the specific captain you are talking about; use *the*. Choice (B) is a correct preposition. Choice (C) is a correct infinitive. Choice (D) is a correct adverb.

157. **(D)** *Food* is a non-count noun in this context; use the singular form. Choice (A) is a correct relative pronoun. Choice (B) is a correct verb. Choice (C) is a correct

conjunction.

158. **(B)** The present tense in the *if* clause of a real condition requires present, future or imperative in the result clause: *we have to cancel* or *we will have to cancel*. Choice (A) is a correct pronoun. Choice (C) is a correct article. Choice (D) is a correct past participle.

159. **(C)** The noun form *responsibility* follows the article *the*. Choice (A) is a correct verb. Choice (B) is a correct conjunction. Choice (D) is a correct relative pronoun.

160. **(B)** A comparison between two things requires the comparative form and *than*: *faster than*. Choice (A) is a correct past participle. Choice (C) is a correct gerund. Choice (D) is a correct article.

Part VII

161. **(B)** The notice is about training possibilities offered through the Professional Education Center. Choices (A), (C), and (D) are not consistent with the information given.

162. **(C)** People should contact the Program Director. Choice (A) confuses the name of the conference center. Choices (B) and (D) are possible, but not efficient contacts.

163. **(B)** A product that irritates eyes and skin is *harmful*. Choice (A) is not consistent with the information given. Choice (C) is not mentioned. Choice (D) is not consistent with the information given.

164. **(A)** Consumers should rinse their eyes with water for 15 minutes. Choices (B), (C), and (D) are contradicted by *rinse with water for 15 minutes*.

165. **(B)** The product should be stored with the lid tightly closed. Choices (A), (C), and (D) are not mentioned.

166. **(B)** If $30 covers the cost of two books, each book costs $15. Choice (A) is the cost of

shipping and handling. Choice (C) is the cost of both books. Choice (D) covers shipping, handling, and books.

167. **(D)** The books should be sent to Denmark. Choices (A), (B), and (C) refer to the bookstore itself.

168. **(A)** *Empowerment* characterizes the new style. Choice (B) characterizes the old style. Choices (C) and (D) are not management styles.

169. **(C)** Employees can make decisions. Choice (A) refers to the old management style. Choices (B) and (D) are not mentioned.

170. **(A)** Employees can take pride in their work. Choices (B), (C), and (D) are not mentioned.

171. **(D)** Complaints peak in January. Choices (A), (B), and (C) all have lower levels.

172. **(B)** The fewest complaints are received in April. Choices (A), (C), and (D) all have higher levels.

173. **(A)** This advice helps prevent repetitive motion injuries. Choices (B), (C), and (D) are not mentioned.

174. **(C)** It should be adjustable. Choices (A) and (B) are not mentioned. Choice (D) is contradicted by *adjustable*.

175. **(B)** It should be at elbow height. Choices (A), (C), and (D) are contradicted by *elbow height*.

176. **(D)** Your eyes and the computer screen should be at least 18 inches apart. Choices (A), (B), and (C) are not mentioned in terms of inches.

177. **(B)** People should work no more than two hours without a break. Choices (A), (C), and (D) are contradicted by *two hours*.

178. **(D)** People like cellular phones because they can take them anywhere. Choices (A), (B), and (C) are not mentioned.

179. **(D)** Some phones work in only one city. Choices (A), (B), and (C) are incorrect

because sound quality and price are not discussed.

180. **(A)** Get another cellular phone number in that city. Choices (B), (C), and (D) are not solutions that allow people to use a cellular phone.

181. **(D)** Cash payments cannot be sent with the registration card. Choices (A), (B), and (C) are all suggested methods of payment.

182. **(A)** A purchase order must be enclosed. Choices (B), (C), and (D) are not consistent with the information given.

183. **(A)** People should make the check payable to Computer Training Seminars, Inc. Choices (B), (C), and (D) are not logical.

184. **(C)** People are more likely to lose your bags when they have to change planes. Choice (A) is contradicted by *change planes*. Choices (B) and (D) are not mentioned.

185. **(C)** People should carry anything valuable on the plane with them. Choices (A) and (D) may be good ideas but are not mentioned. Choice (B) is not logical.

186. **(B)** A list of the contents can help identify the bag. Choices (A), (C), and (D) are not consistent with the information given.

187. **(B)** The article is about keeping statues clean. Choices (A), (C), and (D) are not the focus of the article.

188. **(D)** Each statue is cleaned once a year. Choices (A), (B), and (C) are not consistent with the information given.

189. **(C)** A special team of city employees cleans the statues. Choices (A), (B), and (D) are not consistent with the information given.

190. **(B)** The changes are due to construction at the terminal. Choices (A), (C), and (D) are not consistent with the information given.

191. **(D)** Drivers should park in the satellite lot. Choices (A) and (C) refer to short-term parking. Choice (B) is not logical.

192. **(C)** There are signs at the entrance to the airport. Choices (A), (B), and (D) may be true but are not mentioned.

193. **(A)** You should tell the waiter so he can adjust the service. Choices (B), (C), and (D) might be good ideas but are not mentioned.

194. **(D)** They will leave the salt out. Choices (A), (B), and (C) are not logical.

195. **(C)** You should first discuss it with the waiter. Choices (A) and (D) will not solve the problem. Choice (B) is a possibility after you have spoken with the waiter.

196. **(B)** You should be polite. Choices (A), (C), and (D) are not consistent with the information given.

197. **(C)** It is popular because of its versatility. Choices (A), (B), and (D) may be true but do not necessarily make it popular.

198. **(A)** Experts say most coffee is stale. Choices (B), (C), and (D) are not mentioned.

199. **(D)** Coffee stays fresh for about a month. Choices (A), (B), and (C) are contradicted by *about a month*.

200. **(B)** Gourmet coffee shops in urban areas are sources of fresh coffee. Choices (A) and (D) may also be sources but are not mentioned. Choice (C) is not consistent with the information given.

Answer Sheet – Practice Test 1

Mark all answers by completely filling in the circle. Mark only <u>one</u> answer for each question. If you change your mind about an answer after you have marked it on your answer sheet, completely erase your old answer and then mark your new answer. You must mark the answer sheet carefully so that the test-scoring machine can accurately record your test score.

Listening Section

Part I

1. Ⓐ Ⓑ Ⓒ Ⓓ
2. Ⓐ Ⓑ Ⓒ Ⓓ
3. Ⓐ Ⓑ Ⓒ Ⓓ
4. Ⓐ Ⓑ Ⓒ Ⓓ
5. Ⓐ Ⓑ Ⓒ Ⓓ
6. Ⓐ Ⓑ Ⓒ Ⓓ
7. Ⓐ Ⓑ Ⓒ Ⓓ
8. Ⓐ Ⓑ Ⓒ Ⓓ
9. Ⓐ Ⓑ Ⓒ Ⓓ
10. Ⓐ Ⓑ Ⓒ Ⓓ
11. Ⓐ Ⓑ Ⓒ Ⓓ
12. Ⓐ Ⓑ Ⓒ Ⓓ
13. Ⓐ Ⓑ Ⓒ Ⓓ
14. Ⓐ Ⓑ Ⓒ Ⓓ
15. Ⓐ Ⓑ Ⓒ Ⓓ
16. Ⓐ Ⓑ Ⓒ Ⓓ
17. Ⓐ Ⓑ Ⓒ Ⓓ
18. Ⓐ Ⓑ Ⓒ Ⓓ
19. Ⓐ Ⓑ Ⓒ Ⓓ
20. Ⓐ Ⓑ Ⓒ Ⓓ

Part II

21. Ⓐ Ⓑ Ⓒ
22. Ⓐ Ⓑ Ⓒ
23. Ⓐ Ⓑ Ⓒ
24. Ⓐ Ⓑ Ⓒ
25. Ⓐ Ⓑ Ⓒ
26. Ⓐ Ⓑ Ⓒ
27. Ⓐ Ⓑ Ⓒ
28. Ⓐ Ⓑ Ⓒ
29. Ⓐ Ⓑ Ⓒ
30. Ⓐ Ⓑ Ⓒ
31. Ⓐ Ⓑ Ⓒ
32. Ⓐ Ⓑ Ⓒ
33. Ⓐ Ⓑ Ⓒ
34. Ⓐ Ⓑ Ⓒ
35. Ⓐ Ⓑ Ⓒ
36. Ⓐ Ⓑ Ⓒ
37. Ⓐ Ⓑ Ⓒ
38. Ⓐ Ⓑ Ⓒ
39. Ⓐ Ⓑ Ⓒ
40. Ⓐ Ⓑ Ⓒ
41. Ⓐ Ⓑ Ⓒ
42. Ⓐ Ⓑ Ⓒ
43. Ⓐ Ⓑ Ⓒ
44. Ⓐ Ⓑ Ⓒ
45. Ⓐ Ⓑ Ⓒ
46. Ⓐ Ⓑ Ⓒ
47. Ⓐ Ⓑ Ⓒ
48. Ⓐ Ⓑ Ⓒ
49. Ⓐ Ⓑ Ⓒ
50. Ⓐ Ⓑ Ⓒ

Part III

51. Ⓐ Ⓑ Ⓒ Ⓓ
52. Ⓐ Ⓑ Ⓒ Ⓓ
53. Ⓐ Ⓑ Ⓒ Ⓓ
54. Ⓐ Ⓑ Ⓒ Ⓓ
55. Ⓐ Ⓑ Ⓒ Ⓓ
56. Ⓐ Ⓑ Ⓒ Ⓓ
57. Ⓐ Ⓑ Ⓒ Ⓓ
58. Ⓐ Ⓑ Ⓒ Ⓓ
59. Ⓐ Ⓑ Ⓒ Ⓓ
60. Ⓐ Ⓑ Ⓒ Ⓓ
61. Ⓐ Ⓑ Ⓒ Ⓓ
62. Ⓐ Ⓑ Ⓒ Ⓓ
63. Ⓐ Ⓑ Ⓒ Ⓓ
64. Ⓐ Ⓑ Ⓒ Ⓓ
65. Ⓐ Ⓑ Ⓒ Ⓓ
66. Ⓐ Ⓑ Ⓒ Ⓓ
67. Ⓐ Ⓑ Ⓒ Ⓓ
68. Ⓐ Ⓑ Ⓒ Ⓓ
69. Ⓐ Ⓑ Ⓒ Ⓓ
70. Ⓐ Ⓑ Ⓒ Ⓓ
71. Ⓐ Ⓑ Ⓒ Ⓓ
72. Ⓐ Ⓑ Ⓒ Ⓓ
73. Ⓐ Ⓑ Ⓒ Ⓓ
74. Ⓐ Ⓑ Ⓒ Ⓓ
75. Ⓐ Ⓑ Ⓒ Ⓓ
76. Ⓐ Ⓑ Ⓒ Ⓓ
77. Ⓐ Ⓑ Ⓒ Ⓓ
78. Ⓐ Ⓑ Ⓒ Ⓓ
79. Ⓐ Ⓑ Ⓒ Ⓓ
80. Ⓐ Ⓑ Ⓒ Ⓓ

Part IV

81. Ⓐ Ⓑ Ⓒ Ⓓ
82. Ⓐ Ⓑ Ⓒ Ⓓ
83. Ⓐ Ⓑ Ⓒ Ⓓ
84. Ⓐ Ⓑ Ⓒ Ⓓ
85. Ⓐ Ⓑ Ⓒ Ⓓ
86. Ⓐ Ⓑ Ⓒ Ⓓ
87. Ⓐ Ⓑ Ⓒ Ⓓ
88. Ⓐ Ⓑ Ⓒ Ⓓ
89. Ⓐ Ⓑ Ⓒ Ⓓ
90. Ⓐ Ⓑ Ⓒ Ⓓ
91. Ⓐ Ⓑ Ⓒ Ⓓ
92. Ⓐ Ⓑ Ⓒ Ⓓ
93. Ⓐ Ⓑ Ⓒ Ⓓ
94. Ⓐ Ⓑ Ⓒ Ⓓ
95. Ⓐ Ⓑ Ⓒ Ⓓ
96. Ⓐ Ⓑ Ⓒ Ⓓ
97. Ⓐ Ⓑ Ⓒ Ⓓ
98. Ⓐ Ⓑ Ⓒ Ⓓ
99. Ⓐ Ⓑ Ⓒ Ⓓ
100. Ⓐ Ⓑ Ⓒ Ⓓ

Reading Section

Part V

101. Ⓐ Ⓑ Ⓒ Ⓓ
102. Ⓐ Ⓑ Ⓒ Ⓓ
103. Ⓐ Ⓑ Ⓒ Ⓓ
104. Ⓐ Ⓑ Ⓒ Ⓓ
105. Ⓐ Ⓑ Ⓒ Ⓓ
106. Ⓐ Ⓑ Ⓒ Ⓓ
107. Ⓐ Ⓑ Ⓒ Ⓓ
108. Ⓐ Ⓑ Ⓒ Ⓓ
109. Ⓐ Ⓑ Ⓒ Ⓓ
110. Ⓐ Ⓑ Ⓒ Ⓓ
111. Ⓐ Ⓑ Ⓒ Ⓓ
112. Ⓐ Ⓑ Ⓒ Ⓓ
113. Ⓐ Ⓑ Ⓒ Ⓓ
114. Ⓐ Ⓑ Ⓒ Ⓓ
115. Ⓐ Ⓑ Ⓒ Ⓓ
116. Ⓐ Ⓑ Ⓒ Ⓓ
117. Ⓐ Ⓑ Ⓒ Ⓓ
118. Ⓐ Ⓑ Ⓒ Ⓓ
119. Ⓐ Ⓑ Ⓒ Ⓓ
120. Ⓐ Ⓑ Ⓒ Ⓓ
121. Ⓐ Ⓑ Ⓒ Ⓓ
122. Ⓐ Ⓑ Ⓒ Ⓓ
123. Ⓐ Ⓑ Ⓒ Ⓓ
124. Ⓐ Ⓑ Ⓒ Ⓓ
125. Ⓐ Ⓑ Ⓒ Ⓓ
126. Ⓐ Ⓑ Ⓒ Ⓓ
127. Ⓐ Ⓑ Ⓒ Ⓓ
128. Ⓐ Ⓑ Ⓒ Ⓓ
129. Ⓐ Ⓑ Ⓒ Ⓓ
130. Ⓐ Ⓑ Ⓒ Ⓓ
131. Ⓐ Ⓑ Ⓒ Ⓓ
132. Ⓐ Ⓑ Ⓒ Ⓓ
133. Ⓐ Ⓑ Ⓒ Ⓓ
134. Ⓐ Ⓑ Ⓒ Ⓓ
135. Ⓐ Ⓑ Ⓒ Ⓓ
136. Ⓐ Ⓑ Ⓒ Ⓓ
137. Ⓐ Ⓑ Ⓒ Ⓓ
138. Ⓐ Ⓑ Ⓒ Ⓓ
139. Ⓐ Ⓑ Ⓒ Ⓓ
140. Ⓐ Ⓑ Ⓒ Ⓓ

Part VI

141. Ⓐ Ⓑ Ⓒ Ⓓ
142. Ⓐ Ⓑ Ⓒ Ⓓ
143. Ⓐ Ⓑ Ⓒ Ⓓ
144. Ⓐ Ⓑ Ⓒ Ⓓ
145. Ⓐ Ⓑ Ⓒ Ⓓ
146. Ⓐ Ⓑ Ⓒ Ⓓ
147. Ⓐ Ⓑ Ⓒ Ⓓ
148. Ⓐ Ⓑ Ⓒ Ⓓ
149. Ⓐ Ⓑ Ⓒ Ⓓ
150. Ⓐ Ⓑ Ⓒ Ⓓ
151. Ⓐ Ⓑ Ⓒ Ⓓ
152. Ⓐ Ⓑ Ⓒ Ⓓ
153. Ⓐ Ⓑ Ⓒ Ⓓ
154. Ⓐ Ⓑ Ⓒ Ⓓ
155. Ⓐ Ⓑ Ⓒ Ⓓ
156. Ⓐ Ⓑ Ⓒ Ⓓ
157. Ⓐ Ⓑ Ⓒ Ⓓ
158. Ⓐ Ⓑ Ⓒ Ⓓ
159. Ⓐ Ⓑ Ⓒ Ⓓ
160. Ⓐ Ⓑ Ⓒ Ⓓ

Part VII

161. Ⓐ Ⓑ Ⓒ Ⓓ
162. Ⓐ Ⓑ Ⓒ Ⓓ
163. Ⓐ Ⓑ Ⓒ Ⓓ
164. Ⓐ Ⓑ Ⓒ Ⓓ
165. Ⓐ Ⓑ Ⓒ Ⓓ
166. Ⓐ Ⓑ Ⓒ Ⓓ
167. Ⓐ Ⓑ Ⓒ Ⓓ
168. Ⓐ Ⓑ Ⓒ Ⓓ
169. Ⓐ Ⓑ Ⓒ Ⓓ
170. Ⓐ Ⓑ Ⓒ Ⓓ
171. Ⓐ Ⓑ Ⓒ Ⓓ
172. Ⓐ Ⓑ Ⓒ Ⓓ
173. Ⓐ Ⓑ Ⓒ Ⓓ
174. Ⓐ Ⓑ Ⓒ Ⓓ
175. Ⓐ Ⓑ Ⓒ Ⓓ
176. Ⓐ Ⓑ Ⓒ Ⓓ
177. Ⓐ Ⓑ Ⓒ Ⓓ
178. Ⓐ Ⓑ Ⓒ Ⓓ
179. Ⓐ Ⓑ Ⓒ Ⓓ
180. Ⓐ Ⓑ Ⓒ Ⓓ
181. Ⓐ Ⓑ Ⓒ Ⓓ
182. Ⓐ Ⓑ Ⓒ Ⓓ
183. Ⓐ Ⓑ Ⓒ Ⓓ
184. Ⓐ Ⓑ Ⓒ Ⓓ
185. Ⓐ Ⓑ Ⓒ Ⓓ
186. Ⓐ Ⓑ Ⓒ Ⓓ
187. Ⓐ Ⓑ Ⓒ Ⓓ
188. Ⓐ Ⓑ Ⓒ Ⓓ
189. Ⓐ Ⓑ Ⓒ Ⓓ
190. Ⓐ Ⓑ Ⓒ Ⓓ
191. Ⓐ Ⓑ Ⓒ Ⓓ
192. Ⓐ Ⓑ Ⓒ Ⓓ
193. Ⓐ Ⓑ Ⓒ Ⓓ
194. Ⓐ Ⓑ Ⓒ Ⓓ
195. Ⓐ Ⓑ Ⓒ Ⓓ
196. Ⓐ Ⓑ Ⓒ Ⓓ
197. Ⓐ Ⓑ Ⓒ Ⓓ
198. Ⓐ Ⓑ Ⓒ Ⓓ
199. Ⓐ Ⓑ Ⓒ Ⓓ
200. Ⓐ Ⓑ Ⓒ Ⓓ

Answer Sheet – Practice Test 2

Mark all answers by completely filling in the circle. Mark only <u>one</u> answer for each question. If you change your mind about an answer after you have marked it on your answer sheet, completely erase your old answer and then mark your new answer. You must mark the answer sheet carefully so that the test-scoring machine can accurately record your test score.

Listening Section

Part I
1 Ⓐ Ⓑ Ⓒ Ⓓ
2 Ⓐ Ⓑ Ⓒ Ⓓ
3 Ⓐ Ⓑ Ⓒ Ⓓ
4 Ⓐ Ⓑ Ⓒ Ⓓ
5 Ⓐ Ⓑ Ⓒ Ⓓ
6 Ⓐ Ⓑ Ⓒ Ⓓ
7 Ⓐ Ⓑ Ⓒ Ⓓ
8 Ⓐ Ⓑ Ⓒ Ⓓ
9 Ⓐ Ⓑ Ⓒ Ⓓ
10 Ⓐ Ⓑ Ⓒ Ⓓ
11 Ⓐ Ⓑ Ⓒ Ⓓ
12 Ⓐ Ⓑ Ⓒ Ⓓ
13 Ⓐ Ⓑ Ⓒ Ⓓ
14 Ⓐ Ⓑ Ⓒ Ⓓ
15 Ⓐ Ⓑ Ⓒ Ⓓ
16 Ⓐ Ⓑ Ⓒ Ⓓ
17 Ⓐ Ⓑ Ⓒ Ⓓ
18 Ⓐ Ⓑ Ⓒ Ⓓ
19 Ⓐ Ⓑ Ⓒ Ⓓ
20 Ⓐ Ⓑ Ⓒ Ⓓ

Part II
21 Ⓐ Ⓑ Ⓒ
22 Ⓐ Ⓑ Ⓒ
23 Ⓐ Ⓑ Ⓒ
24 Ⓐ Ⓑ Ⓒ
25 Ⓐ Ⓑ Ⓒ
26 Ⓐ Ⓑ Ⓒ
27 Ⓐ Ⓑ Ⓒ
28 Ⓐ Ⓑ Ⓒ
29 Ⓐ Ⓑ Ⓒ
30 Ⓐ Ⓑ Ⓒ
31 Ⓐ Ⓑ Ⓒ
32 Ⓐ Ⓑ Ⓒ
33 Ⓐ Ⓑ Ⓒ
34 Ⓐ Ⓑ Ⓒ
35 Ⓐ Ⓑ Ⓒ
36 Ⓐ Ⓑ Ⓒ
37 Ⓐ Ⓑ Ⓒ
38 Ⓐ Ⓑ Ⓒ
39 Ⓐ Ⓑ Ⓒ
40 Ⓐ Ⓑ Ⓒ
41 Ⓐ Ⓑ Ⓒ
42 Ⓐ Ⓑ Ⓒ
43 Ⓐ Ⓑ Ⓒ
44 Ⓐ Ⓑ Ⓒ
45 Ⓐ Ⓑ Ⓒ
46 Ⓐ Ⓑ Ⓒ
47 Ⓐ Ⓑ Ⓒ
48 Ⓐ Ⓑ Ⓒ
49 Ⓐ Ⓑ Ⓒ
50 Ⓐ Ⓑ Ⓒ

Part III
51 Ⓐ Ⓑ Ⓒ Ⓓ
52 Ⓐ Ⓑ Ⓒ Ⓓ
53 Ⓐ Ⓑ Ⓒ Ⓓ
54 Ⓐ Ⓑ Ⓒ Ⓓ
55 Ⓐ Ⓑ Ⓒ Ⓓ
56 Ⓐ Ⓑ Ⓒ Ⓓ
57 Ⓐ Ⓑ Ⓒ Ⓓ
58 Ⓐ Ⓑ Ⓒ Ⓓ
59 Ⓐ Ⓑ Ⓒ Ⓓ
60 Ⓐ Ⓑ Ⓒ Ⓓ
61 Ⓐ Ⓑ Ⓒ Ⓓ
62 Ⓐ Ⓑ Ⓒ Ⓓ
63 Ⓐ Ⓑ Ⓒ Ⓓ
64 Ⓐ Ⓑ Ⓒ Ⓓ
65 Ⓐ Ⓑ Ⓒ Ⓓ
66 Ⓐ Ⓑ Ⓒ Ⓓ
67 Ⓐ Ⓑ Ⓒ Ⓓ
68 Ⓐ Ⓑ Ⓒ Ⓓ
69 Ⓐ Ⓑ Ⓒ Ⓓ
70 Ⓐ Ⓑ Ⓒ Ⓓ
71 Ⓐ Ⓑ Ⓒ Ⓓ
72 Ⓐ Ⓑ Ⓒ Ⓓ
73 Ⓐ Ⓑ Ⓒ Ⓓ
74 Ⓐ Ⓑ Ⓒ Ⓓ
75 Ⓐ Ⓑ Ⓒ Ⓓ
76 Ⓐ Ⓑ Ⓒ Ⓓ
77 Ⓐ Ⓑ Ⓒ Ⓓ
78 Ⓐ Ⓑ Ⓒ Ⓓ
79 Ⓐ Ⓑ Ⓒ Ⓓ
80 Ⓐ Ⓑ Ⓒ Ⓓ

Part IV
81 Ⓐ Ⓑ Ⓒ Ⓓ
82 Ⓐ Ⓑ Ⓒ Ⓓ
83 Ⓐ Ⓑ Ⓒ Ⓓ
84 Ⓐ Ⓑ Ⓒ Ⓓ
85 Ⓐ Ⓑ Ⓒ Ⓓ
86 Ⓐ Ⓑ Ⓒ Ⓓ
87 Ⓐ Ⓑ Ⓒ Ⓓ
88 Ⓐ Ⓑ Ⓒ Ⓓ
89 Ⓐ Ⓑ Ⓒ Ⓓ
90 Ⓐ Ⓑ Ⓒ Ⓓ
91 Ⓐ Ⓑ Ⓒ Ⓓ
92 Ⓐ Ⓑ Ⓒ Ⓓ
93 Ⓐ Ⓑ Ⓒ Ⓓ
94 Ⓐ Ⓑ Ⓒ Ⓓ
95 Ⓐ Ⓑ Ⓒ Ⓓ
96 Ⓐ Ⓑ Ⓒ Ⓓ
97 Ⓐ Ⓑ Ⓒ Ⓓ
98 Ⓐ Ⓑ Ⓒ Ⓓ
99 Ⓐ Ⓑ Ⓒ Ⓓ
100 Ⓐ Ⓑ Ⓒ Ⓓ

Reading Section

Part V
101 Ⓐ Ⓑ Ⓒ Ⓓ
102 Ⓐ Ⓑ Ⓒ Ⓓ
103 Ⓐ Ⓑ Ⓒ Ⓓ
104 Ⓐ Ⓑ Ⓒ Ⓓ
105 Ⓐ Ⓑ Ⓒ Ⓓ
106 Ⓐ Ⓑ Ⓒ Ⓓ
107 Ⓐ Ⓑ Ⓒ Ⓓ
108 Ⓐ Ⓑ Ⓒ Ⓓ
109 Ⓐ Ⓑ Ⓒ Ⓓ
110 Ⓐ Ⓑ Ⓒ Ⓓ
111 Ⓐ Ⓑ Ⓒ Ⓓ
112 Ⓐ Ⓑ Ⓒ Ⓓ
113 Ⓐ Ⓑ Ⓒ Ⓓ
114 Ⓐ Ⓑ Ⓒ Ⓓ
115 Ⓐ Ⓑ Ⓒ Ⓓ
116 Ⓐ Ⓑ Ⓒ Ⓓ
117 Ⓐ Ⓑ Ⓒ Ⓓ
118 Ⓐ Ⓑ Ⓒ Ⓓ
119 Ⓐ Ⓑ Ⓒ Ⓓ
120 Ⓐ Ⓑ Ⓒ Ⓓ
121 Ⓐ Ⓑ Ⓒ Ⓓ
122 Ⓐ Ⓑ Ⓒ Ⓓ
123 Ⓐ Ⓑ Ⓒ Ⓓ
124 Ⓐ Ⓑ Ⓒ Ⓓ
125 Ⓐ Ⓑ Ⓒ Ⓓ
126 Ⓐ Ⓑ Ⓒ Ⓓ
127 Ⓐ Ⓑ Ⓒ Ⓓ
128 Ⓐ Ⓑ Ⓒ Ⓓ
129 Ⓐ Ⓑ Ⓒ Ⓓ
130 Ⓐ Ⓑ Ⓒ Ⓓ
131 Ⓐ Ⓑ Ⓒ Ⓓ
132 Ⓐ Ⓑ Ⓒ Ⓓ
133 Ⓐ Ⓑ Ⓒ Ⓓ
134 Ⓐ Ⓑ Ⓒ Ⓓ
135 Ⓐ Ⓑ Ⓒ Ⓓ
136 Ⓐ Ⓑ Ⓒ Ⓓ
137 Ⓐ Ⓑ Ⓒ Ⓓ
138 Ⓐ Ⓑ Ⓒ Ⓓ
139 Ⓐ Ⓑ Ⓒ Ⓓ
140 Ⓐ Ⓑ Ⓒ Ⓓ

Part VI
141 Ⓐ Ⓑ Ⓒ Ⓓ
142 Ⓐ Ⓑ Ⓒ Ⓓ
143 Ⓐ Ⓑ Ⓒ Ⓓ
144 Ⓐ Ⓑ Ⓒ Ⓓ
145 Ⓐ Ⓑ Ⓒ Ⓓ
146 Ⓐ Ⓑ Ⓒ Ⓓ
147 Ⓐ Ⓑ Ⓒ Ⓓ
148 Ⓐ Ⓑ Ⓒ Ⓓ
149 Ⓐ Ⓑ Ⓒ Ⓓ
150 Ⓐ Ⓑ Ⓒ Ⓓ
151 Ⓐ Ⓑ Ⓒ Ⓓ
152 Ⓐ Ⓑ Ⓒ Ⓓ
153 Ⓐ Ⓑ Ⓒ Ⓓ
154 Ⓐ Ⓑ Ⓒ Ⓓ
155 Ⓐ Ⓑ Ⓒ Ⓓ
156 Ⓐ Ⓑ Ⓒ Ⓓ
157 Ⓐ Ⓑ Ⓒ Ⓓ
158 Ⓐ Ⓑ Ⓒ Ⓓ
159 Ⓐ Ⓑ Ⓒ Ⓓ
160 Ⓐ Ⓑ Ⓒ Ⓓ

Part VII
161 Ⓐ Ⓑ Ⓒ Ⓓ
162 Ⓐ Ⓑ Ⓒ Ⓓ
163 Ⓐ Ⓑ Ⓒ Ⓓ
164 Ⓐ Ⓑ Ⓒ Ⓓ
165 Ⓐ Ⓑ Ⓒ Ⓓ
166 Ⓐ Ⓑ Ⓒ Ⓓ
167 Ⓐ Ⓑ Ⓒ Ⓓ
168 Ⓐ Ⓑ Ⓒ Ⓓ
169 Ⓐ Ⓑ Ⓒ Ⓓ
170 Ⓐ Ⓑ Ⓒ Ⓓ
171 Ⓐ Ⓑ Ⓒ Ⓓ
172 Ⓐ Ⓑ Ⓒ Ⓓ
173 Ⓐ Ⓑ Ⓒ Ⓓ
174 Ⓐ Ⓑ Ⓒ Ⓓ
175 Ⓐ Ⓑ Ⓒ Ⓓ
176 Ⓐ Ⓑ Ⓒ Ⓓ
177 Ⓐ Ⓑ Ⓒ Ⓓ
178 Ⓐ Ⓑ Ⓒ Ⓓ
179 Ⓐ Ⓑ Ⓒ Ⓓ
180 Ⓐ Ⓑ Ⓒ Ⓓ
181 Ⓐ Ⓑ Ⓒ Ⓓ
182 Ⓐ Ⓑ Ⓒ Ⓓ
183 Ⓐ Ⓑ Ⓒ Ⓓ
184 Ⓐ Ⓑ Ⓒ Ⓓ
185 Ⓐ Ⓑ Ⓒ Ⓓ
186 Ⓐ Ⓑ Ⓒ Ⓓ
187 Ⓐ Ⓑ Ⓒ Ⓓ
188 Ⓐ Ⓑ Ⓒ Ⓓ
189 Ⓐ Ⓑ Ⓒ Ⓓ
190 Ⓐ Ⓑ Ⓒ Ⓓ
191 Ⓐ Ⓑ Ⓒ Ⓓ
192 Ⓐ Ⓑ Ⓒ Ⓓ
193 Ⓐ Ⓑ Ⓒ Ⓓ
194 Ⓐ Ⓑ Ⓒ Ⓓ
195 Ⓐ Ⓑ Ⓒ Ⓓ
196 Ⓐ Ⓑ Ⓒ Ⓓ
197 Ⓐ Ⓑ Ⓒ Ⓓ
198 Ⓐ Ⓑ Ⓒ Ⓓ
199 Ⓐ Ⓑ Ⓒ Ⓓ
200 Ⓐ Ⓑ Ⓒ Ⓓ

Answer Sheet – Practice Test 3

Mark all answers by completely filling in the circle. Mark only <u>one</u> answer for each question. If you change your mind about an answer after you have marked it on your answer sheet, completely erase your old answer and then mark your new answer. You must mark the answer sheet carefully so that the test-scoring machine can accurately record your test score.

Listening Section

Part I

1 (A)(B)(C)(D)
2 (A)(B)(C)(D)
3 (A)(B)(C)(D)
4 (A)(B)(C)(D)
5 (A)(B)(C)(D)
6 (A)(B)(C)(D)
7 (A)(B)(C)(D)
8 (A)(B)(C)(D)
9 (A)(B)(C)(D)
10 (A)(B)(C)(D)
11 (A)(B)(C)(D)
12 (A)(B)(C)(D)
13 (A)(B)(C)(D)
14 (A)(B)(C)(D)
15 (A)(B)(C)(D)
16 (A)(B)(C)(D)
17 (A)(B)(C)(D)
18 (A)(B)(C)(D)
19 (A)(B)(C)(D)
20 (A)(B)(C)(D)

Part II

21 (A)(B)(C)
22 (A)(B)(C)
23 (A)(B)(C)
24 (A)(B)(C)
25 (A)(B)(C)
26 (A)(B)(C)
27 (A)(B)(C)
28 (A)(B)(C)
29 (A)(B)(C)
30 (A)(B)(C)
31 (A)(B)(C)
32 (A)(B)(C)
33 (A)(B)(C)

34 (A)(B)(C)
35 (A)(B)(C)
36 (A)(B)(C)
37 (A)(B)(C)
38 (A)(B)(C)
39 (A)(B)(C)
40 (A)(B)(C)
41 (A)(B)(C)
42 (A)(B)(C)
43 (A)(B)(C)
44 (A)(B)(C)
45 (A)(B)(C)
46 (A)(B)(C)
47 (A)(B)(C)
48 (A)(B)(C)
49 (A)(B)(C)
50 (A)(B)(C)

Part III

51 (A)(B)(C)(D)
52 (A)(B)(C)(D)
53 (A)(B)(C)(D)
54 (A)(B)(C)(D)
55 (A)(B)(C)(D)
56 (A)(B)(C)(D)
57 (A)(B)(C)(D)
58 (A)(B)(C)(D)
59 (A)(B)(C)(D)
60 (A)(B)(C)(D)
61 (A)(B)(C)(D)
62 (A)(B)(C)(D)
63 (A)(B)(C)(D)
64 (A)(B)(C)(D)
65 (A)(B)(C)(D)
66 (A)(B)(C)(D)
67 (A)(B)(C)(D)

68 (A)(B)(C)(D)
69 (A)(B)(C)(D)
70 (A)(B)(C)(D)
71 (A)(B)(C)(D)
72 (A)(B)(C)(D)
73 (A)(B)(C)(D)
74 (A)(B)(C)(D)
75 (A)(B)(C)(D)
76 (A)(B)(C)(D)
77 (A)(B)(C)(D)
78 (A)(B)(C)(D)
79 (A)(B)(C)(D)
80 (A)(B)(C)(D)

Part IV

81 (A)(B)(C)(D)
82 (A)(B)(C)(D)
83 (A)(B)(C)(D)
84 (A)(B)(C)(D)
85 (A)(B)(C)(D)
86 (A)(B)(C)(D)
87 (A)(B)(C)(D)
88 (A)(B)(C)(D)
89 (A)(B)(C)(D)
90 (A)(B)(C)(D)
91 (A)(B)(C)(D)
92 (A)(B)(C)(D)
93 (A)(B)(C)(D)
94 (A)(B)(C)(D)
95 (A)(B)(C)(D)
96 (A)(B)(C)(D)
97 (A)(B)(C)(D)
98 (A)(B)(C)(D)
99 (A)(B)(C)(D)
100 (A)(B)(C)(D)

Reading Section

Part V

101 (A)(B)(C)(D)
102 (A)(B)(C)(D)
103 (A)(B)(C)(D)
104 (A)(B)(C)(D)
105 (A)(B)(C)(D)
106 (A)(B)(C)(D)
107 (A)(B)(C)(D)
108 (A)(B)(C)(D)
109 (A)(B)(C)(D)
110 (A)(B)(C)(D)
111 (A)(B)(C)(D)
112 (A)(B)(C)(D)
113 (A)(B)(C)(D)
114 (A)(B)(C)(D)
115 (A)(B)(C)(D)
116 (A)(B)(C)(D)
117 (A)(B)(C)(D)
118 (A)(B)(C)(D)
119 (A)(B)(C)(D)
120 (A)(B)(C)(D)
121 (A)(B)(C)(D)
122 (A)(B)(C)(D)
123 (A)(B)(C)(D)
124 (A)(B)(C)(D)
125 (A)(B)(C)(D)
126 (A)(B)(C)(D)
127 (A)(B)(C)(D)
128 (A)(B)(C)(D)
129 (A)(B)(C)(D)
130 (A)(B)(C)(D)
131 (A)(B)(C)(D)
132 (A)(B)(C)(D)
133 (A)(B)(C)(D)
134 (A)(B)(C)(D)
135 (A)(B)(C)(D)

136 (A)(B)(C)(D)
137 (A)(B)(C)(D)
138 (A)(B)(C)(D)
139 (A)(B)(C)(D)
140 (A)(B)(C)(D)

Part VI

141 (A)(B)(C)(D)
142 (A)(B)(C)(D)
143 (A)(B)(C)(D)
144 (A)(B)(C)(D)
145 (A)(B)(C)(D)
146 (A)(B)(C)(D)
147 (A)(B)(C)(D)
148 (A)(B)(C)(D)
149 (A)(B)(C)(D)
150 (A)(B)(C)(D)
151 (A)(B)(C)(D)
152 (A)(B)(C)(D)
153 (A)(B)(C)(D)
154 (A)(B)(C)(D)
155 (A)(B)(C)(D)
156 (A)(B)(C)(D)
157 (A)(B)(C)(D)
158 (A)(B)(C)(D)
159 (A)(B)(C)(D)
160 (A)(B)(C)(D)

Part VII

161 (A)(B)(C)(D)
162 (A)(B)(C)(D)
163 (A)(B)(C)(D)
164 (A)(B)(C)(D)
165 (A)(B)(C)(D)
166 (A)(B)(C)(D)
167 (A)(B)(C)(D)

168 (A)(B)(C)(D)
169 (A)(B)(C)(D)
170 (A)(B)(C)(D)
171 (A)(B)(C)(D)
172 (A)(B)(C)(D)
173 (A)(B)(C)(D)
174 (A)(B)(C)(D)
175 (A)(B)(C)(D)
176 (A)(B)(C)(D)
177 (A)(B)(C)(D)
178 (A)(B)(C)(D)
179 (A)(B)(C)(D)
180 (A)(B)(C)(D)
181 (A)(B)(C)(D)
182 (A)(B)(C)(D)
183 (A)(B)(C)(D)
184 (A)(B)(C)(D)
185 (A)(B)(C)(D)
186 (A)(B)(C)(D)
187 (A)(B)(C)(D)
188 (A)(B)(C)(D)
189 (A)(B)(C)(D)
190 (A)(B)(C)(D)
191 (A)(B)(C)(D)
192 (A)(B)(C)(D)
193 (A)(B)(C)(D)
194 (A)(B)(C)(D)
195 (A)(B)(C)(D)
196 (A)(B)(C)(D)
197 (A)(B)(C)(D)
198 (A)(B)(C)(D)
199 (A)(B)(C)(D)
200 (A)(B)(C)(D)